Ka

No True Love In Tehran

An American Trip to Iran

DARAKEH PRESS

ISBN 978-0-57874-051-5
Available as an electronic book; ISBN 978-0-57874-052-2

Cover design by Dan Tanz
Map illustration by Jesse Maloney
Book design by Kelley Creative

Published by Darakeh Press

www.kareemaal.com

This book is for people who are afraid.

Let the people who never find true love
keep saying that there's no such thing.

Their faith will make it easier for them to live and die.

- Wisława Szymborska, *View with a Grain of Sand*

Fasham

/WN S

Pas-e-Qaleh

Jamshidieh Park

Jajrood River

ame
hran

Sohanak Forest

Saad Abad Palaces

Artesh Hwy.

Lashgarak Rd.

Bagh-é Ferdows

Tehran Birds Garden

Babael Hwy.

Zeyn-od Din Hwy.

Natl. Library of Iran

qasem Soleimani Expy.

NARMAK

HAKIMIYEH

ran Enghelab Hotel

Sorkheh Hesar
Forest Park

ministry of
Foreign Affairs

N 1 mile

Sardar-é Bagh Melli

TEHRAN BAZAAR

TEHRAN

Chapter One

YEARS HAD GONE BY without him killing me. So when my Iranian friend invited me to visit his home country I listened politely before shaking my head once, then twice.

I met Sanjar for the first time on a summer night outside a stinky café in Minneapolis. These were the last days before the citywide smoking ban. From the early morning, patrons began filling the café with smoke that would reach all the way up to its high ceilings. When I walked in at dusk an invisible cloud touched my shoulders, and my clothes slowly filled with the tarry breath of a hundred addicts.

My sister and I sat outside together as we often did, sharing the details of our recent travels. The air was calm, allowing a curl of smoke from her cigarette to corkscrew slowly into the night sky. She had just returned from Lisbon. I had my own tales from the West Coast.

Sitting near to us was an oddly matched crew of Minnesotans. Sanjar was one of them. The group had arranged its chairs in a large circle and were engaged in a light-hearted conversation regulated by a single rule: when someone overcommitted to an argument, their conviction would be undercut with a series of giggles from the crowd.

A fat man, with his legs and arms socketed inside tight blue jeans and a white button-up shirt, squinted playfully at a slight East African who seemed to be kindly ignoring the material world. An Indian woman rattled off a few words to a Scandinavian with gelled blonde hair. The Scandinavian looked at Sanjar, who brushed the tip of his nose with his finger before choking on a laugh that jolted him backwards.

As their stew of talk boiled and splashed, my attention drifted. Across from me, my sister was describing a quest for *migas,* a Portuguese peasant dish made from cornbread crumbs and kale. As she described heading north towards Coimbra on a bus, where I assumed *migas* was available, I heard a man in the circle cry out in affirmation, "Yes! It was the moon. It happened to me too."

I glanced over my sister's shoulder to see a bald man in a thin leather jacket look up accusingly at the full moon. As I was turning back to my sister, Sanjar caught my eye. He invited us over.

There were a few things I had to say to my sister, so I held his eyes for a moment and reluctantly called back, "First things first."

Before turning to his friends, Sanjar crooned, "Oh, I learned something new today. 'First things first.'"

SANJAR LATER ADMITTED to me that he had found my sister cute. When he came up to our table after his friends had left, the disgusted look on his face suggested there were other things on his mind as well. His footsteps nibbled closer to our table, but his body was so energetic that it looked like it was ready to bolt down the street. An arm pinned two books to his chest. His free hand was soon busy animating his case with powerful gestures, like karate blows. It turned out that the book of old Persian poetry in his hand was full of lousy translations.

We offered him a chair in sympathy.

Without wasting a moment, he sat on the chair's edge and launched into a complaint: in one of the translated poems, the moon produced "warts" instead of a "veil of light." I eyed the other book he was carrying. It was a thick white library tome on Ayatollah Khomeini.

A COUPLE OF HOURS WENT by as the three of us sat around the circular wrought-iron table. Our empty cups of coffee were pushed to its center. The roots of a tall elm tree ate up half the sidewalk next to us; patches of its bark were lit by light from the café. The trunk climbed towards the shadowy crown until the whole mass of branches and leaves thrust past the two-story red brick building into the sky.

It was now past midnight. Purple and red perennials had been planted at the foot of the elm and in raised flower boxes. It felt like the three of us were sitting in a private garden. The first hour of our meeting had turned gently towards its sequel—and would blur into a sequence of encounters unknown to us at the time. Strangers inching across the blank texture of night, like watercolors, we had begun to slowly bleed into each other.

A potential friendship did not cross my mind at the time. I was too busy trying to follow an explanation of how Persia came to be known as Iran. A loud group passed us on the way to the nearby Red Dragon Bar. Two sets of pale legs poked out of short skirts and back into cowboy boots. Next to them, artful mustaches asserted themselves on young faces, and a thin T-shirt and tank top half-concealed the black snarl of tattoos, until it all vanished around the corner.

The few cars still on the streets hurtled through the intersection. A yellow light flashed. One car settled to a stop and idled behind the empty crosswalk. The light changed, the sound of an engine drained into the distance, and stillness filled up the block again.

Thumbing through his book, Sanjar had finally found a couple of lines of old Persian verse that had survived the passing of time and the warp of translation. He passed the book over to us. It was a couplet from nearly a thousand years ago:

I will hide in my song so that I may take kisses
from your lips as you sing it.

I did not know what the couplet meant, but I felt it working on me as though it were alive. Smoldering in a hot, jagged orange line, it kept eating its way inside my mind long after I read it. I had been moved by words before but this reaction was different. It was like an Alka-Seltzer fizzing in the depths of my being, a pea-sized hydrothermal vent bubbling up in a forgotten chamber of my heart. It was a private, physical fact and a private mystery. Reflecting on that moment now, I am relieved that the mystery remains despite all the clumsy ways I have handled it. I was reassured and bewildered that even if I did not treat this experience as a secret, it would remain so.

These were the first two lines of poetry Sanjar and I shared together. As sensitive as I have found Sanjar to be, I feel he had only a vague notion of how the words produced a zip of electric chaos in me. Ultimately, it was stranger still to find a man in America who dared to bring poetry out on a Saturday night and not be a bore about it. It was hard to believe as well, that he had no plans to try to sleep with me. It all meant one thing: he was not American.

MONTHS LATER, after we had gotten to know each other, we would spend hours reading, talking, dancing, and drinking chocolate milk from the gas station across the street from the Stinky Café. At the end of one of those nights, Sanjar stepped out of my car. His arm was draped over the open door and his head was still ducked into the car. We were exhausted. A foamy ounce of milk swished in a plastic pint bottle in my hand. The first rays of sun began to sift their way into the weakening darkness.

"Goodnight, man," I gasped.

"Have a great day!" Sanjar answered brightly. When my face contorted, he added, "Man, isn't a day twenty-four hours?"

As the months turned to years, we got used to each other. I even began to dimly apprehend the observations about Iran that he'd present to me in wild, far-ranging monologues.

"Iran is a snake with many heads," he'd say as I plucked the plastic lid of my coffee cup. "The mask is there, but no one knows what is really going on." Leaving me to visualize a colossal and enduring masquerade spanning the Middle East.

One of the hardest claims to believe was that Iran was a country full of poets. A situation, he said, that made it nearly impossible to understand anyone. When Sanjar was finally able to go back to Iran his suspicions were confirmed. Everyone spoke in verse. The older generation was the worst. While at a party in Tehran, he found himself floundering while trying to follow some reference to a thirteenth-century poem. He confessed to me what had gone through his head: "God damn it! Can't you just tell me what you mean?"

He wanted some straight talk.

Thirty years away from his home country, living in the Midwest, meant something else: he *was* American. With one of my parents from the East and the other from the West, I also lived in two worlds. Sanjar and I became friends in both of them.

Chapter Two

AFTER MANY YEARS I finally accepted Sanjar's invitation. I had gone to Iran and come back with all ten toes and fingers. A couple days after returning I found myself driving to a house on Lilac Road in a suburb of Minneapolis. On my back seat was a suitcase full of dried mulberries, pistachios, and figs. The plastic bag on the front seat contained two copies of a book in Farsi. These were gifts for Sanjar's brother Naveed, entrusted to me by their father in the Islamic Republic of Iran.

The highway was smooth under my wheels that afternoon. I turned the air up high, and radio higher. Hitting my exit, I coasted to the stoplight at the end of the ramp. The safety and quietude, the greenery and spaciousness of life in Minnesota pressed upon me as I considered the orderliness of the neighborhood. It was a wealthy suburb where days of dread and perfection teetered on a knife edge. Yet, as I conjured a memory of pensive Iranians on a Tehran subway, this America glided ahead on a sheen of law and plentitude, seeming to embody a superior quality of life.

As I observed the speed limit, my aging Mazda Protegé impinged on the visual landscape and I imagined a patrol car taking notice. It was strange how severe and unfamiliar I felt towards the authorities in America, even though I appreciated what might be called their predictability. As I eased over a hill, I felt a little sentimental for the few encounters with the authorities I witnessed in Iran, where determining who was in charge seemed negotiable, or dependent on variables that were opaque to me.

I took a couple more turns and a big house appeared in my windshield. I pulled into the driveway and called Naveed. No one was home. I rolled my window down, letting the humid August air engulf the interior of the car. My arms started to glisten. I stepped out onto the blacktop and made a breeze for myself by pacing its length.

NAVEED AND HIS FAMILY finally arrived in a black Mercedes. They got out and we greeted each other. There is power in telling a native about the feel of life in their own country, and I questioned my suitability to wield it.

I had gotten to know the family when Sanjar lived in Minneapolis. The two of us would be at a café playing Othello or chess when he would get a call from Naveed. After hanging up Sanjar would gravely say, "Naveed is grilling steak. The best. It's a must-see."

Sanjar promised that if we went to the house in the suburbs our mouths would be rewarded. We would arrive at the house on Lilac Drive at dinnertime. Naveed would be in the dark with a spatula in one hand and cigarette in the other, a grill tuned to medium-high in front of him. Sanjar would kiss him on both cheeks and I would extend my hand. Naveed would grip it firmly, pointing the spatula towards two rows of thick steaks, docked next to each other like aircraft carriers. He would hold on to my hand until I accepted that being there was not a burden to him.

In the driveway, in front of the black Mercedes in broad daylight, a sort of standoff ensued that every traveler must encounter. I bluffed and waved my arms around, not wanting to reduce my experience of their home country into a package of hastily picked adjectives. Naveed and his family were laughing. We stood smiling at each other until I raised a finger and scurried over to my car. I pulled out the suitcase and books.

Upon returning, Farzaneh, Naveed's wife, hit me with an astute first question: "So, I want to know about the girls. Were they flirtatious?"

"Ah ... you know, when I met them, I felt welcomed," I mumbled.

"Welcomed?"

"Yes, welcomed—to join dreams that had little to do with me," I shrugged.

All around the adults chuckled knowingly while their young daughter, Tara, turned to her father. Her beautiful Persian eyes were searching. A feisty mouth paused as the lips started to form a question.

Naveed intervened, "He means they liked him because he was American."

"Did you see any girls wearing short sleeves?" Tara inquired, trying to wrest the conversation back to familiar ground.

"No," I quipped, deciding to lie. How would I explain the time I saw a young woman in a tank top at an apartment in Tehran, her brassiere strap sliding off her shoulder? Iranians generally don't find it necessary to shield children from life's interesting topics, but I decided to wait.

"She's worried about ruining her tan," Farzaneh teased.

Tara would be going to Iran for the first time soon. Their son would stay back while the family traveled. It was the only sure way to avoid any unwanted offers from the army to help serve Iran.

"Tara, we'll only be there two weeks next summer, you don't have to worry," Farzaneh added.

"You're all going?" I asked. "That's great!"

Ignoring my comment Farzaneh looked hard back at me, "So you just stayed in Tehran. No Shiraz? No Isfahan? I'm going to kill Sanjar!"

"Tehran was enough ... better an inch wide and a mile deep," I philosophized.

This time it was the son, Azad, a muscular and driven pianist and sportsman, who cocked his head towards his parents. He had a powerful mind and had given Sanjar a scare at the chess board when he was six years old. When Sanjar and I spoke of our nights out he was always curious, but was willing to accept that despite his intellect, he would have to wait for experience to illuminate certain things.

"Azad, he's saying that it was better to stay in one place and get to know it. He's right." Naveed punctuated his answer with a smile, picturing me roaming around the city he grew up in.

Farzaneh still could not believe we had not left the city. She knew Sanjar though, and smiled, thinking about the activities he must have come up with.

We stood in the driveway talking until the sun pushed us into the shade of the garage. I needed to go, but the hunger to tell and the need to listen made it hard, binding us in some ancient way. Tara got restless, waiting for some fragment of my trip to confirm her fears about her own. Azad grabbed the suitcase of fruits and nuts and hauled it towards the door leading from the garage into the house. A bicep flared as he lifted the case over the steps.

The rest of us stood for a moment, catching our breath before another round of smiling and head shaking. They needed to know so much. And I knew so little, almost nothing. I did not know what I really wanted to say about Iran.

I was resting my hand on the cool metal cover of the grill. Beneath all the smiling, my thoughts were tumbling incoherently. Farzaneh's brother showed up in a red convertible and saw us standing in a huddle in the garage. He was heading to Iran in the fall after three decades away.

"What should I see in Tehran?" The question flew from the open top before the engine was off.

"We went to the mountains a lot … Bame Tehran … that's one to see," I spit out. I felt less prepared to answer him than Naveed's family, but surprised myself pulling out a place name. Hearing "Bame Tehran" out loud caused me to reflect fondly, and secretly, on the place where I thought my life would end.

You can only stand in someone's driveway for so long. Eventually someone comes home or someone has to leave. We hovered in the open doorway of the garage on Lilac Drive a few more moments. Tea was offered a third and final time before I climbed into my car and drove away.

THE SAME WEEK I visited Lilac Road, an Iranian pharmacist who worked with my wife Marie asked to have tea with me when he heard I had just returned. I had never met him before and shied away from the meeting.

The pharmacist had decided long ago never to go back to Iran. He had one sister who stayed behind and was taking care of their parents. Their mother had multiple sclerosis and he had not seen her in ten years. He carried guilt under his white lab coat like an extra rib. Finally, he made plans for his family to reunite in Turkey. He would pay the way for everyone.

IN THE PAST, the Soviet Union used to plant spies in the villages just beyond their borders, including in Iran. Their aim was not to gather high-level intelligence but to check the local atmosphere. Through the dull chatter of everyday life some KGB algorithm would ferret out usable patterns. The moods and expectations of common people gave insight as to how they might be swayed. I did not underestimate the Russian penchant for transforming the fixtures of ordinary life into devices of heroic struggle. One KGB handbook recommends penetrating the high-rise office bathrooms of enemy targets, plugging the sinks and turning on the faucets.

Iranians who had not been back since the Islamic Revolution in 1979 used the information they obtained abroad to terraform a second Iran, a model they created to judge the current life of the place. They longed for fresh spaces to join to their old memories. The sights I had seen in Tehran held precious information, but I had taken them for granted.

I let the invitation from the pharmacist expire, but I had begun to understand that everything older Iranians asked me about my visit really boiled down to a single question: "What remains of the Iran I knew as a child?"

Chapter Three

THERE IS SOMETHING everyone suspects about the world: things are not as they seem. Iranians, steeped in symbolic literature and twisted political circumstances, are more willing to accept this than most. There is a beloved character in the Middle East who appears in stories that attempt to get people to reconsider their perceptions. For centuries his tales have moved easily between borders and cultures—a fool with a king's seal. In Iran he is called Mullah Nasruddin.

Once in a while Sanjar would tell a Mullah Nasruddin story. We'd be in a café or walking along the lake and Nasruddin would suddenly be there, his antics illustrating some point.

Sanjar was in Iran and we were corresponding by computer the last time I heard one of his tales. It was early spring, nearly a year after I had returned from Iran and delivered the pistachios. Another period of unrest had been initiated in the Middle East, and people's minds were busy with the latest headlines. Egypt had just gone through its first upheaval; Iran had weathered its own. The Middle East was being brought to a boil.

Ordinary life was once again cocooned by the silken thread of rumor and intrigue. Outbreaks of violence blinkered the minds of observers and participants alike; attention switched from one atrocity to another, from one hope to another. City squares filled with blood while the elite and the superpowers bided their time. Eventually the crowds, and aspiration, were washed out by the awful tedium of oppression and everyday survival.

I had written Sanjar to ask what he thought of it all, and instead of a clear pronouncement I got Mullah Nasruddin. I took a sip of tea and read the message.

"One night, Mullah Nasruddin was woken up by his wife," Sanjar wrote. "'Mullah, there is a fight out in the street. Go and see what's the matter.'" I continued reading, imagining how Sanjar would bring more life to the story in person.

"Mullah was reluctant, but his wife insisted. So he grabbed the comforter and wrapped himself up to stay warm. He went out and asked the men to stop fighting. They went toward him and took his comforter and ran away. Mullah went back inside. His wife asked, 'Mullah, what was it about? What were they fighting for?' Mullah said, 'The fight was over my comforter.'"

"Life can be very hysterical, and no one sees what is going on to laugh at it," Sanjar wrote beneath the tale. "People are simply too distracted to notice."

I sat in front of the bright screen, Sanjar's message still open. Sanjar thought something else was going on in the Middle East. Iranians always do. Telling this story was his way of letting me know how he felt about the situation.

I wondered what made Iranians so cynical, so convinced that "the eyes make you blind." When I was in Iran, Sanjar's uncle told me a story about the eve of the Shah's overthrow: Inside the palace an American military attaché is standing alongside the Shah, America's supposed best friend in the region, the "policeman of the Middle East." The American looks down at his watch. He then looks up at the Shah and says, "It's been two hours. When are you leaving?"

Of course, the standard version is that Ayatollah Khomeini and his supporters came swooping in, surprising the US. Details that emerge like deadheads from a story we think we know well may have something to do with Iranian suspicions about the nature of events.

I closed Sanjar's message and clicked on some news sites. My eyes scanned different media reports, and I read sure-footed Middle Eastern analysis written by adults. I looked at the cursor zooming around the screen, and then down at the little white device under my palm controlling it on my mouse pad. I thought of the story of the mouse who wins a full-grown cow at the fair. When he picks up the leash in his little mouth, he immediately begins to be dragged behind the beast. All the while he's shouting, "That's right, go left! Okay, straight ahead! That's good, now go right!"

Pop-up advertisements jiggled and taunted on my laptop screen. My focus sagged and thoughts about a topsy-turvy world began to pool. People in authority are people; they carry the ancient grab bag of human beliefs into the sober, rational, settings they inhabit. In America, a certain commander in chief consulted starry patterns in the night sky to guide his executive decisions. Years later another American president claimed to have received supernatural messages encouraging him to invade Afghanistan and Iraq. In Iran, a high-ranking official was accused of being a sorcerer and having links to the "known and unknown worlds." Another official in Iran was deputized to arrest *jinn*, the genies or spirits that populate a hidden dimension of our world according to many Middle-Easterners.

My all-time favorite was when Sanjar told me a mullah he'd seen in a photo was able to tele-transport himself.

The hours passed. My hand was numb, frozen in a claw around the mouse. I was in the sunroom of my house, but the beige shades were drawn down tight on a grey early spring landscape: roads, boulevards, and sidewalks encrusted with road salt and sand, and moldy lawns that had been buried in snow for five months. I looked at the bright yellow and red dots on my empty Moroccan tea glass. Underneath it, the disciplined body of an exercise guru graced a DVD case.

The world is strange, I thought. In time maybe I would learn to take note of it and even smile about it. Yet there was some-thing nagging me about what people say in the West about life. They advise *carpe diem*—seize the day. It is the power and conceit of a culture that believes man can bend life to his will. In the East, power comes through the back door. Fate is a wild bird: you can't grab it, but it might land on your hand if you settle yourself.

"Life," they say: "sometimes the man on the saddle, sometimes the saddle on the man."

SANJAR PROMISED that "nothing" would happen to me in Iran. His family was well-connected, and he had my back.

"They'll love you there. It's so safe you won't believe it. You'll be walking around, and it'll be *safer* than Minneapolis," Sanjar insisted.

One hot summer night, years after I visited Iran, Sanjar would be proven right about Minneapolis.

Accepting Sanjar's invitation at the time meant that I had valued the word of a friend more highly than State Department advisories. Though as I prepared to go, the warnings that greeted me at the US Bureau of Consular Affairs read like a liability waiver:

"The Department of State warns US citizens to carefully consider the risks of travel to Iran."

"US citizens may be subject to harassment or arrest while traveling or residing in Iran."

"Iranian authorities also have unjustly detained or imprisoned US citizens on various charges, including espionage and posing a threat to national security."

"The US government cannot provide protection to US citizens in Iran."

Nothing did happen to me in Iran. It was so hard to believe that I had to stop and write a book to find out what "nothing" looked like. I thought of the solemn, reassuring line of Amin Ul Mulk, a character in James Buchan's *The Persian Bride*, who said: "I have seen the ledger of humanity and it is blank." Inconsequence was all right by me—but even inconsequence has a substance that lets it take shape in the mind.

I thought of the twenty-three-year rule of Antonius Pius in
Rome, about which so little is said—so few and short-lived were
the wars, foreign troubles, and civil strife, and so happy and prosperous the citizens. I had been struck to the heart by Iranians, yet
there were no marks—no trouble and scars worth noting in the
annals of travel catastrophes. What had reached me there?
As a middle school teacher, when I asked my students to write
about their childhood the boys came back with reports of fists,
falls, bites, and cuts. Anything centering the story on the physical
world shielded them from entering the internal. Action provided
the footholds that allowed them to move freely from one unexam-
ined phase of life to another.
I was back in America, my body was whole, uninjured—all the
better to hide within. Sometimes the tiniest of tales pops up to
serve a purpose. It amazes me how such tales find their way out of
the void into a moment that suits their telling. A Turkish friend I
had met at the School of Oriental and African Studies in London
once described to me a crazy old man in her hometown who had
been asked to "touch his heart" by some local jokers. The old man
first placed his hand on his arm, then his leg, head, foot, mouth,
stomach, and knee.
The trip had erased some wall in my heart, and now, like the old
man, my whole body was filling with passion. It was time to take
hold of myself, and drill inside, word by word.

IT HAD BEEN a year since we first met at the Stinky Café and
Sanjar and I had a routine. Each Saturday a friend who worked at
the Minnesota Orchestra gave us free tickets. We took our seats
in the center of Orchestra Hall and closed our eyes. The Finnish
conductor Osmo Vänskä hustled on stage, chest thrust forward.
He raised his baton high above his head. Then, from behind my
eyelids, I felt him leading one hundred of the best musicians in
the world straight into the aurora borealis; the room swirled with
the cold, dazzling fury of classical masterpieces.
After the concert we headed down Seventh Street to the Saturday
Night Danceteria held at a club called First Avenue. Armed with

piles of blue comp tickets we'd found on the counters of local cafés, we never paid to get in. We handed our tickets to a friendly punk at the door, slid two quarters across the counter to buy neon yellow and pink ear plugs, and stepped around the corner into a cauldron of bass and strobe lights.

"Man, I'm drunk already!" Sanjar yelled.

"What do you mean?" I screamed back.

"Just the atmosphere—it makes me drunk!"

Most of the time we were the first people on the dance floor for this very reason: we did not have to wait for the alcohol to sink in in order to be intoxicated. We didn't just bend our knees and paddle our arms back and forth—we spun, jumped, mixed the Russian squat dance with high chorus-line kicks, threw our arms out and carved designs into an energy field, like kids with burning sticks at a campfire.

If I got tired, Sanjar said to keep moving just a little bit, but never stop. That was dancing to us: primitive, unpredictable, insane-looking from the outside but pure and free from the inside. Not the cheap toy of a few plotted moves designed to go viral in the Cracker Jack Box of a cell phone screen.

More than once I was asked, conspiratorially, "Hey, what are you guys *on?*"

After a few hours we sat down to drink some water. I looked up past the DJ on the main stage to a second-floor balcony where a go-go dancer was humping the air, and said "This is not bad."

"It's fun because we're together," Sanjar shouted back over the table.

Dance nights used to be even better at the club according to Sanjar. The defunct Sex-O-Rama on Wednesday nights in the 1980s was the benchmark. For one, there were cages with dancers swinging from the ceiling. Sanjar even went once wearing nothing but his silk boxer shorts. His older sister, there with a crew of Iranians, had screamed at him when she saw him. He defended himself by declaring that a few miles away there was a beach on a lake where shirtless men, in little more than underpants, could be found all summer.

Sanjar was full of stories. He liked to say, "Man, stories. We *live* for stories." This is what made him so frustrated with his father in Iran who had the best stories but was spending his time writing a highly technical academic book.

That particular night at the dance club turned out to be a very good night. Sanjar used to challenge me to get ten girls to say "no" to me by the end of the night. I never could. Though I had all those phone numbers, I could never quite get the sequence down on when to call, what to say, and what to do. I did get better at talking to strangers.

For some reason one number I got that night led to an actual date. Sanjar and I were both excited because the girl was training to be a part of the Minnesota Orchestra as a violinist. The next afternoon I picked her up and we drove to a wine bar. I tried to sit up straight as she talked, knowing she was a professional musician. She had gone to Juilliard when she was fifteen, and her classmates would go deep into New York City every weekend.

"I went crazy. I went *crazy*," she said and looked at me until I stayed with her eyes.

A montage of sweat, streetlights, drugs, panties lost in the folds of sheets, taxicabs, and vomit plowed over my image of a studious musician. She then described an event from another phase of her life: a long walk with a young Senegalese man from evening till dawn through the streets of Paris. I listened and listened until it really was my turn to talk. I had my own international walks under the stars to describe. Instead, I offered a few cryptic lines and started to pick at my napkin.

When the waiter came over, she pointed to her wine glass and said, "I better have another." They shared a smile that seemed to be a code understood by people who date a lot.

The red wine in her second glass was half gone and being swirled around clockwise before going down her throat in gulps. She was sitting back from the table with one arm crossed over her chest, her hand resting on the bare skin of her other arm. Her face was getting pink.

"It's sad. It's so *sad*. You're being selfish with your words."

Soon we were walking towards the car with the sun still high in the sky, and I dropped her off at her apartment minutes later. As my car pulled into traffic, I felt the words, as usual, flowing through me in great generous waves to the tip of my tongue.

Chapter Four

WHEN SANJAR GOT his US citizenship, he returned to Iran for the first time in thirty years. Citizenship meant he could leave and re-enter the US with fewer problems. We were together in San Diego for the ceremony. He had moved there a couple of years before and was living in a tiny room in the house of a Vietnamese family. He got along with the grandfather, who spent all his time tending his hibiscus flowers and herb garden. The old man slept in a separate room from the grandmother—they had split long ago in Vietnam.

The grandmother suspected there was a romance between Sanjar and their daughter and spent a lot of time devising curses against him. One angry night she abandoned witchcraft and engaged in mundane sabotage by taking the license plates off his car. When I came out to visit one spring, I braced for a volley of malevolence launched from one dimension or another.

While I was out there, Sanjar was looking for other places to live. Half the people in San Diego work for the Department of Defense or other security-related businesses. For landlords this infuses the routine of background checks with a hilarious solemnity. We showed up to check on a room at one place, and the owner was describing his daily schedule, which included a shift at some defense company. During the interview he of course found out that Sanjar was from Iran.

An orange, fluffy cat hauled itself onto the dining table where Sanjar was filling out the rental application and answering questions. The obese cat stared at the moving pen. The skinny owner stared at Sanjar. Across his eyes, nestled in a calm face, played a duet of apprehension and civility. The cat fell like a blob onto the floor, leaving a pile of orange fur on Sanjar's completed application.

THE CITIZENSHIP CEREMONY was held in the huge San Diego Convention Center. A couple hundred citizens-to-be stood in line, the final chapters of many years' worth of paperwork in their hands. Sanjar stepped out of line to thank one official who had helped him with some forms two years earlier.

When we left there was an old Marine at the exit congratulating people. Sanjar's first act as an American was to ask him about the soldiers called to stand up first during the ceremony to be recognized as new Americans.

"But sir, is this a country where members of the military are treated differently from average people? I thought I was getting away from that!" Sanjar joked.

The gentlemen offered his thoughts before we cut away to stroll the waterfront. I don't remember what he answered, but the fact that the old Marine felt Sanjar *deserved* an answer said a lot about the country and how it desired to present itself.

On the oceanside walkway we were at ease. Sanjar was a good patriot, a questioner. I wondered if the country would have him. A level stream of sunshine warmed us. This stretch of Southern Californian desert had been turned into a walled garden on Mexico's border. A landscape once ruled by chaparral, a drought-resistant shrubland, was now a paradise filled with jacarandas, eucalyptuses, carrotwoods, flowers, and fountains.

It was America's best example of the good life its citizens had been promised through over two hundred years of advertising the right to "pursue happiness." This right, through the alchemy of money, vision, and violence, was always asserting itself—stretching like the Coronado Bridge over the harbor. A country with still-bright ideals and internal peace, betrayed by the shadows cast by mighty Navy aircraft carriers onto the deep-water harbors where they floated.

SANJAR HAD BEGUN life in the US while I was growing up. His father had sent him and his siblings here for an education in 1977. The bad news took its toll over the years. There was a lot of it from Iran. Filled with anxiety after three decades of scary reports, Sanjar went back to visit with his new US passport.

At the airport in Iran the security officer chided him: "Why have you been away so long? My dear, this is your country."

I wondered how it would be different for me when I arrived in Iran. Bad news does take its toll. I was born just before the 1979 Revolution, and for most of my life Iran had been comprised of two images. The first was the accusatory and mesmerizing seriousness of Ayatollah Khomeini's stare. He would appear on the screen when I watched Dan Rather's CBS Evening News with my parents as a young boy in the 1980s. During one report I saw a box floating above an enormous black sea made of people. I realized the box was a coffin and watched as it started to veer off in a strange direction before falling open. It was Ayatollah Khomeini's funeral.

My father grew up in a small village outside Cairo, Egypt, called Meet Swaid. He told me a story from the village about a savant that lived there. The man himself was non-verbal, but word that he was blessed had traveled the village grapevine. The adults treated him with varying degrees of reverence ranging from letting him be, to kissing his hand. Children were amused by his oddities and teased him whenever possible. On the day of his funeral, there were reports of the coffin lurching from left to right. At one point it began to take to the sky, only to be held down by the efforts of the villagers.

"I was there," my father told me. "The body didn't fly. We were made to believe that something divine had happened. I only witnessed theatrics."

Nevertheless, the man had been outfitted in holy armor by the villagers even before death. If anyone stole from or abused him, the Almighty would punish them.

There are many forms of protection, worldly and otherworldly; I had no intention of testing the efficacy of any of them. From childhood on I had a weird apprehension about even mentioning the Ayatollah, let alone criticizing him. Whether he was divinely anointed or not, people's belief generated a force field around him that was to be respected, and his starkly sober gaze announced to me a presence that was more than willing to *be* respected in return.

The second image of Iran was of yelling men. Yelling men at protests, funerals, elections, and bakeries. They had filled the television screen for as long as I could remember. I felt that if one were to peel the old wallpaper off an apartment wall in Iran, one would find beneath it the spittle of men who had yelled. These men threw themselves into chants and fist pumping with such vigor that one was forced to consider the local Iranian analysis: they were paid to protest. With no dance clubs or heavy metal mosh pits in Iran, street protests weren't just political—they were a form of cathartic entertainment.

MY BACKGROUND had the effect of putting me at relative ease in Muslim countries. While traveling I always thought that if war broke out, I would be Muslim and Egyptian. When I saw the US tanks coming up over the ridge, I doubted whether I would deny being Christian and American. A half is enough to make a whole, I reasoned: why impale myself on an identity that I was unsure of how to define?

The problem with that was the bitterness many Iranians felt towards Arabs. Arabs were the barefooted tribesmen who crossed the desert in the seventh century and destroyed a civilization. They brought with them a religion that many in Iran wear like a costume at best, a uniform at worst.

Sanjar's uncle, a well-known geologist, told a group of friends at work that even Islamic scripture says "Arabs are the worst of the nations." Muhammad lived during what is known as the "Time of Ignorance" in Arabia, when tribes were at each other's throats. Admittedly, the clashes were ritualized battles whose aim was not total victory but acts of bravery; this ensured that the tribes avoided extinction. Nonetheless, Sanjar's uncle was ridiculed for insulting people from the birthplace of Islam.

Sanjar's father, Sepehr, who had studied with the mullahs, sent the uncle back the next day with the passage marked in the Qur'an that says as much about Arabs.

When I told Sanjar's uncle that "Arab" was also a name given to anyone who speaks Arabic, he quipped, "You don't call Indians 'English' because they speak English." No, Iranians had something very specific in mind when they said "Arab."

Egyptians, however, were given a sort of reprieve born from geography and a long kinship in history and demeanor. When I was in Iran, the disdain shown Arabs was always qualified with short, determined speeches absolving Egyptians. "Now translate what I say to him. Word. For. Word," Sanjar's aunt told him, before delivering her own soliloquy about Egyptian exceptionalism.

Egyptian territorial continuity since ancient times, the unique history of their pharaonic past, and (until recently) their Coptic language and culture had made Egypt into a distinct nation for millennia. Many Egyptians, except when suffering from fevers of Pan-Arabism, saw themselves, their history, their culture, and their language as first Egyptian and then Arab.

Iranians also thought of their country as a whole entity with a similarly unbroken past. What they had in common was the self-assurance of belonging to civilizations that were thousands of years old, pre-dating the insecurities and failures of the modern nations bearing their names.

A HEAT DOME was smothering the Midwest when I returned from the citizenship ceremony in San Diego. I stepped out at dawn one morning into a balmy pocket of air. As I pedaled away from my house, I saw a squad car parked at the corner. Coasting past the cruiser, I peered into the window. A thick roll of yellow police tape sat on the black vinyl of the back seat.

Sanjar's words popped into my head: "Iran will be safer than Minneapolis." A few summers later, a man's fate would be caught in a weave of plastic yellow tape threaded from tree to tree.

That morning the tape was still tightly wound, its loose end unraveled from the roll by only a few inches. I looked at the well-tended houses as I glided by and figured that it had been years since the police had had to unroll a long strip of yellow tape in the neighborhood.

Chapter Five

EVERYONE ON THE BUS was asleep—even the chickens were quiet. I scratched my scalp and felt the fine grains of Saharan sand in my fingertips. It was night and I could not see much on the way from Errachidia to Ouarzazate. Without a map I was not sure how much farther there was to go. I had given my guidebook away to an old Moroccan on the train down from Tangiers.

Two more people were now awake on the bus: a mother and her sick child. The girl was throwing up, and soon the thin green plastic bag the mother was using to collect the vomit was filled. She was holding her girl in one hand and the bag in the other.

I offered to take the bag from her. On the roof of the bus was a cracked air vent that allowed cool desert air into the bus, and through which I could see a sliver of starry sky. Trying not to wake the sleeping tribesman next to me, I stood on my seat and reached up. The warm bag swished around above my head. It morphed around my hands as I tried to squeeze it through the crack. The sour aroma caught in my nostrils. I looked down at a rugged sea of dreaming Arab and Berber faces and crumpled jellabiyas.

I thought of Prophet Mohammed's saying: "More harm is done by fools through foolishness, than is done by evildoers through wickedness."

IN MINNEAPOLIS, a few years after my trip to Morocco, there was a British guy named Sameer with whom I would often have coffee at the Stinky Café. His family hailed from the northwest frontier of Pakistan, and he had a fearlessness that I envied. One

25

day we needed to find some camping gear in the city. I ran to get the café's ragged copy of the Yellow Pages that sat like ancient scripture under a pay phone.

Sameer frowned, then scowled, "I'm not someone who uses the Yellow Pages."

I had been thinking something similar when I handed over my guidebook to the old Moroccan, but I had not yet applied it to life in my home city. I closed the Yellow Pages and shoved it back under the pay phone. Then Sameer and I set off to get lost in our own city. The straight line between us and our task began bending and twisting into an afternoon of adventure underwritten by the help of strangers.

ALTHOUGH I HAD BEEN TO NORTH AFRICA a few times, there was a string of years in which I refused to even consider Sanjar's invitation to Iran, in Western Asia. Those same years were an inconvenient time to have a Muslim name in America. Still, I concluded that having an American passport in Iran would be an even more obvious risk.

After all, the few Americans who had spent time in Iran since the US Embassy hostages were released in 1981 were either prisoners or Special Forces. A few tour groups were whisked through the ruins of Persepolis and the carpet bazaars, but, more often than not, they were wedded to guides and government minders.

"When you have a problem with someone, you should talk," Sanjar often said. Not doing so, or setting prohibitive conditions to doing so, could only mean that both sides desired the impasse— as was the case with the American and Iranian governments. It was a schoolyard dance between bully and bullied, and the world had grown used to watching it. The result was that the citizens of each country had little chance to speak with one another and bypass the trolls guarding either side of the divide with their aging arsenals of propaganda.

MY FATHER AND UNCLE could never understand anyone's desire to go to the Middle East. They would take turns saying,

"Everyone is trying to leave, and you want to go?" What they couldn't appreciate was that their lives in America constituted continuous journeys. The pleasures, surprises, and exasperations of their journeys had trickled in on a daily basis since their arrival decades ago. It was plain to see in their interactions with native-born Americans. My dad would laugh talking about his neighbor who would burst out of his house and hop into his SUV, as if there was an impending invasion. He would speed down the street only to return a few minutes later with a carton of milk, or Starbucks coffee.

Even simple observations at mediocre small-town restaurants revealed an enduring fascination. One Mexican place had glued pre-fabricated patches of crumbling bricks to the walls. "Only in America," my amused father said, shaking his head, "would someone try to make something new look old."

Their childhood, spent in a village in the Nile Delta, had had its charms, which they admitted when pressed. An example was their choice of entertainment one afternoon: a radio. Except they did not have one. Their solution was to form a box out of mud and straw and then fill it with wasps. To raise the volume, a stick protruding from a hole in the box was given a stir.

The government in Egypt owned the airwaves and, as with a mud radio, you could not change the channel, only try to adjust the volume and hope to decipher a thoughtful message in the nationalistic drone. They were likely better off with the home-made radio, and the angry song of wasps.

The story became more bittersweet as the boys got older and the family moved to Cairo. My father got a job managing a mango orchard on an island in the Nile. The Jewish man who founded the orchard brought in the Alphonso mango variety from India—the only kind my father will eat to this day. The orchard was eventually sold to an Egyptian prince. My father lived on the island and, incredibly, had his own cook. The only problem was that his entire monthly salary went towards buying the food *to* cook.

There are two foggy episodes from that time that elicit responses from my father similar to those of President Reagan at the Iran-

Contra hearings. Whenever I seek more detail, he claims he "can't recall." The first is about the accusation that he killed a white donkey. The second is a romance and engagement gutted by tradition and class.

Idiotic wads of bureaucratic paperwork began to gum up and jam around my father, smothering his ambition and talent: a papier-mâché prison, familiar to anyone from a hot, developing country. He began to plot an escape.

In time, my father's youngest brother also soured on Egypt. As a teenager, excited to just be skipping school, he was cornered at an anti-government protest. President Anwar Sadat had sent in the thugs. My uncle was taken in and lined up with common criminals. Enduring wild cursing by a security officer, he offered a fatal personal protest: "You can curse all you want, but not about my parents." They took him to "the room," where the officer responded with baton blows that masked his own insecurity—the flaw of men who make up the blunt tools of any dictatorship. Broken and confused, my uncle looked up as the officer walked out and slammed the door; he spotted a young guard sitting in the corner, wiping tears from his eyes.

Soon after came the flight to America—first my father, then my uncle. They started families, and—in the way that immigrants from Third World countries do—pushed on doors and found them opening.

MY SISTER AND I grew up learning that we had it good. One lesson from our father came from a story about what constituted a special treat in Meet Swaid; a walnut-sized piece of sugar divided between seven brothers. As we got older, we were encouraged to not look away from the American underclass, whose dignity was like a lantern overturned in the rain.

So it was that a couple of days after September 11, I put a Qur'an in a duffel bag with a change of socks and bought a forty-five-day Greyhound bus pass. It was a surefire way to spend time among the underclass. I also wanted to see what the country was made of during a fragile time. The wounded thrashing about, the vengeance, had barely begun when I walked downtown and climbed aboard a bus headed west. I never took the Qur'an out. It just sat between T-shirts like a weight, a silent passenger, a stowaway. Instead I read Doris Lessing's series *Canopus in Argos: Archives*. Science fiction novels written on a scale of time and space so expansive that, in their pages, the holy books themselves become brief whispers in a stream of heedfulness, spoken through the millennia in a thousand different languages.

On highways in the middle of the night, when the passing landscape was walled off by darkness, I would pick my head up from my book. By my overhead reading light, I saw the scarred and nicked up faces of the poor: seventeen-year-old lovers eloping from Alaska, migrant workers slumped under hats, a gay cowboy wobbly with lust, and a red-eyed trombone player from Detroit, his limp body keeping time with the contours of the asphalt.

I felt the humble range of possibility within passengers in transit through a dazed country gathering its venom.

Wherever I was, the verdict kept coming back to me: not guilty. I checked in and out of cities. Trouble quickened under the surface, in places and among people I didn't know. Around the country, patriotic zealots, noticing the keepers had left the gates open a bit wider, paced and eyed the grazing grounds expanding into new reaches of American law and life.

MY BUS TICKET listed my Muslim name. As I passed it to drivers at stations in Portland, San Antonio, Macon, I hoped any misgivings they felt remained hidden to the passengers. They were ordinary Americans at work, with enough to worry about getting through the day. In that way I passed quietly through the hinterlands, hitting veins of trusted friends west to east.

I fell in love with a land that could hold their different lives and desires.

It was still dreamtime for young Americans of a certain class, who named and created as they moved. They took each direction, path, and job with confidence and ease, knowing they were laying out one of many lives.

In San Francisco, there was a friend with the seedling of a publishing career and a futon for my tired body. We took the long way back from a day trip to Santa Cruz. The dark distance was filled with a half-hour description of how her mother made matzo ball soup, which often required my friend to take both hands from the wheel. The car swerved and was hauled back onto a straight line before she began describing how the chicken boiled through the night. We laughed about the candid farts of her mother, the mighty midget, the first I had heard by a woman unrelated to me. A milestone.

In Salt Lake City a friend was trying to make it in professional indoor soccer. He had fallen for a judge's daughter, and the two of them took me to camp in the Wasatch-Cache National Forest, a low place in the high mountains. On the way, his mouth opening wide and eyes gleaming, he told me how a teammate marveled at a tornado that bypassed the Salt Lake City Temple, only to have a temple in another town struck by lightning and burned to the ground the following week.

In Savannah I stayed with an artist, a friend of a friend. I sampled the rhythm of wealthy art school students who breezily dipped here and there, to pick up an album, to watch the glow of algal blooms on the Atlantic surf, to stand around in an ocean parking lot tempting the next act of beauty. There was a girl from New Orleans who said in her Southern accent, "I could just die for a popsicle!" The words were so outrageous that I stiffened all over while another guy bounded into the passenger seat of her car.

I was reading *The Sentimental Agents in The Volyen Empire* from the *Canopus* series when the Greyhound entered Washington, DC. I sought out an old friend who worked at an economic think tank, who was living out an international dream with a cast of foreign boyfriends and roommates. When she left for work in the morning, I wandered the deserted city. At the stairs of the Capitol, a plump official in a tailored suit was giving an interview. A security guard tucked his head into his shoulder and said something.

Suddenly the guard took the official by the arm and walked him to a waiting black Cadillac. The genial confidence drained from his face. His cheeks jiggled as he left off what he was saying and climbed into the SUV, while the rest of us stood on the sidewalk exposed to whatever danger lurked.

I looked up at the Congressional Building and saw black-clad figures on the roof, like crows scanning for a glint of metal.

Inside the building a forced air of casualness reigned until I took a wrong turn down a hall. Well-dressed people lost their composure and began to wrinkle their suits to get my attention. "Sir, sir, SIR! That is a restricted area ... this way please."

I sat down to watch a legislative session, during which a senator recounted the long friendship between the United States and Pakistan. In the House, a representative pleaded for a small Pacific island that had outlasted its use to the military.

In New York City, ignoring the distaste of my host, I clamored to the smoking ruins of the Trade Center and witnessed civilians nosing along the edges of the battlefield. What were they looking for? It could have been fiery shards of emotional sustenance, or forbidden awe at a wounded giant. Or maybe it was a bridge back to reality. The tangy aluminum air wakened the senses, but around me, people still wavered hypnotically like strands of sea kelp in the current. As we rode back to his apartment, my friend described a charred hand on a roof found several blocks away from the site.

Returning from Montreal, my last stop, where my sister was living European-style at a discount, I anticipated some remarks from the border patrol. The agent who unpacked my bag asked the same question twice and caught me with two undeclared sweaters. They were the kind with big collars that make you feel French. The thick green book with Arabic writing was turned briefly in another agent's hands and shoved back in my bag.

A climate had been cast in America. In Eugene, Oregon, early in my American trip, I had walked down Main Street one warm evening and heard from storefront speakers a loud rebranding of enemies by the President of the United States: after bubbling menacingly on the back burner under a policy of isolation, Iran was now officially evil.

Nearly ten years would pass before I would be able to see for myself if this were true.

Chapter Six

THE ROOM SHOULD have burned down. After the Christmas concert I went to lock up my classroom and saw a single candle still burning in the dark; a tendril of green butcher paper floated within inches of its flame. The chalkboards of the room were made out to look like the brick wall of a Persian garden. Green paper had been carefully cut to resemble hanging vines. Kebab skewers sat in a pile that could have filled a quiver, stripped of their meat. A few crumpled Dixie cups on a large metal tray soaked in the juice of a few leftover pomegranate seeds. It was our school's yearly celebration, the Festival of Lights, and my classroom had chosen to represent Iran.

Weaving through the room was a path, and every few feet was a chapter of the story of Scheherazade: the young woman who educates and tames the rage of a jilted king through storytelling. Having been betrayed by his first wife, the king took a new wife each night and beheaded her in the morning. After marrying him, Scheherazade delayed her own fate by telling him a story that gives birth to another story that does not end before he falls asleep. In the morning he lets her live because he must hear the ending of the tale that night. Like a sort of Hydra of stories Scheherazade's story grows for one thousand and one nights.

Josh, one of my students, had stayed up all night writing it out on large paper and illustrating scenes. He wanted to be a writer and his shoulders were always held high as if they were being coiled to launch an idea. He was the kind of student that circles about the confines of a classroom like a hawk, scanning for suitable perches for his intelligence. To set the tone by the door he had the science teacher, a polymath, draw the king's executioner in expert gory bombast.

That night, when the parents and students arrived at the door during their tour, they were greeted by the drawing of a huge ax dripping blood. Then they followed the candle-lit tale episode by episode in rapt clusters. I saw two girls walk through three times. Josh spent the night in the darkest corner of the room, tapping gently on a drum.

AS A SPRING RITUAL for a couple of years, I would restart my quest to obtain a visa for travel to Iran. I had gotten over my existential foot-dragging. Now it was time to face the bureaucratic hurdles. In what turned out to be a smaller challenge then expected, I discovered there was no Iranian bureaucracy to face in America. The Iranian Embassy sits shuttered in Washington, DC.

Therefore, all visa applications are processed in the Pakistani Embassy by the Interests Section of the Islamic Republic of Iran.

When I tried to get through to the Egyptian Embassy, to see if I could enter Iran as an Egyptian, I got three answering machines and a wrong number. Talking to an Iranian was fairly easy at the Interests Section. With my first call I reached a patient gentleman who told me they needed a visa authorization number. I could get this through a sponsor in Iran who petitions the Foreign Ministry on my behalf.

When I mentioned this to Sanjar, he had one of his father's employees go to the Foreign Ministry. The employee went there numerous times, but had no luck.

Another option was to go on a pre-packaged tour. The groups have guides and government minders. The tour company advertisement "Visit Friendly Iran" in a popular American magazine confronts presumed attitudes head-on with a picture of three smiling girls in hijabs. "Friendly": a shameful adjective under the circumstances, equivalent to saying "my black friend who is a real nice guy." A trip where you know all the stops ahead of time is like watching a movie with someone who has already seen it twice.

With such tours, drama and possibility have been leached out for safety's sake. I kept looking for other ways to get a visa.

THE IDEA to try going by way of an academic conference came from my Canadian brother-in-law. It was the spring of 2009. I was in Minneapolis talking on the phone to my sister. She was living in Halifax, Nova Scotia, at the time. We have a tradition. Every so often we reassure each other through incantations of exotic destinations.

Nova Scotia was not one of them.

However, it did not matter where we were. The tradition lived because of where we would dream to find ourselves. When I was studying in Iowa, I got a postcard with an update on her life. Looking closer, in tiny print, I saw the words "Taj Mahal" isolated like an island in the white space under the address. If I went to India the giant gravesite would not be high on my list of things to visit, but the name was alluring. When she was working as an office temp in the catacombs of a downtown skyscraper, she got an e-mail from me about the best land route from Samarkand to Bukhara. I sent it from a student computer lab in the Midwest.

A trip to Iran had begun to look far-fetched, and I was ready to add it to the list of magical destinations carried through mundane life like a talisman.

That night, on the phone, I spoke to her about the book *The Persian Bride,* by James Buchan, which I had read a couple years before. It tells the story of a ragged young British man pulled through the last third of twentieth-century Iranian history. He is on a quest for a young beauty that had been shimmering in his hand. They married but were separated by the upheavals of the Islamic Revolution. Roaming the ruins of a country that was once the pride of the Middle East, he settles in Esfahan, the city where he first came to teach English. Crippled and destitute, uniden-tified lines of Persian poetry run through his mind. Grief keeps him company but joy and luck skim past his life like prayer beads through the fingertips of an atheist.

ONE DAY AT THE Stinky Café Sanjar had seen me reading the book. It had a bare ankle and foot on the cover that he enjoyed, but he recommended getting a "real" book on Iran. I loved it but read the rest of it trying to figure out what was missing.

My sister and I had been on the phone for an hour and my ear was mushy and red like a gummy bear. I was letting a honey-storm of longing for a broader world flow right through the line. The balm of our tradition was gradually cooling me down. Then I heard some sounds in the background. It was her husband muttering something. I forgot that it was two hours later on the East Coast of Canada. My sister mentioned that he was in his sweatpants as if to temper the credibility of what he was saying.

He is a professor in the humanities, and had received a message requesting paper submissions for a conference in Tehran on "Education and Global Literature." Enter an abstract and I could become a presenter or participant. If the abstract was accepted, the organizers would help me get a visa authorization number.

THAT NIGHT I sat down to write an abstract for a paper that did not exist. By dawn I submitted it and was on my way to becoming an "independent scholar." I was accepted as a participant and told to wait for an authorization number. After a month and a half with no answer I halfheartedly plotted land routes from Turkey. The border crossings there, according to European travelers, yielded a trickle of visas, but absolutely none for Americans.

When I checked my messages again a month later, I found an authorization number at the bottom of a long message. The conference would begin in ten days, and I had to get the visa from Washington, DC, and arrive in Tehran before it started.

My friends and family were silent. I thought they were sad to see me go. Now I think they were all just holding their breath.

A COUPLE OF DAYS before my flight, I was reading a Marco Polo picture book to my five-year-old son Khalil. Marco has just returned to Venice after twenty-four years of traveling. As I turned the pages, Khalil kept searching the pictures for the young boy he had seen at the beginning of the book.

Wanting to be useful, Marco becomes the captain of a ship and sails bravely into battle when Venice is attacked. He is captured and placed in a crowded Genoese prison, and languishes in chains with a group of skinny men in white loincloths.

"Baba, did they give them food?"

"Stale bread and some watery soup probably."

"What are those?" Khalil was pointing at the little grey blobs at the feet of the prisoners.

"Rats."

"Why rats?"

"Because they're in a dungeon and that's where rats live."

I saw Khalil's eyes drift off the pages of the book to his desk, lingering on a Lego man holding a spear twice its size. Then Khalil glanced back at the picture book, where Marco was standing in the prison cell dictating his stories to Rustichello.

"Where are their chains?"

"Right there. See, they're just hard to see."

"Baba."

"Yes?"

"So why did they even keep them alive?"

Chapter Seven

BEFORE FLYING TO DUBAI en route to Tehran, I spent one night in New York City.

Self-importance: that is the scent in the air of New York. I had a twenty-four-hour layover to spend insulated by the crown jewel of the Anthropocene. Concentric circles of photo-snapping tourists emanated from Times Square, documenting the influence of our species. I was content to meet up with one old friend.

I knew Rob from the School of Oriental and African Studies in London. Our friendship survived ten years with the occasional phone call and a retelling of our introduction to Pancake Day in the United Kingdom. While out in London one night, we had heard about the holiday. As we made our way home from a pub, through a narrow alleyway near Kings Cross Station, we found our path blocked by a biological feature that rose a full half foot into the air. Someone had failed to observe Pancake Day in moderation. Now, their earthy farewell to the festivities was piled across the width of a seventeenth-century alley.

A lot of Rob's teeth show when he tells the story. I missed Rob and his teeth and was eager to see what was new in his life, and hear the story retold in person.

Rob picked me up from the airport in a light blue pickup and we headed to his apartment in Brooklyn. Grant money had dried up for his documentary work, so he had some free time. As we drove, he pointed out one of his favorite views of New York: a cemetery with Manhattan in the background.

He told me of his Iranian-American friend who had just gone to Iran for the first time, accompanied by his aging mother. Their reactions matched those of other travelers from different generations: the younger fearing what they will find, the older fearing what they will not. After a month the man was fulfilled and energized, the mother drained and distraught. They flew home early.

AFTER DROPPING OFF my bags, we went to an Italian restaurant where scenes from *The Sopranos* had been filmed and talked about our lives. Two men in checkered suits sat at a table across the dim wood-paneled room. At the table was a buzzer for the waiter. We didn't need it: an ancient Italian in a tuxedo appeared every few minutes to fill our water glasses.

Rob had fallen for a girl. He told me the whole story, from the heroic first smile while waiting for the elevator with her, to the ordinary life that took hold as months went by without seeing her. When they ran into each other again one day, she remembered him. She asked him, "If you hadn't smiled that day by the elevator, things would be different, wouldn't they?"

I squashed a clump of stewed tomatoes with my fork and the description of his feelings for her sunk in. I imagined the man in the funny checkered suit raising a pistol and shooting; then I imagined watching a single bullet sailing across the room, over the saucy remains of my cannelloni, and striking the buzzer at our table to confirm Rob's Italian heritage—the gesture of a people who take big gulps of life.

A glint of light hit the name tag of our waiter, Luchino. In his hands were two tiny cups of espresso. We drank them down and promised to be friends forever. I would be on my own for the remainder of the afternoon and night. Rob had to go visit his sister in Connecticut. He passed me his apartment key and the light blue pickup found its way out of the city.

TO BE IN NEW YORK was like dating the prettiest girl in school. The excitement of being by her side was outpaced by the anxiety of keeping up with her. I spent eight hours in Central Park trying not to be possessive of the city's spirit. As I sat on a bench, the sexy, bored lives of the people in the windows rising over the treetops started to take shape. A bike wheel spun in a patch of dirt. The electricity of that daydream gave way to thoughts about women as I edged towards Iran, a place that is held up as one of the exemplars of chauvinism.

Before leaving town, Rob had coached me on how to get to JFK, drawing a little map on the back of my printed e-ticket. The train ride was easy, followed by a comfortable flight.

I arrived in Dubai on Friday morning. The metro was closed down for the time of communal prayer. To make use of the few hours of the layover, I headed out of the terminal to find a bus. Every city is fabricated, but in Dubai, the speed and volume of the fabrication help bring that fact home. The smell of paint and cement, the fully intact surfaces of buildings—everything struck me as I stepped outside.

At the airport bus stop, I shuttled between the signs of different bus lines while weaving between South Asian workers, roasting in their white *shalwar qameez*, the baggy pants and tunics of their homelands. The temperature was nearing 110 degrees. I was wrinkling my face at the posted bus schedule until I resembled the eighty-year-old next to me who was doing the same. A Filipina barista on her way home responded to my confusion, took mercy, and swept me into a bus idling nearby.

We took seats in the "Women and Families" section of the bus, which was heading toward the Mall of the Emirates. We got along. At one point I told her a story that made her laugh so hard I barely caught the offer she made me under her breath.

The bus brakes screeched as we pulled to a stop. Nodding to a side street she asked, "Do you want to lie down with me in a room?"

The offer expired by her next breath and she was on to another topic, the bus lurching back into traffic. I blinked very slowly and wrapped a strap of my backpack around my hand.

SANJAR HAD ARRIVED in America when he was a teenager. One afternoon in those early days, he found himself with one of his new American friends sitting on the couch watching television. One hand gripped a chocolate bar the size of a VHS tape while the other broke off chunks and hurtled them towards his mouth like meteorites. A tall glass of milk on the coffee table reflected the orange and brown colors of a sitcom from the late 1970s.

From behind Sanjar a hand flew through the air, compressing the dark curls on his head for an instant until it landed heavily onto the back of his skull. The hand belonged to Naveed, his older brother. Upon entering the apartment Naveed and his Afghan friend had found the scene: Sanjar snacking on chocolate while a pretty girl sat next to him. Naveed's hand remained at his side, but the message was clear to Sanjar that an unwritten rule of after-school behavior had been broken: get your appetites in the right order.

THE FILIPINA and I made our way out of the family section to the second level of the bus. The first row was open. A large wind-shield dropping past our feet divided us from the hot air. As we settled in our seats her chest heaved under her tight black Costa Coffee shirt. Her physical frankness suggested sex without drama. I ignored the epiphany that this is the promise of time with a pros-titute. In Dubai there are many, some working full time, others augmenting meager salaries.

I appreciated her shamelessness. Her loud voice in the conser-vative silence of the bus drew attention, but she carried on with ambassadorial immunity. I felt the eyes of some of the roasted South Asian work force in the back of the bus staring with antic-ipation, indifference, lust. Many just stared out the window, exhausted from six-day workweeks, missing their families.

A pothole jolted our jaws. The conversation went quiet.

This silence set off what would become a nuisance throughout the trip: waking nightmares. In this episode I imagined a balmy, shadowy room, the smell of dust, and the feel of it on sheets. I am adrift on brown mounds of skin. I look over and a Costa Coffee

T-shirt is draped on a chair. There's a loud crash. We jump out of bed. Someone has kicked in the door. Silhouetted in the doorway are the flowing robes of the Virtue Police.

Another bump in the road snaps me out of it. She's beside me texting in Tagalog.

In Dubai, around the time I was there, a British couple was imprisoned for a month after kissing in a restaurant. The by turns pious and delusional norms of a modern Arab society were being exposed. The man, from a Muslim family, should have known better (the story goes), but the woman was found guilty as well. As an American, I found a devilish amusement in the spectacle's reversal: a white woman had violated the purity of a brown man.

AN HOUR LATER we were in the mall walking towards a Carrefour. She described the contract she had signed with Costa Coffee, how much she made, other details about a guest worker's life. It was not international business, but nor was it Saudi domestic work, a hell that trapped many South and Southeast Asian women on the Arabian Peninsula.

She had lent a friend $150 to visit the Philippines. Now she was feeling short of cash. The coins scattered around her apartment would not add up, she decided, unless they could be put into a cute piggy bank. I got bored following her around the store, for no reason other than a suppressed hope that she would repeat her offer.

She joined a group of countrymen standing near the mountain bikes, and vanished behind a force field of rapid-fire Tagalog consonants and vowels. I left and stumbled deeper into the gilded lunar colony of the Mall of the Emirates, embarrassed, and wary of a reckless horniness.

I FOUND A COSTA COFFEE, ordered an Americano, and looked for a seat. I searched for that rift that develops inside me when I travel. The psychic adjustment to unfamiliar surroundings that lets me become new again, a stranger to myself. Becoming a stranger to promises and responsibilities back home was the gamble that came along with it.

Huge black leather chairs faced each other alongside a four-story window looking onto Ski Dubai—an indoor slope filled with real fake snow. I pressed my cargo pants into some shiny leather across from a beautiful Ethiopian woman.

All things being equal, which they are not, man meets a woman halfway. He answers the time she spends buying a push-up bra and arranging her breasts in a blouse with a low-cut neckline with the duration of his gaze. As I became enamored with the rounded triangle of skin under her white suit top, equilibrium, not shame, was settling in. Not interested in skiing with her three British friends, she was drinking her iced mocha and dawdling on her cell phone. She was open to talking. I found out she had immigrated to Finland but owned a hair salon in Abu Dhabi, successfully working the jet stream of money and style.

"*Poika. Kahvi aika!* Boy. It's coffee time!" I sputtered the only phrase I knew in Finnish as an impromptu test for her back story. When I described her to Sanjar in Iran, he asked if she was Russian. When I said no, he responded, "She probably wasn't working then." In Dubai, businessmen will sometimes assume that women who are sitting alone are prostitutes, but she was a *businesswoman*. I had started the conversation and she had more money than me. The situation turned inside out, and who I was became the question.

"POY-kah," she corrected me. Then her own suspicion appeared at the corners of her eyes. "How do you know Finnish?"

"Believe me, it's stranger to hear you speak it," I replied, recalling the lessons Marie's mother had given me while we ate cardamom bread over a game of Scrabble in northern Minnesota. "Do you like it there, in Finland?"

"I do. I've been there since I was fifteen years old, so now it feels more like home than Ethiopia."

"Really?"

"Yeah, but I spend most of my time away in London now, and I have to take care of the business here." She typed a quick reply on her phone and said, "My sisters and mother are in Helsinki, so I go back all the time."

"Sweet." I watched a skier circle back to the quad lift that churned towards the top of the mountain. "Do you have an apartment here for when you have to work?"

"I stay at my friend's flat. It's really nice actually."

"Yeah?"

"Yes. She has these Italian silk sheets on her bed," she said leaning back. Wriggling her straw to the bottom of her cup, she added, "They are *really* comfortable."

"Okay, Helsinki is for family. London and Abu Dhabi for business. So, what is Dubai?"

"Dubai?" She looked down into her cup, where light-brown traces of milk, coffee, and chocolate were laced around the ice cubes. "Dubai is for fun."

I swallowed hard and reached in my pocket to fondle the few crumpled dirhams in my possession. It was enough for a metro ride back to the airport.

I FOUND THE METRO station at the end of the mall. Friday prayer had ended, and service had resumed. Like much else in Dubai, the mall was empty bright space, shielded from the desert sun by glass, metallic surfaces, sharp angles, and the best temperature control money could buy. To my eyes, the spotlessness signaled death—a mausoleum of perfection, like the mansions in American suburbs.

On the train platform I stared up at the sign reading "To Jebel Ali." In the film *Code 46* the near future is a world divided into rich urban centers called the "inside," and the underclass with their barren lands on the "outside." To move from the outside to the inside, you need to obtain *papeles*, travel documents—easy for some, impossible for others. Two lovers flee to a place called Jebel Ali in the Middle East, where special travel clearance is not required. A place where anything is possible.

I had thought all along that it was a screenwriter's made-up city. I jumped on the train and rode in the direction of Jebel Ali.

At the Burj Khalifa, currently the tallest tower in the world, I was obliged to take a photo. Its final height was kept a secret until completion to foil rival blueprints from Jeddah to Shanghai. From a distance the tower looks like a mirage; from up close it remains a mirage. Despite its majesty, it was just another exercise in purchased virility. The odd case of having something big and not knowing what to do with it: Arab wealth in a nutshell.

The other use concocted for oil wealth was worse: keep the Iranian regime dangerous so that frightened Arab monarchs keep buying Western arms. At least, that was the knowing analysis of Iranians I spoke to.

The role of dutiful customer was once played by the Shah of Iran, who had a weapons fetish. He read all the tank and gun magazines, and personally placed orders for the army. When Iran was a US ally, it was strong enough to "stand in front of the Soviet Union" for two weeks if necessary, according to Sanjar. Now Iran was supposed to be the menace, a reputation created by its own bluster and regional power plays more than any real military capabilities. Scary stage makeup applied by the United States also helped secure the hostile image.

IT WAS NOT FAIR in the end to single out the self-conscious grandeur of the Burj Khalifa. Many cities have plans to stay on the map by rising up to a mile above it—the reported height of the proposed Jeddah Tower in Saudi Arabia.

I got off the metro at the station below the tower, smelled my melting skin, confronted the structure with my camera, and wondered how a reach so high, so flooded with light, could anchor a civic life that was apparently subterranean. At its base, looking around, I saw paused construction projects, precious clumps of green landscaping, waves of heat coming off all surfaces like radar echoes, and not a single person. It was a Friday afternoon, but I still felt that German engineering combined with relentless sunlight had purified the landscape of the creep and crawl of organic life. This land was fit for either spiritual asceticism or untethered modernity; Dubai's former desert nomads, drinking bottled glacier water somewhere in the bowels of this air-conditioned future, were planning for both.

The metro delivered me back to the airport. From Dubai, an emirate careening ahead on a titanic wave of steel and glass, frighteningly limitless, I turned towards Iran, a place restricted by sanctions from importing bicycle parts.

ITALIAN, FRENCH, SPANISH, German. I was dreaming of an international life with my arms full of language books at the downtown Minneapolis library. Each day I had waited at its doors at 9:55 a.m., along with homeless people and stay-at-home mothers with strollers. The smell of smoke, seasoned crotch, and armpit mixed with perfume and baby powder in the packed lobby. The Farsi language book had been left on the shelf because another year since Sanjar's invitation had passed with no hope of a visa.

When the doors opened, I raced up the stairs to occupy one of the beautiful private study rooms: a desk, lamp, outlet, and window looking out on and masking the sounds from Hennepin Avenue.

Again, I found my favorite room taken by a teenager who for the past two days had been poring over a huge purple *Guinness Book of World Records*. As I was staked out at a table near the room, I heard him talking to himself: "Goddam! Motherfuckin' broke-ass headphones again." The kid sat under a baseball hat so high on his head it looked like a ten-gallon cowboy hat.

When he got up to go the bathroom, I felt all the tingling prejudices that are embossed on the American soul rising up to my lighter skin. When he walked his legs swung wide and loose so his pants would not fall down. He returned, entered the study room, and disappeared behind the huge purple book. It was his favorite room too.

On the third day of waiting with the hobos and mothers, experiencing the full panorama of human odors, I ran up the stairs and smack into the big purple cover of the *Guinness Book Of World Records*. I figured he was getting the vicarious thrill of looking at a picture of Michael Jordan soaring above the rim with his sack at eye level. I had seen a handful of my students easing their minds from time to time during class in the sanctuary of basketball stats and photos.

Maybe he was reading a thumbnail biography of Roger Bannister, who was told that breaking the four-minute mile barrier was impossible. I got up, walked down one level, and found an open room.

Behind the wall at my back, a homeless man was at the concert grand piano of the library's private music room. I read to myself the little placard on the desk stating that rooms are intended for those seeking a quiet place to study and write.

Three stories below was a bus stop I could see from the huge window that reached from the floor to the ceiling of the study room. On the bus stop bench, blocking a real estate agent's picture and phone number, was a bald white man in a red satin jacket buttoned tight against a big belly; next to him was a lady with Dwarfism, both her feet pointed sideways in the same direction, the suitcase beside her matched her height. A black man with fraying cornrows and raw indigo denim shorts, his elbows on his knees, was also seated on the bench. The way his hands were clasped in front of him, he could have been leading a prayer for all of them.

The homeless man pounded louder on the keys and I could hear his voice now. It was Lionel Richie's song "Hello." It began to sound better and better.

Chapter Eight

SHE GLANCED AROUND every few seconds. It was night near Darakeh, a popular mountain path in North Tehran. I had been in the country nearly a month. Finally, she lifted her eyes past the poplar branches to the sky and kept them there. The sky was bleached with city light and only a few stars flickered.

"In Iran you feel like there are eyes always looking," she whispered to Sanjar.

I knew the feeling. The first time I had felt it was in the boarding area for my outbound flight to Tehran from Dubai International. In my mind, everyone was a potential spy, tasked with observation. I found myself gauging the movements and motives of every passenger. Between then and touching down at Imam Khomeini International, any series of false moves—the jerk of a backpack, a twitch of the head, a mistimed glance—would expose either me or them. I sought refuge in the airport bathroom. There was a knock on my stall door. I concluded that it was not a vacancy check but Iran's secret police giving me a brief reminder that they knew my shit stunk.

I was so close now to Iran. Although I've never fallen victim to a panic attack, I began to sense my mind and body as a collection of distinct pieces floating eerily away from each other.

Returning to the boarding area, I focused on safe targets for my vigilance—casual, internationally recognized ones, like the television and dyed blond hair. Two young women, their hijabs not on yet, sat next to their plastic shopping bags. A few children bobbled drunkenly out of range of their parents and then found the environment impoverished—tired, distant, and tense adults, and grey immobile chairs. Soon they cuddled back into their mothers' arms. I rested my eyes on them and associated with their innocence.

SITTING THERE with my hands folded on my lap at Dubai International, I thought about personal connections that would incriminate me in the eyes of Iranian security.

I could only think of people I knew in the US military. A cousin who is an Army recruiter, another in the Marines who flew sorties in Cobra helicopters in Iraq and Afghanistan. I thought of a friend who joined the Navy and worked on a nuclear submarine, packed into a metal tube beneath the Pacific for months at a time. All I had was an unflattering description of life underwater: fresh food gone within two weeks; oxygen released in batches each day, its manufactured freshness dealt a deathblow by the rancid socks and briefs of young service members. He had spoken about how the close quarters could dull depth perception. To counteract the effect, the submariners would take turns standing at one end of the compartment through which the missile tubes passed, focusing and refocusing on a ping-pong ball held at the other.

Back on land he left the Navy and got married. I showed up at the wedding in Madison, Wisconsin, without having returned the invitation.

"I have trouble with paperwork," I told him, attempting to apologize.

"Is that how you ended up at a college in Des Moines for two years?" The retort was sharp but true.

A strict code of silence about his missions meant I had no good intelligence about trips under the Strait of Hormuz to trade for my life in the event of an interrogation in Iran. So instead I analyzed that old conversation we had at his wedding. "Paperwork" was a minefield and it had hurt me before, hitting my life unexpectedly from beneath the surface. Living in Santiago De Compostela, Spain, I planned the next years of my life with an 800-*peseta* calling card, to return a message I got from a college soccer coach in Iowa who had tracked me down. I was lazy and indecisive, but mostly I did not want to figure out the series of stamps and signatures required for another visa extension to stay in Spain. When my car was loaded for college in the driveway that August, I had an expression on my face that my father waited a few years to tell me about. The folk meaning of De Compostela is "field of stars," and I had haphazardly consigned myself to a state on the other side of the Atlantic known as a national park for just that: fields and stars.

As is the case for most people, my crimes in the past were against myself. They took the shape of minor lapses in affection and will. These quiet things imperceptibly changed the course of life until suddenly a girlfriend was gone, or an address in Des Moines became mine.

In the departure terminal in Dubai, I finally found the mirrors that enabled me to see the face my father had seen that day. When I scanned the waiting area, I saw Iranians returning from all over the freer world: Paris, Berlin, Vienna, Geneva, Milan. Social media was in its infancy, still an obscure term invented by a marketing strategist, but the shadow on each face was the unmistakable trace of FOMO, fear of missing out. I would like to say that many saw through the West's sparkling commercial shell, which accounts for some of its allure, but judging from the quantity of the shopping bags next to each of the passengers, they were yearning for it with every fiber of their new outfits.

I remembered that Dubai, before the discovery of oil, had been famous as a port where pearl oysters were collected from the shallow banks of the Persian Gulf. Young men had left their camels and date palms to work on one of some twelve thousand dhows, diving for oysters. Eventually families and whole tribes settled by the coast.

A flowing stream going through a date garden used to be the definition of luxury for a Bedouin family. What was done with wealth and freedom, once won, was a question inadequately answered by the both the Mall of America and Mall of the Emirates. They loaded the present with stuff, like they were barricading a door through which the past was trying to enter. They worshiped the future, but neither culture knew what to do with it.

IRAN LOOMED. The impression of a broader, lighter world—the carefree images that form the compelling holographic ideals of Western life and liberty—began to recede. I felt the myths of the West being internalized unreflectively, even spitefully, within the most stylish of the waiting passengers. What was left were three hundred glum faces. Sanjar's mantra came to me: "You want what you can't have." How different it was for me sitting there, scared, but feeling I was on the trail of shiny treasures, not leaving them behind.

We all boarded. A ginger ale and croissant later, we were descending into Imam Khomeini International Airport. I hadn't packed any English books, and now decided I'd leave my American magazines on the Emirates plane when we landed. I didn't want to risk being called a subversive when customs found the photo of the bare thigh in the pop-star profile in my copy of *The New Yorker*.

ANDREW WAS on a Fulbright Scholarship in Cairo, studying at Al-Azhar University, and had also found the conference his only way into Iran.

He was the only other American on board the flight, but I did not meet him until customs in Iran. He wore a brown tweed sport coat and had mousy but sharp brown eyes. A disciplined modesty and politeness guided his behavior—an acquired demeanor of the supersmart that hides nuanced views from the bludgeons of the ignorant.

Being young and American guaranteed us some extra attention. Upon arrival we were led away from the customs area down a hall. His Arabic was lively, but splintered against the ears of our Farsi speaking host. When our passports were taken, I watched the soldier walking away with them. I felt like Hansel, his bread snatched and sealed in a ziplock baggie, with the footsteps of the soldier carrying it falling trackless on the marble floor. For a few minutes there was not a single person or sound in that branch of the airport.

The airport *had* once been abandoned.

For over twenty years it sat, the American architects and contractors who envisioned another Dallas Love Field having fled after the 1979 revolution. I meditated on the tiny trickle of activity in the airport. As the hall reverted to that hastily instituted silence, I wondered what else about Iran was frozen in time.

I KNEW A THOROUGH background check was occurring behind closed doors. A security algorithm applied to our names would decide our fate—one constantly fed inputs such as changing geo-political alignments, upcoming international summits, the quality of the kebab, and the post-dinner mood it produced in the security official working that night.

I discovered during that long wait that I am an optimist.

The wait, in fact, was not painful. Although the phantom limb of the U.S. Embassy hostage crisis did throb in the shadows, fed by a steady stream of ghost stories about Iran in the media, the situation lacked true foreboding.

Far from haunting, the dim halls at that late hour began to summon the sleepy ease of an inefficient country. A floor below we heard the echoes of a group of soldiers. They were 18- to 22-year-old conscripts returning from dinner. They slouched and joked up some stairs, straightening their backs just so as they passed.

A man in a dark navy suit eventually appeared. Directions to follow here, sit there, were given without contempt. It was a welcome change from the vibes I felt at Dubai International from the dour young sheik manning the customs gate. It is always a lottery, the people encountered on a journey. Good and bad must be stitched together into a pattern that provides some kind of guidance.

In our new waiting area, a skinny soldier passed by serenely. On his face was the strain of plodding through his few words of English: "How...are...you?" Sanjar anticipated that I would experience some discomfort at the airport. He said I would then appreciate his ordeal whenever he re-entered the U.S. The discomfort though, was not materializing.

After being fingerprinted, Andrew and I carried on. Our passports were taken out of the plastic bags and handed back to us. We were relieved but a little disappointed by the civil treatment. Andrew described the six-hour hassle he had had to go through trying to get into Lebanon.

As we cleared the gate, I joked, "If people continue to be nice here, what will I brag about back home?"

SANJAR MET ME at the airport with a cab driver he trusted. We gave each other a muscular, unsentimental hug. Seeing Sanjar felt very normal. It was just another setting in which we were friends. I quickly looked at some signs in Farsi to remind myself I was in Iran. Andrew went with a representative from the conference. Right then our trips diverged. We would enter into two different versions of the country. Andrew would be subject to the airtight scheduling of the conference organizers, and I would be following the jazz soundtrack that is Sanjar's life.

Sanjar and I ended up spending the first two days with Andrew anyways, hanging out in the hotel lobby, eating, and bussing to and from the National Library, where the conference was held. Sanjar said it was worth staying in touch with him. Andrew was a future ambassador.

At Al-Azhar he had been immersed in Islamic thought, a good-natured attempt to embrace a point of view and see if it felt rational from the *inside*. He seemed fatigued by his review of one thousand years of jurisprudence. At one point he turned to me in exasperation and said, "I've tried to get it, but I'm getting to the point where I'm going to have to say that I understand—but do not agree."

DRIVING BACK TO TEHRAN from Imam Khomeini International took a couple of hours. I had time to sit in the backseat of the taxi and enjoy that sweet spot of arrival: the feeling of calm after thousands of miles, and a lingering view of myself from up high. The weight of the planet moaning to a new stop, and my feet gently stepping onto a destination, the worth of its lode expanding in sync with my own exploration of it.

The countryside flew by outside the window, unbroken but for the massive Holy Shrine of Imam Khomeini, glowing like a giant otherworldly ship in the deep ocean of night, four lit minarets climbing ninety-one meters high like elevators to the surface. Farther along a bus-sized statue of a hand, inscribed with Qur'anic phrases, thrust up from the side of the highway, waving to its head eleven thousand miles away on Easter Island. Sanjar and I just giggled about being in Iran together, in between his Farsi banter with the driver.

Imperceptibly Tehran began to emerge. The taste of the air changed. Soon, like the arid desert cities of Cairo, Dubai, Damascus, and Baghdad, which straddle and cling to the edge of mountains or rivers, Tehran eased out of the dry night on the horizon in a suave mellow-orange bloom.

Pressing my face to the window, I listed off mundane sights—supermarket, billboard, family, apartment—marveling at their presence like a person checking a newborn for all its toes. They were all there. Tehran was inhabited by humans.

Sepehr, Sanjar's father, was awake when we got to the apartment after 2 a.m., having just returned from a party at their family garden. We had met a few times in Minnesota, and he seemed just as amused as Sanjar to see me standing in Tehran. We sat and had fruit and tea in the living room. Though both big talkers, Sanjar and his father were quiet, allowing my last bits of energy to be spent on tasting the superior sweetness of green melon from Persia.

THE NEXT DAY at noon we went to the Hotel Enghelab to register for the conference. I had one hundred sixty dollars in cash and a Visa card. The registration was two hundred dollars. No problem, I thought: I had shown up in Morocco years before with only a debit card, wielding it like a capitalist lightsaber.

Walking into the center of Tangiers from the port, I knew I'd hit an ATM. Would-be guides trailed behind me. They struggled for pole position while trying to discredit each other's record of deeds on Earth.

"He's a thief. No go with him. I help with everything!"

"Amigo? Mon ami? Friend!"

"I am Mustafa. You can trust me. Alone—they eat you like wolves. You go alone, they eat you and you say, 'Mustafa was right.' I'll take you."

When I found a bank, I realized I had forgotten my PIN number—so long had it been since I had withdrawn cash. Being in the *Al Maghreb*, it shouldn't have startled me that the sun was beginning to set.

Mustafa was waiting behind me, in his rags and grime, soft—nothing like a wolf—but I didn't care to go with him. Arab culture wouldn't allow him to let me spend the night on the streets. But the thought of spooning with Mustafa in a crumbling *riad* inspired me, and I punched in the numbers.

Days later I was twenty miles outside Erfoud, sleeping in a mud hut at the shore of the Sahara. I had traded T-shirts for *tagine* and was without a single dirham, an absurd moment for someone with a debit card. A Bedouin came by with some items wrapped in cloth. He unfolded them to reveal fossils from the time the Sahara was a sea full of life. He left with my backpack and a couple 500-peseta coins I was going to keep as mementos. In my hand was a rounded stone that split open to reveal a trilobite and a 475 million-year-old dream of water. I gathered my belongings into a plastic bag, wrapping my new treasure in my last change of socks.

The young men running the place couldn't believe I had no cash. Youssef, the manager, poked fun at my amateur con while playing chess by candlelight. Opposite him was a German man who was vigilant about organ robbers who took poor Africans away by night. Enormous green bugs with flimsy wings miraculously appeared from the sand to die in the single flame.

After my stay, I was driven—or rather, given a civilian sample of tactical evasive driving methods—to get money. The road blended with the cratered desert through which it ran. We stopped in Rissani, where I was dropped off at an ATM, sand dunes still in view.

I kept trading my possessions. In Tinghir, my Walkman and Frank Sinatra cassette were exchanged for a decorated yellow plate, which was so lousily crafted that the sands of time should have buried it on the shelf where it sat. I just liked the thought of the young Berber listening to "Strangers in The Night" as two backpacking girls from California emerged from the dingy hostel across the street. One by one I lost the rest of my belongings as they fell out of the ripped white garbage bag.

COMPARED TO THE SOUTH of Morocco, the area around Hotel Enghelab in Tehran was like the financial services sector of the City of London. Sanjar and I left the hotel to the imagined quick fix of international finance. We smacked up against bank after bank, none of them able to help. Bankers were divided as to whether Visa was operating in the country. As in other Middle Eastern countries, Iranians, helpful but also eager to seize a morsel of authority, have a hard time admitting they don't know something. Through the answers of half a dozen bankers who didn't say no but couldn't say yes, it was at last pieced together definitively that Visa was banned from doing business in Iran as part of the economic sanctions. Sheepishly I turned to Sanjar.

"No problem man, I'll cover your ass."

When we presented Sanjar's money at the registration table I was told that one of the main organizers was "mad" at me. It had been years since I had been around a scolding Muslim woman. Decades ago, I attended Arabic class on Sundays in Minnesota. A lady there was fond of shrieking, "We are no Jesus! We are Muslim!" Powerhouses like this woman convinced my father to personally take care of any and all religious instruction. There was the obvious problem that Jesus is a revered prophet in Islam and a fully credentialed "messiah."

I braced myself for the second coming as I walked over to talk to the short woman in full chador.

With my shoulders hunched and head bowed I learned the nature of my offense. The e-mail message she had sent with the "visa authorization number" had gone unanswered for months. She told me she assumed I wasn't coming. I feigned boyish aloofness, but it was unnecessary. This is what I had done: I had not given her a chance to arrange my lodging and side trips adequately. This prevented her from doing the professional job that she wanted to do. I waited for her to tell me that I couldn't just stay with Sanjar, that I needed to enjoy the soft sequester of the Hotel Enghelab, and the guide-monitored tourist excursions.

I waited, but instead she hurried off to make sure the hotel restaurant had turned up the burners under the *ash-e-reshteh*, bean and noodle soup. Lunchtime had arrived, and we were expected to eat well.

Chapter Nine

THE CONFERENCE fit my brother-in-law's description of academic conferences: well organized, devoid of revolt (its absence filled by coffee breaks and cookies), and lame.

The only interesting exchange during the panel discussions came between two Brits over the definition of "honor killings." The woman pointed out that men routinely kill women in the West over harm done to their honor. It's just not formally encoded in the culture. Suppose a husband walks in on his wife and her lover. In an instant he writes his own code, and two shots are fired. Often a third to his own head, as the husband completes the cycle of his own justice. The male professor countered that killings sanctioned by a culture merit special condemnation. Like many academic discussions, it was a set piece used to frame displays of verbal skill, like a trumped-up offense on a city street corner that leads to a lively rap session. If Washington, DC, is Hollywood for ugly people, academia is Hollywood for the articulate.

Sanjar and I attended a short story workshop run by a devoted Iranian teacher named Parviz. It was supposed to be about short stories related to religion. Parviz seemed to care more about good writing. I imagined him tacking on the "religious" moniker to his seminar disingenuously, like fruit to a Happy Meal.

Parviz was well prepared, and endowed with an intelligence that he must have insisted on and carried forward through a university system eviscerated by politics. After the 1979 Revolution, universities were closed for three years. The purification of students and lecturers supportive of the Shah would have claimed him. As it was, he crept along, young enough to have entered the system after the violence of the early years. I can see him, like many others, surveying the scene, pushing when he could, pulling back when he needed to.

In the workshop he chose an American short story to share. In it a married man and his eighteen-year-old mistress are riding through the countryside in his truck. When they pass another car on the county road, she ducks out of sight. With her head down below the car seat, the girl notices the smell of damp floor mats, stale coffee, cigarettes, and age.

The cozy social surveillance Americans found themselves under in small towns was something the young Iranians related to. A legacy of post-Revolution venality was that a crooked whisper to the authorities could bring down an entire family.

During a writing exercise, we were to describe rooms in our houses. I volunteered and began to read my passage out loud. Sanjar lost it and started shaking as a burst of laughter pounded to free itself from his ribs. I spoke of a place with one hanging light bulb. There were old cobwebs, slackening and drooping in the corners. There was nothing in the room except a cement floor and four brick walls with a small door. It was the room where I practiced the deadly arts.

"Ha! The *deadly* arts. I know what you're talking about. Karate! He's talking about KARATE!" I still don't know why Sanjar thought this was so funny. I think he was covering for me in some way, assuming that I was talking about my bedroom in a disguised way.

At the front of the room Parviz was expertly guiding the class from start to finish. When it was time to partner up, he made sure Sanjar and I, being the semi-foreigner and the foreigner, were paired up with the young women. The reasoning: the young Iranian men would get too excited about the rare partnership with girls outside their families.

Our task was to pull up the earliest memories we could. My partner was half-Iranian, half-Filipina. She had a wide face framed by a cream-colored hijab. From her lips came a faintly British accent. My elbow pressed against the dark leather of my padded armrest as I leaned towards her voice. She began describing herself at age five, standing before an apartment window. I don't remember if she is planning on jumping, looking at the street below, or daydreaming. Her father appears at her back and lovingly tries to explain to her, "People can't fly." She becomes angry and confused.

Then she turned to me, her eyes widening as she looked through me to her past: "I just could not understand why *not*."

I ONCE WROTE A COLLEGE TERM PAPER in a language I didn't know very well. The professor hadn't required it. I just anticipated that by using English, the words would have done all the thinking for me. Technical terms could stand in for any effort at original thought. Like a child's battery-operated toy that talks and moves, and essentially does the playing for them, I distrusted my native tongue.

A beginner in a language has more innocence and clarity than a fluent speaker of the language. I wanted to be like an old shepherd using what I truly knew in simple strokes, and these could be made by the modest collection of Spanish words I knew. In the novella *The Little Prince*, there is an admonition from the narrator: "Being witty makes you lie." I figured it was harder to lie using a second language.

I suspected that a shepherd was wiser than a sophisticated man. The shepherd considers the world that touches him: rain, sun, earth, and the grass that will feed his animals. The sophisticated man can't let the world touch him because he wants to consider it first. Words build thoughts in his head that can't be turned into footsteps leading back to the ground. They are no longer a bridge to reality, but a collection of selfish symbols that divide the body from the soul.

The shepherd doesn't entertain thoughts out of their correct time. Since his thoughts emerge from his life, he avoids making false moves. When he needs a doorway to another world, he can tell himself a story. Stories are where the sophisticated man and the shepherd can harmonize. In the subconscious, symbols are shared and everybody is literate.

THE DJ HAD the right touch. He was playing songs from the 1980s that none of us had heard before, but which sounded like the hits we all loved. However, the armpit sampler that had become the dance floor's air supply had become overwhelming. My friend Dan and I stepped out onto the patio. There was an unoccupied corner and we took it. A string of white lights traced the top of a high wooden fence enclosing the herd of smoking and drinking Minnesotans. It was the summer after my trip to Iran. Life was peaceful: the biggest threat was the sweat, beer, and spit misting from the body of an oafish hipster when the DJ hit upon an obscure David Bowie track.

A woman who was nearby began to collect a harem of artsy guys who were pretending they didn't want blowjobs. They talked about Mexico City and the cinema. There was nothing to do but join in.

"Tell us a story," Dan abruptly asked the woman. His bald proposition dispersed the horny boys disguised behind thick-rimmed glasses. The woman, wearing a black spiderweb top, had a boyfriend who was enduring her free spirit by composing a Russian novel on his cell phone. She dabbed out her cigarette.

"All right."

Dan and I leaned forward and peered at her through a forest of green and brown empty bottles that covered our table.

"I'm from Raleigh, North Carolina. One day it was time for us to move north. I was sixteen years old. We loaded up the truck and were ready to drive out the next day. We were standing around our yard feeling sad. Then my dad told me he had a present for me."

"Wait, don't tell us," Dan stopped her. "What would a dad give his sixteen-year-old daughter?" We guessed while she stirred her straw and shook her head. "Okay, tell us."

"He rolled up his sleeve and on his arm was a tattoo of me."

After dropping Dan off I thought about her story. Getting a tattoo of your daughter on your arm seems like a stunt necessary for someone going to prison. The ink from her image poisoning the very blood he shares with her.

It troubled me that the vessel that holds what is inside might also begin to alter what is inside. Laurence Olivier, the famed actor, would prepare for a role by working from the outside in, beginning with a hat the character might wear, transforming himself in reverse. I felt I was closer to understanding why Sanjar used different names sometimes: to keep the pitcher from contaminating the water.

IN TEHRAN, a young man at the workshop was being persistent in his efforts to be a great host. He was stocky, with a large greasy face molded onto his head. It sat in a plump square on his shoulders like a hunk of wet clay. His vocabulary was atrocious. His thoughts transferred in his big head from Farsi to English, and came out of his mouth lumpy but recognizable, like a botched teleport in Star Trek.

"It is honor for me to welcome you to my country. I very feel good to have you with me at my side. Please accept my welcome home."

I loved him—not because he was unequipped to take me to task for U.S. policy: even Iranians with spotless English weren't interested in doing that. It was because the feeling of his wish fit the few words he could speak it with.

The other conference attendees were harmless, though less charming than him—perhaps by design. Academics used to the territoriality of departments stayed within their lanes without much fuss. When an ayatollah or mullah (there was at least one on every panel) spoke in Farsi, and professors from around the world scrunched their eyebrows, this could be interpreted as the strain of listening to the English translation through headsets rather than criticism.

A retired professor from my old university in Wisconsin (where he taught a course called "Malevolence in Religions") was there. He had arrived on another flight. After three decades as a professor of religious studies and chair of various departments and centers, he was getting his first chance to visit Iran. In his excitement he had prepared a lengthy discourse on "concealed feminine powers in past and present religions."

He was a gentle, soft-spoken man, and had been even in his younger days. His technical, dryly-read paper disappeared into the depression of sleepy and inattentive attendees. Halfway through the paper, the moderator began signaling that time was up. The professor read on, making the aside, "I didn't know time would be so short." Again, and again, he was given verbal cues. Each time the moderator edged his way closer to the stage and then the lectern. Was an important figure due to speak next? Was an authority troubled by his description of the folk popularity of Fatima, mother of Hussain, in Shia traditions?

Sanjar kept marveling at how well put together the conference was. It seemed *normal*, and this was a giveaway for an Iranian observer. For Iran, given its current state, putting an event on in this way was a big deal—lots of money and thought went into it. It may be that the moderator was simply doing his job, following the schedule and keeping order. It was not fair to say that the good professor was shut down because of the content of anything he was saying. In fact, I even heard myself mutter "*Alhamdillah,* thanks be to God," when he closed his thick manuscript and sat back down.

AT ONE POINT during a question and answer session, a young woman shot up and began an agitated plea for liberty. As people tossed and turned in their seats, Sanjar turned to me and smiled, "I think she's at the wrong conference."

Her passion ran out of oxygen while we held our breath.

We were all on our best behavior. She was allowed to finish. No security force, no screaming and being dragged out of the auditorium. With all these witnesses, it took nothing but gravity to lower her to her seat. Perhaps a check mark went next to her name in a notebook resting on a lap in the back of the room. Perhaps she was ignored. I wondered which was worse for her.

There was a photographer who worked diligently to capture the proceedings. He was everywhere: the Hotel Enghelab, the cafeteria, the conference hall. His camera was extra large, like a hulking black Transformer robot. I thought about how quickly context weaponizes objects: I pictured super-spy Jason Bourne, cornered in a Tangiers bathroom, throwing shampoo bottles and loofahs to stop his would-be assassin. Each day the photographer's photos would be posted in the main hall of the National Library, but I couldn't shake the feeling of being under surveillance.

While standing in line for lunch, the photographer bent his knees and took fifteen shots of Sanjar, Andrew, and I. Each click of the shutter felt like an incision in search of my intentions in Iran. I tried to control the expressions on my face.

I relaxed when I could start filling my plate with saffron rice and kebab. Next to me was a young man training to be a mullah. His burqa-clad wife and darling daughter sat at the next table. I waved at his daughter, forging a tenuous alliance with Iran's future through the use of goofy faces. I heard the man drop the names "Metallica" and "Guns N' Roses." His head dipped closer to his plate for a gulp of rice, and I wondered if I was listening to an indictment or a confession.

Chapter Ten

I WAS STANDING in the doorway of Saleh's second-story apartment. I had left college with my friend Ted Storm to play soccer in Spain. After Ted left for Madrid to fly home I had drifted south where I met Saleh. Now he was gently mocking me, waiting for me to make a decision. He walked back into the shadows of his kitchen. When I turned back outside, I was dazzled by the Andalusian sun covering a green hillside. On the top of the hill stood The Alhambra of Granada. Saleh's voice called from deep inside his kitchen.

"*Me voy. No me voy. Me voy. No me voy.*"

Saleh fussed with the dishes. I teetered in the old doorframe.

The evening before, I was sitting on a bench in a square below the Moorish palace. Cafés were filled with gorgeous Spaniards. I was woozy after two encounters with gypsies. First, I had helped one push his motorcycle up a hill that only the metric system disqualified from being a mountain. At the top he offered to read my palm to thank me. He studied a crease.

"It will take a long time for you to come into your own. *Mucho tiempo.*"

I was out in the world trying to ferret out the makings of my adult life. Now my big fear was being repeated back to me: I would have to return home. I was still a child.

The motorcycle gypsy and I parted ways. On the way down I saw a path that followed along the edge of the Darro River. As I walked, I heard some wailing coming from the other side of a deep ravine. It was a pre-historic sound, ripping into the air like a spear.

Peering across, expecting to see *Homo habilis* gnawing on a giant bison thigh, my eyes fell upon a leather-clad gypsy crouched on a small rock outcropping. One hand was raised high above his head. Suddenly it swung down towards his guitar. His fingers slashed the strings and a weeping voice repeatedly penetrated through my body, like a lover storming out of a bedroom yelling, and then storming back in to yell louder still.

I sat on a stone and took the beating.

When the gypsy again raised his hand high above his head like a scimitar to begin the next song, I got up and stumbled down over the cobblestone to the square.

I stood at the edge of the Plaza Nueva plucking the strings of my makeshift backpack—Ted's old laundry bag. Saleh was on a nearby bench. I set my bag down and took a seat. We spoke for a time. I said I was interested in Granada's Islamic past.

"Then I will sing a special Islamic song for you," Saleh replied.

That was a strange offer. I wasn't aware of any of Islam's greatest hits.

"But first, we should have some tea at my home."

A short walk brought us to the entrance of the Albaicín, the medieval Moorish quarter. I followed him through narrow laby-rinthine streets, halfway up a hill, then up some stairs to the door of his apartment. I entered. It was filled with the books and mementos of a well-traveled man. One lamp lit the room, creating a shadowy, expectant atmosphere. It was hard to make out what any one item actually was. They breathed; a living pattern made out of the artifacts of a man's life.

Saleh was like a jewel hidden during the *Reconquista*, softly emanating the glory of Moorish Spain. Inviting me to stand next to him, he faced east, ready to sing the Islamic song. I stood next to him. He cupped both hands, held them in front of each ear and sang the most sonorous rendition of the *adhan*, the Muslim call to prayer, that I had ever heard.

Night fell in the Albaicín. Eggs sizzled in an iron skillet that looked like it could have shielded Saleh from the sword blows of Catholic holy warriors five hundred years earlier. We sat down to a late supper in the dim kitchen. We ate silently, passing each other dishes from the red and white checkered tablecloth. The taste of a spoonful of cucumber and yogurt salad hit my tongue. In the warm, greasy room, the salad cooled my head. Across from me Saleh contemplated his last bit of bread. After the meal we moved into the other room where he took out some Spanish- and Arabic-language books.

"With me you'll know Spanish and Arabic in one month."

He had lit a pipe of hashish. I declined, but it was useless. Soon the smoke filled the room. I squinted through the clouds of smoke at a picture frame on a desk. Saleh noticed my stare. "She's in Sevilla now."

My attention floated slowly over the desk. When I looked next to me Saleh was gone. Turning back to the desk I found my view blocked by a steaming glass of tea. I took it gingerly with two fingers. When my grip was sure I wrapped the rest of my fingers and my palm around the glass to feel the heat and keep myself alert.

Saleh walked to a bookshelf and brought down a photo album. In it were photos of Saleh in different cities around the Muslim world. There were many of him in Mecca, the holiest city in Islam.

"Have you been to Mecca?" he asked.

"No. I was thinking I needed to learn more before going there."

"You learn *by* going there."

He flipped through a few more pages. I noticed that many of the pictures were of handsome young Muslim men. One wouldn't hang about with women in the capitals of the Islamic world. Still, I glanced down to make sure a thick piece of *tortilla española* would fit between us where we sat leaning against his bed.

There was a picture of Saleh on a mountain path with a fine-boned young man. In the background I was able to make out a tower, blasted with sun and dust. I would see this very tower, the Milad Tower, when I climbed the mountains and looked out at that very city years later.

Saleh pointed at the picture: "Tehran."

⟿

THERE ARE MANY ways to continue a journey once it has begun. In Iran it was harder to think one could control when and how it would end.

I was glad that I hadn't blown off the conference, not only because it allowed me to meet Andrew and Parviz. Another reason was that it gave me a chance to meet the Vice President of Iran and make a gamble for a new beginning to my trip.

After a day of speeches at the conference, we climbed on the bus at the National Library and were driven to the Iranian Institute of Philosophy. Night was falling. The mountains that ring the city, so dominant by day, were being ironed into the darkening sky. We arrived and followed the energetic organizers into a one-story building. In a large room a buffet had been laid out for us. The hungry scholars filled their plates with kebabs, roasted vegetables, and saffron rice.

We sat across from an American professor who had taught at a university in Iowa. I wanted to commiserate with him, but it turned out he had a better attitude about the place. I had the feeling he was based in California now; he had the ease of a modestly successful man who took the time to exercise and got enough sun.

I watched as he baptized a hunk of chicken in a dollop of *maast-o-khiar*, cucumber yogurt. Then he put it in his mouth sending it on an unholy pilgrimage to his stomach. He licked his fingers and asked, "What do you think of Tehran?"

"It's so clean. I mean the roads are in good shape—no potholes—and there's not a lot of trash around."

I wondered if my answer was too enthusiastic, as if enthusiasm was a sign of inexperience. I found out later that these fine roads were the fruits of extremely high unemployment. Infrastructure work sites all around the country were stocked with low-paid crews in blue overalls.

"Have you been to this part of the world before?" he asked.

"Yes. I mean compared to Cairo or … Cairo was crumbling. It's strange, but that's what I notice: very smooth roads."

I tried to present my worldly credentials the best I could, struggling to find an interesting insight. I had the feeling I was talking about an oil change with a mechanic: there was the risk that the topic would quickly rocket beyond my understanding to carburetors, pistons, and struts.

There was an alert professor from Holland next to him. She had brown Billy Idol hair that spiked out and a tremendous mole on her cheek. Sanjar wanted to ask if she knew German, but she had already started talking with the American professor. They were in each other's league. Their minds were going now, teasing out theories from all the silos of academia, and recklessly merging them in a sexy discourse.

All the American professor had to do was rely on his vocabulary, and muscle mass, to hold steady as a flow of erudition left her lips and tested his mettle. Technicalities would beget technicalities until logic short-circuited in a spasm of hypertextual moans and groans. Seeing his moment passing, Sanjar wrote her a note on a napkin and passed it across the table. It read, "I want to talk with you." The two professors looked up, disoriented.

WHILE WE ATE, the guest of honor, whom Sanjar could not identify by sight, began a short speech. It was Dr. Mehdi Mostafavi, then Vice President and Cultural Advisor to President Ahmadinejad. Dr. Mostafavi began by saying something about his wish for cultures to have a space to interact outside of politics. These academic conferences, though serving as public-relations events for the government, were for all their flaws made up of people interested in understanding culture, rather than using its markers to sow divisions. This was one reason why it was one of the only ways left to get into Iran for Americans.

Scholars, the hope was, had different agendas than their governments.

I was barely listening to the speech, but the translator, a pretty news anchor from Tehran, was someone we had met at the conference, and eventually her voice brought me to attention. I slowly realized that Dr. Mostafavi was actually saying something. The gist was that people needed room and time to communicate: when and where would they find it?

WHEN THE DINNER ended, the Vice President took up a position by the door with his entourage to form a receiving line. They were crisply dressed in suits and white shirts without ties. Sanjar encouraged me to speak with Dr. Mostafavi about my seven-day visa that was set to expire in a few days.

On my first day in Iran, we had driven around looking for an office whose address had been posted in an "Iran visa" thread on a travel website just a few weeks earlier. As we jerked and maneuvered in the private taxi, we realized not only that the office did not exist, nor did the street where it was supposedly located.

My next attempt to get an extension was to give my passport to the conference organizers, who would bring it to the Foreign Ministry. The following day, they said they had been told that none of the foreign participants could get an extension.

I was an American desperately trying to find the right authority to allow me to stay in Iran. Yet it was not a question of "the right authority." That would imply a functioning system. I needed an individual with *enough* authority to have formed his own system, one that I, with luck, could access and pass through. Sanjar understood this and had told me it was a key to understanding how things worked in Iran.

Being on the radar of the security detail of a high-ranking government official was not the best way to keep the low profile I wanted. I have heard of Iranians in Los Angeles who are reluctant to join the National Do Not Call Registry because of the memory of being on various lists of the Iranian intelligence agencies.

I had enjoyed the anonymity of being part of the broader conference group. Now I needed to be known, and was pulled into the spotlight by Sanjar. We didn't know we were going to see the Vice President that day, and had not dressed for the occasion. Sanjar wore cargo pants, a baseball hat, and a T-shirt. I stood at his side in an untucked, crumpled linen shirt, my own cargo pants bulging with the photocopies of my passport that I carried everywhere as insurance.

Sanjar spoke first to Dr. Mostafavi, and as an Iranian citizen he had better reason to lay low. Afterwards he would joke, "I probably have the attention of a few intelligence agencies already, going back and forth to the US, so what's a few more!"

THE CONFERENCE PHOTOGRAPHER raised his heavyweight camera to his eye, and I stepped forward to meet Dr. Mostafavi. The moment angled sharply against the brief handshakes from attendees who quickly disappeared out the door and onto the bus. The room was empty of foreigners. The security guards edged closer.

The body-conscious feeling I had in the airport in Dubai returned. I had a ferocious itch in my left nostril. Dr. Mostafavi had a short, neatly-trimmed white beard. Next to the tougher types around him, he had a gentle face. It was this kindness that distinguished him.

"Hello sir, very nice to meet you," I said.

"And you. Welcome to Iran."

THERE IS A DIFFERENCE between the portraits of former Presidents George W. Bush and Barack Obama that goes beyond the obvious. Sanjar noticed it when he waited to be questioned in customs and immigration offices at US airports. Once he had seen the visionless pinch of President Bush's face; this was followed by the open features of President Obama's serene composure. The demeanor, style, and talent were different—if not the corporate agenda.

Leaving aside the policies behind both masks, Sanjar's anecdotal story supposes that one can judge how welcoming a country is by the expression of the presidential face hung on the wall. For brown people who arrived at US customs the relief may have been the simple warmth of skin. But I can imagine a rivulet of decorum trickling down from the top as well.

I PREPARED MY CASE for Dr. Mostafavi to consider. Standing in front of the Vice President, weathering the lethal affections of his security detail, I asked him if he could help me. "I love Iran but I can only stay for seven days. I would love to stay longer and learn more."

"Yes. Thank you."

Dr. Mostafavi glanced at Sanjar, and I leaned closer.

"Sir, is there any way I can stay longer?"

He and Sanjar then spoke for a while in Farsi. He said that he could not do anything about that kind of problem.

"In your speech you spoke of the greatness of Iran and its people," Sanjar began, "and now we are making my friend leave after a week. Let him stay and see for himself how good the Iranian people are. And, sir, who is going to say no to you?"

He smiled and told us to give his office a call, saying, "You have my number."

Sanjar, finding himself in the strange position of telling a public figure that he did not have any idea of how to reach him, answered, "Yes, sir."

After a humbling moment for both men Dr. Mostafavi said, "Do you have a pen?"

"I have my phone."

Sanjar reached slowly into his pocket. I noticed subtle recalibrations of body weight occurring in the security guards as Sanjar took out his phone. Sanjar entered his pass code, at first incorrectly out of nerves. The Vice President, the guards, and I stood limp for five ridiculous seconds.

He gave us the number of his office and said he would see what he could do.

Turning to me he said, "I wish you luck." We shook hands again. I blurted out, "I love Iran."

I wanted to give the mild-mannered politician a pep talk. Shore up any hard feelings felt by Iranians due to worldwide sanctions and alienation. But his guards and handlers were shutting down the petition more forcefully now. Up close I felt the dense energy of well-paid men, with bodies like sand wrapped in sheet metal. We hustled out the door.

Boarding the bus, we found the other conference attendees all waiting. Taking our seats in the very back, we looked at each other. We had the number of a big guy.

Chapter Eleven

OVER THE NEXT COUPLE of days, Sanjar left messages at the Vice President's office without getting any responses. In slow motion my trip crunched up against another bureaucratic wall; on its opposite side my departure date sat without a scratch.

The night before my flight home, we went to Bame Tehran, a popular mountainside promenade. On the way down, we sidled up to a small group of guys and girls headed by a pointy, energetic man. The leader swiveled from youth to youth with jokes and comments timed according to prompts emitted from deep in his solar plexus. He resembled a DJ at work on the turntables, adjusting frequencies and holding off the beat drop. Sanjar and I spoke with him in French as he quickly translated our conversation into Farsi for his friends. We took on his carefree buoyancy as if we were charging up the Butte Montmartre, after a night of dancing, to hang out on the steps of the Sacré-Cœur.

"Who is he?" I asked Sanjar.

"*Un guide.*" Sanjar was still in French mode. I heard "ahn geeed," and was puzzled.

"Just tell me. Who is he?"

"Euh ... *il est un guide*," Sanjar replied and left it at that.

BEFORE I REJOINED the roving band, I had to give rational thought to the term "guide." Analysis: the brittle obligation of the Western mind, good for running cities, terrible for the mysteries of love. Un guide. For whom? To what? To where?

I thought of the story of the boy who becomes fascinated with a butterfly. Eventually, wanting to discover the trick of its flight, he pulls it apart.

One of the young guys, who let loose a horsey laugh after each massacred syllable of English, was determined to set Sanjar up with his sister. She was a heavy girl, un-preoccupied with getting a new nose as was the fashion in Iran. She radiated a sexy, embracing good nature as she swung her long hijab around like a Janis Joplin wig. Another guy, unable to speak English or French, sustained a broad smile as if he received clandestine payments from the American Dental Association. He sat like a little brother on the rim of the proceedings.

We were skipping and laughing down the paved mountain road. Then, inexplicably, not to demonstrate for or against anything, five or six of us began to hold hands.

I WENT BACK in time and saw a young man with messy hair and a brown flannel shirt moving between the dark stacks of a university library. There is a blue cloth-covered volume in his hand. The figure steps inside a private study cage. There's a metal chair. It's hard and cold. I know because it's under me. My forearms rest on a metal desk. A porthole looks down five stories. It's night but I can make out the movement of water through the trees. The book is open to an Omar Khayyam poem in Arabic, French, and English. I turn on the desk light and the pages brighten. The French does not make sense to me; the Arabic looks more beautiful and incomprehensible. I place my finger under the first English word:

To what end do you concern yourself with life?
Why trouble your heart, your mind, with vain desires?
Happily live, joyfully pass the time,
After all, if you will exhale the breath just now inhaled,
You do not know.

SANJAR NOTICED my gaze lingering on the young group of friends up on Bame Tehran. The petite and playful young woman who had been at my side smiled as she spun and walked backward away from us, disappearing into the parking lot. The jamboree of fellow feeling ended. The event dispersed into space with the reach of a solar flare: measurable, potent, and invisible.

Ringing in my ears was the taunting *gimme gimme* chorus of my acquisitive culture. I wanted those friends, their guide, and that feeling for keeps. I imagined myself running around with a butterfly net at the dawn of creation. There's a sticker on the handle. It reads, "Made in the USA."

"You'll leave Iran with the taste on your tongue!" Sanjar, with this quick, precise remark, broke my dark trance.

We walked to the car silently. Within hours the expiration of my seven-day visa and flight home would wheel into alignment. Wrapped in a steel tube 30,000 feet in the air, this eclipse was set to cast a lone shadow on my heart.

PROFESSOR MEMON was a grouchy man. He wore a white Harrington jacket, and would stand at the front of the room with his arms folded. His grey goatee would move, and puffs of air would deliver an even, unamused Pakistani-British accent. I think he held some doubts about how well we were understanding Islamic mystical poetry.

Years before I met Sanjar, Professor Memon strained to unlock the intricacies of Persia's great poets for a room full of kids at a university in Wisconsin. Hafiz, Saadi, Rumi, Jami, Attar, Sanai: when I hear them listed, they sound like prescriptions I was on during my college years. When State Street filled with drunks on Saturday nights, I was hiding in a café or library trying to get divinely intoxicated with those old poets. While young couples discovered details about each other's bodies in dorm rooms, I was trying to interpret the passions of Persians that had been dead for 800 years.

Professor Memon was impressed by one student in class. He too wore a casual white jacket every day. Instead of a bald head and short-trimmed goatee, he had unwashed blonde locks to his shoulders. One day Memon allowed him to deliver a lecture on the number seven and its holy place in different religions. For some reason when Memon introduced the student he mentioned his place of birth: Racine, Wisconsin.

That night, I passed very purposeful kids heading to the bars, and stepped into a café. I held a container of honey above my cup and counted to five as it poured out. Popping the wooden stir stick in the corner of my mouth I sat alone with a book. When I reached to sip my coffee it was cold and too sweet. I forgot about the day in class.

A year passed.

I was back in Minnesota at the Stinky Café. In my hands was the book *Le Petit Prince*. I came upon the word *racine*. I looked it up. Finding out that it meant "root," I feverishly developed a wild theory that somehow Racine, Wisconsin, was the mystical center of the Midwest. Memon said there were many meanings to every poem. As I contrived to understand my life as a poem, I tried to unlock the significance of *racine*.

Over the years I've grown to have my doubts about making any pilgrimages to Racine.

My mystic quest, embarked on with the skill of an amateur sleuth, led me swerving back and forth between the charged nibbling of revelation and embarrassment. In the middle of the semester when I was in Memon's class, a street hustler basically hypnotized me on the promise that he had something that would "open up all the deepest places" inside.

I handed over forty dollars, dazed with spiritual striving. It didn't occur to me that he was talking about drugs. I waited for him on a bench outside of Walgreens. When I snapped out of it, I left very quickly.

A few days later, the fast-talking medium chased me down and said, "Man, I've been looking all over for you. Don't you want your stuff?" As they say, there is counterfeit gold because there is such a thing as real gold.

⁓

THE PERSIAN GIANTS of poetry became quiet monuments, covered in the vines of a bygone era of my life. The new English translations available were fatally infused with the soft-focus of Californian spiritualism. Part of the natural impulse to make their meanings as easy as buying scented candles. Those years in college, when I pressed against their sealed inner depths, never led to profound insights, but I jealously believe the effort strengthened me in some way.

Some years after college, while reading a book of stories collected in the East, I did come upon a line that was hard to vandalize through lousy translation: "An hour with a man of learning is better than a thousand years studying on your own."

I thought about that dart of a man and his little group on Bame Tehran. *Un guide.* A group of young people who were not drunk, enjoying the up-anchored thrill of intoxication. He must have known how to handle the ecstatic using some doctrine of sobriety.

At Bame Tehran I felt closer to and farther from those old poets. I had arrived in Persia; there was poetry, mysterious strangers, and a longing that moved like a riptide beneath the faces around me.

MY BAGS WERE PACKED, and I sat in front of a glass coffee table in the living room. Russian MTV was on a big, new flat screen. The Russian host introduced a Swedish song, "Dancing on My Own." The blonde singer, Robyn, lurked through a discotheque singing about a big black sky over her town. Sepehr, Sanjar's father, worked on his book on a huge dining table. Medieval Persian texts were splayed all around, each one selected from the bookshelves that ringed the entire main sitting room.

I was eating pistachios at a trembling clip, as if an Iranian drug lord had ordered me to smuggle a kilo in my lower intestine. The phone rang and Sanjar went into his bedroom to answer. I was sipping my tea when Sanjar came into the room holding the phone, doing the who's-the-man head bob in his boxers. With his long neck stretched and chin jabbing out it was the chicken dance of paradise.

We had gotten verbal permission to extend my stay from Dr. Mostafavi's office. I was elated, but before I canceled my flight, I wanted an ink stamp on my passport. I wanted it in writing. In the East the spoken word still has a place of honor, but my Western side would not rest until I had it on paper.

"You *were* going to leave with the taste of Iran still on your tongue. Instead ..." Sanjar let out a playful snigger that registered ominously in my ears.

IT WAS A GRIM plight: three young American hikers were accused of illegally crossing the border after a foot soldier supposedly led them from the Iraqi border into Iranian territory. Isolated inside Evin Prison, they faced charges of espionage. I still wondered how three Iranian backpackers on the forested Canada-US border would be treated.

As an American in Iran, I was not sure how many rights I could claim. It was a place where you had to rely on people—not a system—if you wanted justice.

If I overstayed my visa without getting a stamp, I would be exposed to fines if the official at the airport strictly followed the law. The reality was that if they wanted to detain me for political uses, they could make up any excuse. I began to look at Dr. Mostafavi's word as my bypass of both law and people: a king I could petition, should I run into trouble. In old stories the king is often the most forgiving, pardon being a greater form of power than violence.

There were other stories that did not comfort. The stories where the king, Dr. Mostafavi in my case, remains in the dark.

Take the story of the common man who, during the time of the Shah, named his cat the *Shah-e-Shah*, or 'King of Kings.' He was taken away by the secret police, disappearing into the maze of torture and prison. There was little chance the Shah ever knew of the offense, or the punishment.

MR. MOSTAFAVI'S OFFICE did in fact call the head of the Ministry of Foreign Affairs, and it was there that we were supposed to get a letter, to supplement his word.

My visa had been expired for a day when Sanjar and I headed for the Foreign Ministry in central Tehran. We left just after dawn. I felt like a piece of rotten fruit that might be identified by the greengrocer at any moment. To access central Tehran, you need to take one cab with all the right licenses or get out at certain points and switch cabs. These perimeters have more to do with reducing congestion than security.

At the Bagh-e Melli compound where Iran's Ministry of Foreign Affairs is located, the only guns I saw were painted on the stones above the huge wooden gates. They were next to a green, white, and red Iranian flag. A gold lion in the center of the flag, painted at the time of the Shah, had its head and body covered by a white band of paint added in 1980. The lion's paws and tail stick out below the white and into the red band of the flag, a color signifying sacrifice. A passing man happily pointed out these features. I pulled out my camera.

After taking a few pictures, we walked in. A huge empty courtyard stretched before us. A lone man in a suit stood outside a guard booth. Reza Shah had had the complex expanded by German architects. Cut into huge blocks, the dark grey stone it was built with looked immensely heavy.

It was still early morning, and the Consul General had not arrived yet. We went back out to the courtyard to talk with the man in the suit. When a caravan of three cars arrived from another entrance, he brushed us back.

"Who was that?" Sanjar asked.

"That was the Foreign Minister," the guard replied.

WHILE WE STOOD next to the guard, a darkness imposed itself on my imagination like a thick pair of curtains. Then they parted, and one of the waking nightmares began.

I saw myself on a grainy satellite image.

A small group at CIA Headquarters at Langley gathers around a screen. I am standing there in the sun with my friend, talking quietly with the guard. The monitor lights up the face of a pasty technician who asks, "Why are they there?" His glasses glow with the reflection of the screen. "Wrong place, wrong time, such is life," another agent says and nods his head at the technician. His finger passes over the keys until it snaps down on one. A second passes. Then a high-pitched whistle sounds over my shoulder and the rip and crunch of a missile impacting wipes past and future clean. My senses focus and another whistling metal tube flies over our heads. The heavy stones slowly lift into the air, still whole, float to the ground, and crumble into blue-grey dust. The Foreign Minister's caravan jolts into reverse and disappears out of the gates of the compound. Both places appear in my dream, the screen split, and my mind works to put my body in one or the other.

I blinked, looked up, and saw the blue sky. The stones sat in neat rows, stacked upon each other, untouched. After taking a breath, I thought about how easy it is to bewitch yourself with fear.

The Consul General arrived, and Sanjar was allowed into his office. When Sanjar emerged, he spoke about the handful of low-level diplomats from poor West African countries that were present in the room: Benin, Ghana, Niger. The Iranian government had given these countries aid money, and they sent officials to visit Tehran from time to time.

My friend Rob, working on a documentary for USAID, observed this relationship. When he was in the impoverished countryside of Togo, he saw signs that read, "This project brought to you by the Islamic Republic of Iran." When President Obama arrived in Ghana, an ambulance at the airport read, "Donated by the Islamic Republic of Iran." The Africans still vote in line with the United States at the United Nations, but the arrangement grants them cash and isolated Iranian officials influence and the sensation of a normal existence on the international stage.

We traced our steps out of the building, past the four offices we had been misdirected to on our way to the Consul General's office. In the end, Sanjar had gotten his signature on a letter approving my visa extension.

IN THE VARIOUS offices at the Foreign Ministry where we had been waiting, breakfast was being served to officials and secretaries—tea and a type of Turkish peasant bread. The mediocre quality of the bread at this important government office caused more alarm in Sanjar than the mild confusion of the staff when he asked simple questions.

The secretaries at the Foreign Ministry were all men with stubbled chins, which shed light on the shortcomings of Iranian statecraft. Many of them were ethnically Turkic. An insignificant observation until Sanjar told me that many powerful officials were of Turkic ancestry. Some Iranians fret about the *Turkification* of Iran, part of Pan-Turkic economic ambitions stretching from the Bosporus Strait to the Xinjiang Uyghur Autonomous Region in China.

To get an idea of this expanse I had to make an analogy. I imagined a clan from the Ozark Mountains. They would have to swell in number, pride, and sense of destiny. Banjo picking would have to turn into a national anthem, shotguns into Kalashnikovs, a backcountry honor code into a transnational creed. The pale faces would have to multiply from New York to California. It's a three-thousand-mile sweep of fellow tribesmen. Only then did the scope and presence of Turkic peoples in Western and Central Asia sink in.

The Azeri, a Turkic tribe, are the second-largest ethnic group in Iran. There is worry that immigration of Azeris from Azerbaijan, and relocation of ethnic Azeri-Iranians to gas rich regions, are part of a scheme by Turkic power holders in Tehran. The Kurds in the southwest and Baluchis in the southeast feel neglected and are subject to agitation. Iranians believe these groups are "tickled" by foreign powers, like Iraq and the US, to turn grievances into revolt.

Many Iranians are suspicious of dwelling on the tribalism of their country, seeing it as a ruse by others to divide and conquer the country.

What I saw was another stratum of Iran. The Azeris were a lithified layer of Iran's historical ethnic flux. The current situation allowed them to show their pride, to transform. Through the grinding of political forces from within and without, they were surfacing like fresh rocks from deep within the geologic mishmash of ethnicities. Now, the tribe's modern sons were seated in some gatekeeper posts in the government.

THERE IS A TREASURE HOUSE of ethnic faces in Iran, as it is, collected over a couple thousand years of Persian Empire.

Sanjar once called out "*Ni hao!*" only to have the "Chinese" man answer in Farsi that he was Iranian. The ancient Persian Empire did touch 3.4 million square miles, from the Indus Valley to the border of Greece. Persian soldiers spread their DNA across that expanse, and conscription added to the mix. There is dark and light skin, Asiatic and European faces. The large Persian nose still dominates the genetic stew, leading to a booming business in plastic surgery.

Depending on the political agenda, the boundaries and populations of ethnic groups expands and contracts, but most people strongly identify as Iranian because of the geographical and cultural continuity of Persia. For those needing religious confirmation, Ayatollah Khomeini himself deemed the concept of "ethnic minority" contrary to Islamic doctrine.

That decree has proved an inconvenient foil for geopolitical facelifts attempted by Russia and the US. For example, the Republic of Mahabad was created by the Soviet Union as an attempt to attach northwestern Iran to itself. The Soviets supported a group of Kurds, who enjoyed the arrangement as long as the Soviets kept the Iranian army out and gave them economic support by buying their entire tobacco crop.

When the Soviets pulled out after World War II, support for the leader of the new republic dwindled as they became isolated by the West. The life span of the Republic of Mahabad was less than one year.

More recently a bus carrying eleven Revolutionary Guardsmen was bombed by a Baluchi separatist group. Evidence of US involvement in the attack has been located by American reporters.

AT THE TURN of the twenty-first century, a vintage absurdity was caught on film across the border from Iran. At a press conference in Baghdad, a US general complained about Iran meddling in Iraqi affairs.

The preoccupation with America in Iran is justified and at the same time self-defeating. The US pushes its weight around as much as it can, just like any entity with power. I purposely tried to avoid political talk in Iran because I did not want to deny, justify, or condemn this reality.

One afternoon at a park called Jamshidieh, Sanjar and I met a young man who told us, "If the US economy became like that of the third world, the country would quickly split into warring tribes along color lines." One look at the tribal outlay inside U.S. prisons, where vulnerability requires a raw racial dictation of what defines brotherhood, reveals the truth of his words.

I remember Sanjar providing commentary once while we drove through the neighborhoods of Minneapolis: "There goes the Chicano Tribe. The Somali. And here we have the African American Tribe. Over there is the strongest and most heavily armed tribe, the only ones who can move easily through the territory of the others." He was pointing at a police cruiser containing two white officers.

I've rarely felt informed enough to go head-to-head with someone over politics, but I decided to preach to the young man in Park Jamshidieh.

"Poor Americans have always been in third-world conditions!" I told him.

"No, no. Not like the real third world," he replied.

"Yes. They do their best to hold it together, but poor black people have always been living in near wartime conditions. They have the wartime statistics to go along with it: higher birth rates, and infant mortality, undernourishment, raids, curfews, broken up families, many adult males in prison camps."

The man stared ahead. I was up against the still-potent myth circling the globe that in America money and opportunity can be picked off the ground if you have knees that bend.

WHEN WE RETURNED to the apartment from the Foreign Ministry, triumphant, Sepehr and Sanjar's uncle were having tea. We had entered the heart of bureaucracy, faced down a series of stubborn male secretaries, and worked loose a result.

"How was the office?" Sepehr asked, himself a decorated veteran of bureaucratic struggles.

"The bread they were having for breakfast was very lousy," Sanjar said as a catch-all for the incompetence he felt pervaded the office.

"Well, they did everything they said they would. Didn't they?" Sanjar's uncle, a geologist who had worked for the government, did not like the whiff of ungraciousness.

Sanjar is rarely silent. When he is, I know someone has said something true.

If I looked into Dr. Mostafavi's profile on the Internet, I could find reason to condemn him. A photo of him shaking hands with a certified despicable character from the international stage. Searching my own memory, I find how he treated me, and the fact that he kept his word.

IN GRANADA, SPAIN, I was sitting inside a cloud of smoke, wondering how I got there. Saleh held the mouthpiece of a water pipe in his hand. Finding the beginning of a journey is not so easy. It was late and I wouldn't be returning to the pensión where I had rented a room. In Middle Eastern culture, which Saleh was a part of, male friends hold hands, get battered at Turkish baths together, and are altogether more affectionate with each other. This was my reasoning when Saleh offered to give me a foot massage and I accepted.

The socks that I had been wearing for two weeks were peeled from my feet. Anyone willing to touch them was a saint, and worthy of some trust.

After a few minutes Saleh said, "I have an idea." He disappeared into the bathroom and came back with a strong-smelling lotion.

The hashish was swirling, but I was hanging in there, conscious of consciousness. It was without a doubt the greatest massage I have ever received. I lay back and enjoyed some of the attentions that have bonded men for millennia, with one hand ready to cover my zipper.

In the morning we sat on his balcony for breakfast. Two cups of bitter black coffee steamed in the Andalusian sun. I looked at a spoonful of sugar above my cup before dropping it in. As it dissolved, I realized someone was shouting.

"Saleh! Saleh! *¿Dónde estás?*"

We both peered over the railing. Two stories below was the image of a biblically proportioned white beard, a red face, and two excited eyes. We waved at each other.

"*¡Dos horas, amigo!*" Saleh answered him. The man seemed satisfied and bounded up the hill with giant strides.

"I am going with some friends to take a mud bath this afternoon. You can stay and we'll go together," Saleh said to me.

This was an invitation to live a completely different life. I would learn Arabic and Spanish and make journeys around the world. I could learn each story attached to the artifacts that filled Saleh's room.

"Me voy. No me voy."

I turned towards the Alhambra. Saleh gave me a good hug and wished me well. I walked down the steps, my laundry bag backpack slung over my shoulder, and made a private vow.

The late morning sun plunged over the uneven tenements and landed on the narrow cobblestone streets of the Albaicín in jagged waves of light. The curve of the stones rippled under the worn rubber of my shoes. For a moment I felt I was standing in the clear water of a mountain stream.

From an open window I heard the polished first note of a Sade song. I turned my head up. Beyond red petals in a window box, and through the frame, I saw the darkened angles of a stranger's room. As I passed, the first few lines of the song were clear, before my stride opened and only the melody remained. She was not going to pretend to stop living, or that she was able to forgive. I could only hum the rest.

"If you die without seeing the Alhambra you have not lived." I was on a train to Sevilla. I had copied those words, author unknown, on a small piece of paper. I had gone to the palace at sundown—it was beautiful and deserted. Saying no to Saleh was haunting me more than the lonely Moorish ruins. I tried to say "yes" to as many things as I could in the following years.

True invitations are rare, offered in life a few times, and sometimes only once.

Chapter Twelve

A PIECE OF BREAD the size of a welcome mat covered the kitchen table. It was sangak, a staple of Iranian daily life, and now of mine. Its low price made it a vanquisher of citizen unrest. There were plates piled with feta cheese and fruit. In front of us were hot glasses of tea. The samovar on the stove held a day's supply of hot water, and in a pot above it tea leaves brewed.

"Iran is below Iraq and Afghanistan in Internet speed," Javid spat out of the blue. He was the son of the family cook, and a friend of Sanjar's.

"Well," Sanjar answered, "would you like America to come here and fix it for you?"

We had gotten up early to go to the Visa and Immigration Office to present the letter from the Foreign Consul and get my passport stamped.

"The way business goes in Iran makes it so bad." Javid had a green piece of melon in his hand. He postponed eating it so he could argue.

"Hey man, America will gladly come," Sanjar said and chuckled, with a mouth full of *sangak* and feta.

"In America companies fight each other; in Iran customers fight each other. In the neighborhood you fight like hell for the wire to come to *your* apartment. Then you still sit to wait one hour for the Internet to come on."

"Your tea is getting cold." Sanjar nodded at my steaming cup.

I soaked the ball of *sangak* in my mouth with a swig of tea. The bowl of sugar cubes had been refilled by Hamid, one of the family's workers. The night before I had eaten them like popcorn with five glasses of tea. I took two cubes and put them in front of me. It felt good to just sit with Sanjar and Javid. I put a sugar cube between my teeth, then melted it into my mouth with the rest of my tea.

Javid's cousins were packing up Sepehr's huge library in boxes—the family was preparing to move apartments. Volumes in Farsi, Arabic, French, and even Russian filled them; law books, philosophy, Persian classics, history. Sepehr remembered most of the things he had read. In front of this sort of learning, you don't expect to have conversations. You sit back and listen.

This did not stop people from approaching Sepehr with questions and requests. And people did show up before Sepehr with requests. It had happened Sanjar's whole life growing up, and now I saw it myself. Young and old people at the door with their heads lowered a touch. One advantage they had was knowing they were in the presence of a generous man. They would be invited to sit and have tea and fruit. After some unknown timer—signaling decorum had been observed—went off, they would begin, "*Agha*, I have this problem …"

My type of problem, however, was out of his purview, and we would have to make the trip.

IT WAS A SHORT WALK to the private taxi stand where we went to catch a ride downtown to the Visa Office. We passed giant sycamores and poplars, grateful for the quiet streets of North Tehran. Soon we would be in the agitated city center.

The taxi stand owner, sitting in this modest office, was surprised to see us. Business was an abnormal part of the day. He and Sanjar had a conversation that sounded more complicated than necessary. When I saw this simple exchange—money for a ride—become an orchestral point and counterpoint, a line from Bruce Springsteen's song "Hungry Heart" popped into my head. The gist of it being that you just put down your money and play your part.

The man nodded at one of his young drivers, who turned from his buddies, looked at us, and walked in slow motion to his white taxi.

WE ARRIVED at the Visa Office, which was squeezed between two clothing shops on Valiasr Street. A green paint job framed the aging gold lettering of its name, "Visa and Immigration Office of the Islamic Republic of Iran." Two scrawny members of the *Artesh*, Iran's regular army, slouched at the door.

We went down some steps into a dim room filled with light-brown people, black hair, and hijabs. It was crowded but calm. This was a time when the vice grip that characterizes Iran's geopolitical situation surfaced locally. Standing in the line, which stretched in front of and behind me, were Afghans and Iraqis.

With almost no help from the outside world, Iran hosts the world's third largest refugee population. In the games of the great powers, humans were batted back and forth over borders like ping pong balls. Iran had to turn victims into guests, cheap labor, and something less than a burden. They were all around me: the anxious, humble faces of people forced to ask for help. Refugees from conflicts seeking help from a country that might be next on the hit list.

The US military's invasion of the countries on Iran's eastern and western borders made it hard to blame Iranians for their watchful demeanor. In fact, the Iranians should have been the happiest of all to have the Iraqi regime sacked. They had been attacked with poison gas in the Iran-Iraq War. Desperate for soldiers, the Iranian Army drove around "party" busses. Boys would be invited on a heroic trip. Once on the bus they were driven to the front where they were made to clear minefields with their bodies; the morbid reality was that the party was in paradise via martyrdom.

"Let me tell you, I hate the guy, but still I didn't want the U.S. to go in," Sanjar had said back in America about Saddam Hussein. "War is like surgery: it unbalances the whole system."

Muslims believe the community of the faithful is one body. When one part is hurt, the rest of the body feels it. To Sanjar, that body was humanity: the shock of war that inflamed the tissue around the incision in the Middle East went all the way to the trembling hand of a veteran watering his lawn in North Carolina. The US disruption of the Taliban also supposedly benefitted Iran. The Iranians had almost invaded Afghanistan themselves after the Taliban's execution of diplomats at the Iranian Consulate in Mazār-i-Sharīf in 1998. The result of the US invasion, though, was more chaos and refugees.

For ordinary Afghans, Iran had for decades been a place to find better wages and health care. It was also a refuge from Soviet brutality, civil war, tribal violence, and now US drone strikes. Poor and with less formal education, Afghans were welcomed on religious and humanitarian grounds rather than as a legal obligation, and were treated as second-class citizens.

For many Iraqis who were Shia (a branch of Islam), Shia-dominated Iran was an understandable haven, given the nastiness of Iraq under Saddam Hussein, who was Sunni (a different branch of Islam). Iraqi Kurds fled to the northwest, Iraqi Shia Arabs to the southwestern border. Viewed as wealthier and more educated than Afghans, the Iraqis enjoyed more rights in Iran.

They also arrived in a place where the phrase "nothing good comes from Iraq" was still on people's lips. I first heard it used to describe the waves of dust blowing east across the Zagros Mountains. It likely reaches back to the Muslim invasion of the Persian Empire, which originated in Arabia, collected itself in Iraq, and rolled on to military and religious, if not cultural, triumph in Persia.

A FRIEND OF SANJAR'S in Iran got married on a weekend. For the wedding he gave himself a close shave. Then he added two days to his honeymoon to give himself time to re-grow his beard before returning to work at a government post. Loyal revolutionaries make up a good portion of government employees, and might look at a smooth face as a broken mirror upon which to assert their piety.

I had read on an "Iran visa" thread on a travel website that everyday details could influence the likelihood of a visa extension—a shirt that is too nice or not nice enough, word choice, the hair on your chin. In a land with loose laws, this divining had become a pragmatic art. The mastery of this art might have mattered more in the end than the political details of a refugee's situation.

When it was time to send in a picture for my visa application back in America, I had curls that tumbled off the back of my head like a wild rapid. I imagined my hair marked as a decadent Western attribute, a freak flag, in the eyes of a stern Foreign Ministry official.

Sanjar recommended that I keep it a little shorter when I came. It turns out that in Iran, having long hair does not raise assumptions among security officials about your politics, but about your romantic preferences.

"PEOPLE'S BRAINS are in their eyes!" I had heard this line from Sanjar before. This time it was during a Minnesota spring, when warmth and the sight of skin make driving around fun again. At a stoplight, Sanjar had greeted the girl in the next car.

She offered a toothy sneer. The light changed and she sped off. Sanjar looked ahead.

"God, maybe if she spent less time whitening her teeth and more time cleaning her heart ..."

Sanjar would encourage people to acknowledge the superficiality of the world. More than once I heard him say, "Man, the best style is a fit body. Then any clothes look good."

Sitting in my old Mazda Protegé, Sanjar shifted around on top of the crumbs that covered his seat. I caught him looking at the empty coffee cup that I had turned into a fruit cocktail of banana peels and apple cores.

"Look, you should get a nice new car," he told me.

"I don't need one."

"You'll see what I'm talking about."

"This one's okay. It runs and I don't have to worry about it getting stolen."

"No, no. You see, if you show up in a nice car, all of a sudden you'll wonder why everyone likes you, and why they are laughing at your jokes. People are so fucking stupid. Like a bunch of sheep. I told you their brains are in their eyes!"

"But I'm a public-school teacher ..."

"Just think about it."

AT THE VISA OFFICE in Iran, there were worries that went beyond hair and teeth care. I looked around at documents being clutched in each and every pair of hands.

An Iraqi man had made it to the counter with his paperwork, his wife and three children dropping in height successively behind him like the tale of a once-mighty dragon.

He leaned toward the glass in a tortured bow. In his hands were two folders full of stamped documents of all sizes. The officer thumbed through the pile and frowned: there was a piece missing in the application. He handed back the folders.

Time was running out for the Iraqi. He needed to stay tolerable to the officer.

Faster than a magician, his thick fingers ripped through the files. His wife lunged forward, pecked a half sheet of paper from the side of a folder, and handed it to the officer. By some combination of effort, luck, and timing, they oiled the gears of a great creature (half man, half paper), and lurched forward with their lives.

CLUTCHING MY LETTER from the Foreign Ministry, I stepped to the counter, the stakes so much lower for me than for the Iraqi family. The officer had a round, dark, whiskered face. Sanjar told him the story of Dr. Mostafavi and our trip to the ministry, dropping so many names that the man behind the glass interrupted him with a smile.

"Sir, you're always mixing up names."

Sanjar did not let up, implying a mandate of importance and official backing for my extended stay. The officer shrugged and looked back down at the letter.

"You didn't have to do all that. You could have just come to see me."

"Yes, sir," Sanjar answered.

The letter was small, a half sheet of paper, but the name on it mattered. It got me the stamp on my passport, and I kept it in my cargo pant pocket for the rest of the trip. Sanjar, as an Iranian, appreciated its alchemical properties.

"You have no idea what the word of a big man means, what this letter means. It's the only reason we are being treated this way, the *only* reason."

As we walked out of the immigration office with the visa extension, the words of Sanjar's uncle returned to us: "They did everything they said they would do."

Valiasr Street was sunny. It was midday and people filled the sidewalks. We all had to dodge the occasional motorcycle escaping the traffic jam. Leaping to the side of the motorcycles in unison with the men and women of Tehran, I felt like I had won a role in the epic musical of Iran's megacity.

We strutted down Valiasr Street. We got an ice-cream cone to celebrate, and stood around. Passing my camera over the counter to the vendor, I stood with Sanjar and straightened my back. Sanjar was dubious. The juice vendor snapped the picture and handed the camera back over the counter. We looked at the digital image and Sanjar let out a puff of derision. A bowl of bananas blocked half of me, while a box of straws cut off Sanjar's chin.

"See. Lousy."

I read it as part of Sanjar's ongoing and general condemnation of the way citizens of Tehran had lost a touch of class in his eyes.

But our business was finished, and it was time to walk the city with renewed confidence. We carried on down Valiasr. I noticed that despite the sun none of the men were wearing sunglasses.

"How come?" I asked Sanjar.

"They don't want to look like they have something to hide," he answered.

"I feel the same way."

I WAS SITTING on my parents' porch in Minneapolis and the mail arrived. I got a postcard from my sister. She must have been in Portugal when she sent it. It was a black and white photo of an ancient boat decomposing on a beach. For an afternoon, the three-by-five-inch stock paper would become my magic carpet.

I looked through the grey fuzz of the porch screen and floated away to the streets of Lisbon hours after midnight. A New Year's party had ended. Two long tables overflowed with empty wine bottles so that not one inch of tabletop remained—a bed of nails for the last drunk.

My sister and I were with friends from the island of Cabo Verde. I see us walking quietly together. Guilherme, a sinewy philosopher with thick glasses and a nasal drone, was there. Ana, a young dancer who was sick from the wine. Antonio and Simão, friends who each claimed they would go to the end of the world to deliver the other an ice-cream cone.

"Everybody wait," the nasal hum of Guilherme's voice called out in the dark. He was gripping the top of an iron gate. Sleepy, we shuffled to a halt like cattle. His head was tilted toward the sky. "You will remember this. You were standing here with Guilherme in Lisboa.

Here with Guilherme, this night, you were looking at the moon."

The summer afternoon came back into view. Through the grey fuzz a huge pink hibiscus flower bowed twice in the breeze. On the bottom of the postcard, in the space under the address, were the words "But you have to choose: to live or to tell." I recognized it as a Jean-Paul Sartre quote my sister had probably carried away from a college course.

There were reasons why I was taking hardly any notes in Iran. I wondered if one of the reasons was the command I read that afternoon.

Chapter Thirteen

THREE OLD MEN were singing ballads on the side of the mountain path. A few couples were standing around listening. The heavy chanting easily found a way into my sunny mood.

"Man, old Greek politicians and scholars would write their speeches and then hire young men to deliver them." Sanjar was talking loudly.

"It sounds alright," I said.

"No. What are these guys doing? Moaning and bitching! Can't they teach their sad songs to a pretty girl? Then at least it'd be something to look at."

We kept walking until the bend of the hiking path silenced their voices with a limestone wedge of the mighty Alborz mountains.

It was the start of my second week in Tehran, and we had a routine going. The first step was *sangak*, feta, fruit, and tea in the morning. Then, if we didn't head for the mountains, we would go on a short expedition into the city, to the bazaar, a museum, or a café.

We were always back to the apartment in time for Neda's lunch. Neda was the family's trusted cook. When the afternoon got hot, we would take a siesta. When night fell, we would call Roy, Sanjar's Iranian friend, because in the night there was all that could still happen. With Roy, there was a chance it would.

Most of life is spent between points A and B. In Iran I didn't cover much distance. What was between points A and B was not miles but time. Not much happened but the passing of time—in between rounds of tea, waiting for a minibus, or in a traffic jam. It made the miles we walked up and down the mountain path near Sanjar's apartment feel grand and sprawling.

I remembered the American writer Kurt Vonnegut, whose wife pestered him as they ambled to the post office and waited in line to buy a single stamp.

He said to his wife, "I tell you, we are here on Earth to fart around, don't let anyone tell you different."

WHEN I TOOK my first hike to the top of Darakeh, I kept my eyes on the rocky path. Then, stopping to look back down, I saw smog clinging to the city below. But up ahead the blue sky met the mountaintops.

It was when I turned to keep walking that I got a good look at Evin Prison.

The site had an effect. A high stone wall runs along the first mountain ridge in jagged steps. Beyond that is the prison built into the mountain, eight stories deep according to reports. I lowered my eyes, not wanting to invite in the reality of the prison. Even from the outside, the agenda within its guarded walls imposed itself, clearly and publicly. It was part of the point. Evin was one of the choice symbols of power and oppression in Iran.

While ascending Darakeh, a parallel descent into Evin shadowed me.

IT IS THE CONCENTRATION of injustice that powers the grim reputation of Evin. Constructed in 1972 and initially run by the dreaded CIA-trained SAVAK intelligence service of the Shah, its holding capacity has grown from 320 to upwards of fifteen thousand. So many intellectuals have circulated there that it has acquired the nickname "Evin University."

The American hikers, one of whom grew up in my home state, were in there at the time. Conspiratorial and mainstream versions of events are indistinguishable in Iran. One such version is that there was no reason the hikers, each of whom spoke one of the region's languages, should have been so close to the border. That must make them spies.

As I stood a thousand yards from Evin, I found myself reflecting on American prisons. That was where you could find many of the strongest, best-looking, smartest black men in America. America has its share of political prisoners, but they are not categorized as such. Many potential business and political leaders of the black community are taken out early and often. Culture clashes with the white middle-class school structure, suspensions, and juvenile detention lead to tattered academic records. On the streets, microscopic property offenses or fleeting macho moments were given immortality on state rap sheets.

This amounted to digital shackles, which were dragged into a future in which a potential employer's mouse click would reveal prior convictions or a lack of diploma, releasing the guillotine's rope before an interview could even take place. Execution by machine: quicker and less painful for both the executed and the executioner, just as the humanitarian inventor of the guillotine intended.

Then there were the other executions. The numbers were not good for Iran: 180 were carried out one recent year, second only to China. The United States executed forty-six people in the same year. If one dares to cast a black light on the global terrain, another number can be added to the US total for the year: targeted killings by way of drone strikes reached into the hundreds. As nasty as some of those targets were, they were, in effect, executed. There were ways to warp the numbers, and I knew I was guilty of it. I wanted the statistics from America and Iran to neutralize each other so I could find equanimity standing next to Evin.

IN HIGH SCHOOL I paged through an atlas and found a place called "Magic City" outside
Amarillo, Texas. The first chance I had, I got in a car and drove there. The atlas was from the early 1970s and stained with coffee. When I pulled over where the town should have been, all I found on the side of the road were the brick foundations of a ruined building.

The local sheriff passed by and found me standing off the county road staring at a pulverized armadillo. He confirmed the town was now a ghost.

I drove to a restaurant in Amarillo. A Coke was placed on my table by a waitress wearing the last ration of white and neon orange spandex in Texas. I made nice and after her shift she told me to follow her. She speeded to her friend's trailer. In the dark I followed her up a wooden ramp to the door. It was locked. We looked through the window into the shadowy room: a katana sword sat on a coffee table next to a pair of red Converse high-tops.

We got in our cars and drove to Denny's. She made a vibrant crayon drawing of mythic flowers on the back of a placemat. She said she wanted to try *everything*. It terrified me. Her friend showed up warbling about a job interview at a video game arcade. She slid the drawing over to him.

She followed me into the parking lot. The night sky of the desert was bigger than I expected. There was room to move towards the east, west, north and south. I picked one and said goodbye to the waitress.

The windows were rolled down and Pink Floyd was playing on the cassette deck. It was a live recording, and I felt close to the people cheering between each song as my headlights pulled me through the darkness.

At 3 a.m. I entered Palo Duro Canyon. I wondered if she had had the key and if it had been her trailer—if a dip of silence as we looked at the sword, or my off-tempo movements of inexperience, had changed her mind.

The outdated map, with Magic City still circled on it, had brought me to a canyon in West Texas, where I was walking down a dry riverbed with a can of baked beans and a sleeping bag. A rock shelf on a ridge was lit by moonlight. I crawled under. In the morning I dusted myself off and rubbed my eyes. A red can of beans sat on a rock with its circular lid upright in the air. Beyond that two deer puzzled their bodies into a light-brown landscape and froze.

꠲

DEAD MAN WALKING is a film that came out the same year I drove to Texas. It is about a man on death row in Louisiana and the nun who tries to guide him towards redemption. The death penalty was being debated again on television.

All the while I was chatting to the sheriff, tip-toeing up to a trailer with a waitress after midnight, wandering in the desert—acts equal to a simple hike up the mountain in Darakeh—I never once thought about the huge number of executions carried out in Texas.

I did not think about the number of prisoners in America, a country in which one of every hundred adults was incarcerated. Nor did I think about roaming around in the most heavily-armed place in the world. For every hundred people there were ninety guns.

An assumption about the rule of law in America was what gave me peace of mind in Texas: there was some recourse for those un-befriended by wealth or privilege. By contrast, it was imprisonment and violence done in the name of the law that I feared in Iran.

THE LACK OF A COMPETENT public-relations sense damages Iran's leadership. Ill-advised acts, when they happen, are managed poorly. The arrest of the hikers, flag-burning street parties, militiamen on mopeds wildly swinging sticks at protesters like deranged polo players—all give the impression of unpredictability and amateur score-settling. When a government official redirected a river to water his pistachio patch, it projected lawlessness at a comical level.

A review of American actions still shows similarities with Iran that even American public-relations efforts can't shine and buff away. I took the case of the hikers and compared it to the case of the 12- and 89-year-old peasants turned in to US soldiers for cash rewards in Pakistan and Afghanistan, respectively. These peasants were known to be innocent, but they were held in Guantanamo for years because their release was "politically impossible" according to a US administration preparing the public for another war.

I compared the shooting of protestors in Iran with the case of an Iraqi insurgent vaporized by the United States Military Forces. Suppose an American missile had flattened his house and killed his family. Holding a homemade peace sign on a bridge every Wednesday evening at five would not suffice as an expression of dissent. But his protest in the form of picking up a weapon to expel the invaders would make him an enemy combatant and a 'fair' target.

In the US, brazen corruption is otherwise known as campaign contributions.

As for police shakedowns, they are smoother and more civic-minded in the US. Cash-strapped cities issue more speeding tickets, on average, than rich cities. The city gets the money, but the city pays the police.

TEACHERS AND PARENTS worry about children swearing: "shit, fuck," "fuck, shit," or any other combination. Those words are mischievous grunts compared to the "bad words" adults use (without realizing it) when talking about places like Iran. Words like "sanctions" (actually the suffocation of entire generations), "collateral damage" (a deft linguistic downgrade indicating the murder of women and children), and "terrorism" (which frames resistance of any manner as a cowardly abomination).

Most deceptive of all: "freedom," the sleepy word designating a thing you can claim to have without ever bothering to check if that is what you actually have, want, or can tolerate.

And that was it: Evin Prison.

Understand Iran, condemn America, or vice versa, it was an elaborate, selfish mind game to put myself at ease as I walked past the prison.

Eventually, Evin came close to being just another name to me. Evin, after all, is a commercial and residential area in North Tehran. Whenever we jumped into a cab or bus, Sanjar asked the driver if it was heading to "Evin-Darakeh." This never failed to bring with it enough double feeling for me to spook a horse. I am not a data type of guy, but I ran the numbers comparing the likelihood of imprisonment and death in the US to Iran and liked them.

Still, the prison would remain the touchstone of the worst that could happen in Iran.

WE KEPT ON walking up Darakeh that first day. Eventually I lost sight of the prison wall. Breathing in the fresh air, I began seeing Iranians climbing over smaller walls. They were the crumbled and benevolent walls that steer hikers clear of steep drops to the Darakeh River, which runs alongside the path for its entire length. On its banks were spots of shade, each one suitable for a picnic. One after another, we passed scenes of families and friends spread out on rugs with the samovars, lunches, and gheliyuns (water pipes) they had hauled up. I finally saw Iranians having some fun in public.

The coffee shops along the way each formed their own installations of Eastern dreamscapes. Raised platforms, long and wide, were covered in red Persian carpets and shelves lined with *gheliyuns*. Watermelons ringed the edges of cool fountains. On the hour men in blue coveralls with would appear with buckets and hoses to keep down the dust.

It was a weekday, and the hikers and picnickers became fewer and farther between as we climbed higher. We went up to the second level balcony of a coffee shop, where it was possible to take a nap undisturbed. Sanjar drained his tea and settled in.

I gave it a try but lying down on the dais I couldn't sleep.

One eye opened and focused on the silver bowl of sugar cubes sitting on the tray and then the green leaves off the balcony behind it. The leaves belonged to a grove of walnut trees. When I sat up and opened my other eye, a hazy view down the ravine unspooled.

Sanjar had his arm over his eyes next to me. He was never really asleep. In his old first-floor apartment in Minneapolis, his friend Ferris, having ripped a hole in Sanjar's window screen, would get him up in the middle of the night, with a few knocks, to play chess at Perkins.

The service at these cafés was usually terrible, the responsibility of young men, usually Afghan, who made it very easy for us to disappear into a corner. Customer neglect was a godsend.

It is one of my great pleasures in life to be left alone at a café. In Iran, it had a special sweetness.

With both eyes, I could just see through the dust and smog below to where development in Tehran was clawing itself halfway up the skirt of the mountain. The people who made it to rugged Darakeh made their own harmonious temporary society, cut off from the jaded social terrain of the city.

GETTING READY to go out to a club or around the lakes in Minneapolis, Sanjar and I would joke, "Let's go look at hair!" It was our private joke to remind us to appreciate America.

The amount of hair showing beneath the hijabs of young Iranian women was the equivalent of cleavage in the US: the subject of conference calls in front of bedroom mirrors.

At Darakeh I saw some incredible feats of balance with scarves basically serving to cover only a woman's ponytail. If we walked farther up the path, some scarves hung untied under the chin. At a certain altitude the scarf disappears into a purse: flags taken down from an enemy fortress with new blonde, black, and brown banners of hair flowing in their place.

THE AWKWARD appeal of being American in Iran became evident in Darakeh. It turned out that a few words of English had the potential to bend time. A woman out for a stroll might choose to reposition herself as loyal wife by the time I finished saying "How are you?" Such was the desperation and ambition to find a way out of Iran.

Many Iranians were bilingual. They used one language for public life and the other for private life. Avoiding political trouble required such discipline and vigilance that it really did necessitate two languages. This made many people multi-lingual, with the addition of English, French, or German. The intelligence of so many of these women was so fierce, having been gained at such a great price, that with the smallest of English vocabularies they could discuss anything.

"GREEN CARD!" Looking over I saw a boy smiling. Women were not the only ones drawn in by the sound of English. We had encountered a group of junior-high kids sitting on a stone ledge.

"Green card!" He called out again.

Knowing bursts of laughter came from his buddies. Seeking out pen pals for my own students, I tried out some English. It was clear that none of them knew much. Even their "hellos" had to muscle their way past mouths half-closed with insecurity. These were 12-year-olds: did they already think their future rested outside their own country?

Walking on I heard celebratory shouting in Farsi, this time from voices older and stronger. When I saw Sanjar smiling I demanded a translation.

"He's telling his friends, 'I've found a foreigner!'"

Soon a group of university students formed an entourage around us. I said I was from Spain, not quite ready to represent US interests. We strung together a conversation made up entirely of names from the Spanish national team.

"España, yes, Iniesta, Xavi, Fabregas."

"Pedro."

"Ahh, Pedro."

"And Puyol." At this point the Carles Puyol doppelgänger among the bunch was pointed out.

"Ha! Puyol!" I saw the strong chin and cheekbones of the central defender reflected in their pal's face.

Sanjar shook the hand of their leader. "You're a cool guy. I like you."

They whipped ahead, laughing and clowning. As they got farther away, they resembled a single organism, fearless and optimistic. The way it is with good friends.

SANJAR WAS SPEAKING to himself. We were on the narrow streets of the old Tehran suburb just below Darakeh. We had stopped to visit Sanjar's friend, who owned a bookshop, and no one was there. The shop was the size of a telephone booth shoved into a wall.

"Where is Hooshyar? Where is he? Is he *banging* someone?" The door was locked and Sanjar peeked around the corner. The shop used to be higher up the mountain, but the price of land was increasing there.

A moment later Hooshyar appeared. There was just enough room for the two of us to sit. Hooshyar boiled tea on a hot plate behind a tiny desk and offered Sanjar various wagers on chess matches. The Farsi titles lining the walls put me in a dumb trance. I recognized a huge volume of Saa'di poetry and some basic English readers on a top shelf.

"Hey mister!" Sanjar was trying to get my attention. Hooshyar had his chin in his hand and was sizing me up. "How's your ping-pong?"

"I'm the best. When they taught me the game, they didn't teach me how to lose." I touched a finger to my own chin.

"He wants to play you—for money."

"No problem. I'm ready. I didn't come all the way to Iran to embarrass people at the ping-pong table. But if he insists." I remembered a beautiful volume of Saa'di that Sanjar had won from Hooshyar in chess.

Sanjar reported my answer to Hooshyar and he rubbed his hands together. Behind his small glasses his eyes gleamed. Sanjar liked to visit him. He said he was lonely and that it was so hard for Iranian men to meet women. In all of our visits to Hoshyar, only one man ever stopped in the store—to ask directions.

TWO SISTERS SAT on a wall above the Darakeh River waiting for customers. They were
Sanjar's other bookselling friends. Their shop was out in the open, spread on a blanket under a plane tree. Polite and tough, they would come a couple days a week to make money for their

family. They were Lors, from the region of Luristan. The Lors, like the Afghanis, did much of the manual labor in the country. When they saw Sanjar they leaped from the wall and walked two huge smiles over to meet us.

There is something about teeth that tells all there is to know about the past and future of someone's material prospects in the world. One of the great cruelties of life is that the people with the worst teeth are smiling the most through life, while those with rows of perfect white Chiclets flash them briefly and often disingenuously.

Sanjar had fallen for the older sister. She was lean with a freckled face. I could see her easily managing a huge bundle of firewood tied to her back. The yellow pages of her teeth told a story of poverty and a life lived with little room for lies. Sanjar was picking on her about boys. Her smile got wider. She was engaged to be married to a youth named Mohsen. He was gone for a few more months performing his military service. Sanjar tempted her with the young American next to him.

Nodding to me, she said, "I've seen faces like that before, but *my* Mohsen!"

My vanity spiked and I had a quick, evil fantasy of carrying her away to America and bringing her to a dentist.

More people stopped to browse this open market than Hoshyar's shop, expecting cheaper prices but also titles that a shop owner would be more hesitant to carry—political titles, and complete versions of novels that had been heavily censored. In a sweep by the authorities a few months back, many of the sisters' books had been confiscated.

To me, that type of excitement over books was otherworldly.

I had to give the authorities credit—they knew people could get a hold of what they wanted to read; and what was read had power, even poetry and novels. Once a book was out there it was impossible to make it disappear. Therefore, raids occurred, but more energy was spent going after authors and potential authors. Stopping the leak at its source, as it were.

Many well-known writers have fled. Others are imprisoned or under some regime of surveillance. Some have been murdered with cinematic brutality. A poet was such a threat he was grabbed off the street while on the way to the grocery store and executed. At first, this was bizarre to me. Poets in America were depressed people, safely sequestered in graduate school workshops—champions of insignificance. I wondered if I had more in common with the censors in Iran's Ministry of Culture, believing as they did in the explosive potential of puny words. Then I thought about one of the heroes of hip-hop music who had been gunned down, Tupac Shakur: he was a poet, and he became dangerously relevant by showing up behind his words as he sang them towards the truth.

A police visit to vendors like the two sisters from Luristan was theater. In the audience were authors of unwritten books. In an essay called "Censorship," Doris Lessing describes not the victims who are famous writers, but the "wasted" or "disappointed" ones in apartheid South Africa:

> In the evenings he sits at a table where his mother and then his wife have cleared the supper things, he lights the oil lamp, he gets out his exercise book, he takes up his biro, and then—he stops. What he would like to write about are his daily struggles, the miseries of poverty, the attentions of the police, the efforts of his women to feed him and the children, how it feels to watch and—this is the worst—how his talented children are going to waste. He knows that simply to describe his life could be seen as an act of sedition ... He sits on, staring at the bricks of his wall, which he may have built himself. Would he have to leave his home, his family? Who would look after them? His exercise book remains empty. His own talents, let alone his children's, will remain unfulfilled.

THE SAME THREE old men who had been singing poems of loss on our way up the mountain had attracted a dutiful crowd on our way down. The old men were still singing from a set list of the top-forty folk songs fossilized in amber.

Sanjar couldn't figure out why people liked listening to them. When we passed the little concert, I noticed people squinting from the hot light off the rocks, eyes almost closed. I believed the crowd just yearned for forgetfulness, the kind shared in the moment with others, during live music.

Songs and stories flow everywhere within the skin of a culture. They are the blood of an open circulatory system, the heart pumping them not into narrow veins but all the cavities of the body, keeping the values, traditions, and dreams of a place alive. Sanjar just felt that a transfusion of fresh expression might pep up the culture.

Translated rock and roll lyrics are valued in Tehran. They are like specks of pigeon poop on the edifice of Persian literature—but they are new and besides, pigeon guano has an honorable history as fertilizer. One of my favorite moments in rock 'n' roll history was when Bruce Springsteen and Bono shared a stage at an awards ceremony. Bono was giving a long, serious introduction to a song, saying that rock 'n' roll is about liberty and this and that. The Boss walks over to the microphone with his guitar and says, "Let's add a little fun to that too!" The drums kick in and they begin a duet of the song "I Still Haven't Found What I'm Looking For."

I could hold my head high as an American when it came to music: new blood, new beats, the past not on repeat. Tradition and elders weren't so much disrespected as ignored.

The young Iranians, sitting there on stones with the ancient words rattling past them from dry throats, were respectful and conscious of their elders and tradition, but when you looked closer there was a touch of distrust for them both.

Chapter Fourteen

GIVEN THE CONSTRAINTS on the lives of young Iranians, it was easy to overlook the fact that the country's seemingly glorious past could also feel oppressive. It was like having a father with championship rings on all his fingers—a legend bearing down on you. For Iranians there were daily reminders, in rhyme and meter, of those who had said it first and said it better one or two thousand years ago, from a place of confidence and vigor.

Persia had once been a grand empire, fanning out from the Indus Valley in the east to the northeastern border of Greece in the west. The imperial memory in the back of the Iranian mind sent distant but audible counterpoints to each folly of the modern nation.

Even the words of the Achaemenid king Darius I seemed to provoke the religious authorities while mocking the discontent of Iran's youth. At the National Museum of Iran we saw his statue, carved in Egypt 2,500 years ago at his request, then found in 1972 at the west gate of his palace in Susa. The inscription on his robe had these words written on it:

A great god is Ahuramazda, who created this
earth, who created yonder sky, who created
man, who created happiness for man, and
who made Darius King.

AFTER I HAD READ the translation I looked up from the inscription. Scattered about the museum were guards and a few shuffling visitors. Workers and guests in a ruined economy. Anxiety about cash flow was written in the cursive of wrinkled brows. They were preoccupied with their next move: the one that would get them through the week.

Ahuramazda, the god that "created happiness for man," worshipped by Darius the Great, did not seem to have many believers in modern Iran. The headless statue of Darius was an artfully lit hunk of greywacke rock at the far end of the museum. In the folds of his sculpted robe was brownish reddish paint—the sandblasted traces of what was once a coat of many colors.

I TOOK A SUGAR hunk out of the bowl and bit it in two. I dropped the smaller half into my tea glass and twirled. The inspired molecules of the hot water circled the crystal hunk until it dissolved. We were back from a hike up Darakeh and sitting at the apartment having a snack.

"You have time now. Think of a plan," Sanjar said, with his hand above a bowl of fruit.

"What about Esfahan or Shiraz?"

"Esfahan has a square, with some shops around. You go there, then what?"

"Come on. That's it?" I replied, while eyeing a piece of feta.

"It's interesting if you go with a good guide."

"Persepolis?" I asked half-heartedly.

Sanjar plucked a big hunk of feta and added it to the collection of fruit on his plate.

"Who wants to go see a bunch of old stones?" He tore a piece of *sangak*, reducing its size to that of a king-size quilt. "If someone is there to tell a story then it's worth it. They can bring some life to those old stones."

Playing with the idea that we had to visit another city turned Tehran into a place situated on a point that could only lead to another point. It made me anxious.

I thought of the ruins of Persepolis. Even the history of the world is nothing without a storyteller. I put the bigger half of sugar in my mouth and washed it away with tea.

THE NEXT DAY we had an ambitious plan. We would stay in Tehran and take a ride on the metro. Sanjar was getting ready and I waited in the living room. Sepehr was working on his book. German MTV was on, adding a sense of motion to the large room. A girl was sitting on a beach in a bikini with a large microphone. She introduced a song and the video came on. The sound was off. I watched the red lips of the singer moving silently along two rails of white teeth. Sanjar came in and kissed his father goodbye.

We strolled the quiet streets to the taxi stand where our arrival was met with disbelief and confusion. We lingered until our presence produced the miracle of service. One young guy peeled away to lead us to his car—jeopardizing the momentum of the conversation the drivers were having on the sidewalk.

We rode out of North Tehran. I felt that there was something wrong, then I realized it was the taxi: it had seat belts. We muddled through the morning edition of the twenty-four-hour gridlock. Wing mirrors were folded so motorcycles could squeeze past. After an hour of traffic, we arrived at the metro station where we would start our trip.

The Tehran Urban and Suburban Railway Operation Company had swept and shiny floors in its stations. We walked down the stairs from the street, and I could see the fresh polish gleaming below.

"I'm going to hit my head," I told Sanjar as we went down.

"A Chinese construction company built these stations."

"What? They made the ceilings low because Chinese people are short?"

"No man, this is what it's like here. They wanted to save money on materials."

We reached the bottom and the shiny floor spread out to ticket windows, walls with Persian-style mosaics, and an empty kiosk in the corner.

"What's that for?" I asked.

"A mullah will sit there."

"To do what?"

"Give advice." Sanjar stepped forward to talk to the ticket seller.

The kiosk looked like a metal fruit stand. I imagined a man with a robe and turban sitting behind it while a pious commuter approached to ask whether he was going in the right direction.

SANJAR HANDED ME a ticket that said "One-Way" and we squeaked along the floor to our line.

As I inserted the small blue card to pass the turnstile, the words "one-way" brought a dark smirk to my face. Later, I would keep a bright orange metro card that said "Two-Trip Ticket" in my pocket as a talisman—wherever we went in Iran I wanted a way back.

Inside the train car I didn't feel like sitting and kept changing my grip on the handrails to keep from falling. Normally I like public transportation. It is a chance to see what the population of a city looks like. On the Tehran Metro, though, I felt like a captive. If we didn't speak, I passed as Iranian. As soon as the English began it was like helium, filling the ears and lifting the heads of those nearby, until they were staring at us. It demonstrated how rare Western visitors were in Iran.

Sanjar did not seem worried about who was around us, so we started speaking in English about things we saw through the window. Drowsy with incomprehension, most heads turned back to private thoughts.

In a country where privacy could be violated on a security agent's whim, the spatial intimacy of a train ride might have called for delicacy. The parts of the government that are vigilant about troublemakers rely on the fact that people never know who among them is an agent.

The reality was that the diabolical intentions among the passengers were plotted out solely by my prejudice. They were like skulls marked in red pen on a transit map showing routes of the most ordinary of commutes. Sanjar had struck up a long and intense conversation with a man in tinted glasses. Their voices would drop into whispers at times. At one pivotal moment in the conversation they were so close that their chins were almost resting on each other's shoulders.

"Man, what are you guys talking about?" I finally asked.

"He knows ..."

"He knows what?"

"Where to go."

"When? To find *what*?"

"A street market where I can get designer clothes at knockoff prices."

IN TIGHT SPACES there was a physical familiarity among strangers in Iran that was interesting, in a litigious way, to an American. Upon boarding the train cars, new passengers casually placed hands on knees and shoulders to steady the way to their seat.

Once seated they balanced each other psychologically by muttering absentminded comments on the political situation. Sanjar would translate and feed me occasional excerpts. When the talk became overtly political, I squirmed and shut down, not wanting to encourage subversive topics. I listened with fascination, and my body took on the ridiculous shapes of a teenager at the mall with his parents, affecting both indifference and disapproval.

A skinny man with his briefcase in his lap muttered to Sanjar like he was talking in his sleep.

"We wanted the Revolution. I myself was there yelling in the street," he said limply.

His eyes flickered up out the window at a ramshackle neighborhood. A jumble of grey cement squares pieced together with a web of drooping utility lines floated by. His eyes went back to Sanjar. "This is what we get. We did it to ourselves. Still, I don't want to see another revolution."

The passengers talked and complained. There was a sound barrier beneath which most comments were acceptable. The point at which commiserating became a threat to the government— at which bitching became a challenge to policy—was unknown to me. Older people looking around for someone to blame for their situation often turned on one another. I wondered if this was what caused the distrust among young people that Sanjar had commented on. It had trickled down from their parents.

There was a current of feeling among Iranians that deeply saddened Sanjar. Stressful circumstances had fused together into an emotion that was altogether too strong. I didn't believe Sanjar when he said it.

"They hate each other now, but they will be so polite to you, because you are from the outside."

THE TRAIN WAS heading deeper into South Tehran before Sanjar realized we had missed our stop. South Tehran is the poorer and more religious part of the city. Predictable and civil, but not in ways I understood. Or in ways Sanjar understood. He never went to that part of the city and didn't use the metro even though his aunt helped run the company.

Away from the center, the passengers had thinned out. Two young men in tattered blue military coveralls remained, studying the conversation in Farsi Sanjar was having with a businessman. The businessman looked back and forth from Sanjar to me before speaking.

"Why do you look so serious?"

"Do I look serious?" I struggled to gain control of my face, as if I had suffered a botched face-lift.

"Yes." He pointed to a wrinkle between his eyes and drew two fingers down over his mouth.

"I'm always like this. I have a serious camel face. It's in the genes. But I thought it only scared people in America—not in Iran."

"Smile," he ordered.

"It's hard to do on command, you know. But really, I'm *happy* … and I love Iran!"

MAYBE IT IS IMPOSSIBLE to love a nation. A nation is a fiction we agree on for decades or centuries. It can be loved as much as a character in a novel can be loved. They tell teachers that praise for students that is not specific is meaningless. Love for something abstract, like a nation, expands rapidly before it becomes diluted, unless it is filled in with the precise details of what is loveable about it.

I remember walking with Sanjar to a pizza shop run by Egyptians in Minneapolis. We had walked past a loud street preacher wielding the word "Jesus" like a battering ram, telling us that Jesus loved us. Sanjar had no problem with private, humble worship, but showy displays irritated him profoundly. He had muttered under his breath, "You *don't* know."

We arrived safely at the next block. Our reflections followed us in the long window of an Italian restaurant. Inside, well behaved alcoholics sipped their way to oblivion with the nightly "bottomless" glass of wine special. The marquee of the Uptown Theater was up ahead—a scroungy neon placeholder in the big-money makeover happening all around. Sanjar was rattled.

"I don't understand how someone can say they just love God or Jesus when they don't even know how to love another person!" Sanjar blurted out.

"Okay."

"Look, we don't even understand the number one."

"What do you mean?"

"Suppose you have a glass of water. Is it one glass of water?"

"Yeah, it's one." I was often the involuntary straight man in these conversations that would crop up with Sanjar. We were outside the pizza shop, stepping to the side of the doorway to finish our conversation.

"Is the glass filled up all the way? Is it still one glass of water if it's half-full? If it's broken is it still one glass? When you pour one glass into another bigger glass is it still one? You see, to different people it's different things. To the man dying of thirst in the desert the glass of water is life, he doesn't care what you call the damn thing."

"That makes sense."

When I caught on, there were a few seconds to confirm my understanding before moving on. Sanjar didn't indulge when it came to ideas. We would pick them up, turn them around, pass them back and forth, and carry on. We were not there yet.

"There's a game they play in theater class," I added. "It's called 'Anything but a Chair.' You make a circle around a folding chair and take turns acting out something with the chair. It could be a crutch, hedge clippers, tool for a lion tamer, whatever you think of."

"That's right."

A pink Hummer stretch limousine rounded the corner. A girl popped out of the sunroof and hooted; inside the limo a muffled chorus hollered back. She dropped back down like a sparkly prairie dog, and the vehicle sped down Lake Street.

"What about in math?" I asked Sanjar.

"What?"

"The number one."

"Only in *pure* mathematics do you have 'one.'"

We stepped into the pizza shop, where a young Egyptian met us behind a glass showcase of greasy slices. He took our order and glanced out the window.

"The weather is nice?" he asked.

"Yeah, it's pretty good," I answered.

"Soon, we'll be able to do all the things we have missed," he replied. He turned and slid a large slice of cheese pizza off his spatula into the oven.

WATCHING IRANIANS on the metro and conducting a brief appraisal of their angst, I was confused by how loyal they were to the country. I never heard (as I do from young activists in America) that their country was too big or had outlasted its purpose. No one openly fantasized about secession, as politicians do in Texas and California. The loose bad-mouthing of the federal government that is popular in America is disconnected from the selfsame critics' idea of an Empire America that is untouchable militarily and economically. I saw it as the idle talk of a more secure and prosperous people.

A nation is shaped by strange creators: a colonial official's doodling, a dotted line of blood separating tribes in a forgotten war, the square mileage of circumstantial terrain framed by mountains and rivers.

Once it has its shape, the beast only needs to be named and fed. It's an omnivore, its hunger making it blind to food and fuel that may not be healthy for it. It grows, and even the gravity of small countries becomes too strong for the balances of traditional human life within its borders. When a poor country progresses, wealth attracts farmers and fishermen to cities that are not ready for them, and people pile up in shantytowns along the cities' edges.

Loyalty to specific people was tenable, but loyalty to a political entity, a country, a cause, took imagination. It was a fiction that nations found useful for fighting wars. Loyalty was so vague and blank it could do the bidding of hate and greed: a soldier seven thousand miles away fires rounds into a mud hut, or sets the timer of a homemade bomb in a city on the other end of that seven thousand miles; only when there is silence can he question what the wreckage—and the satiated bank accounts of arms dealers or egos of militant leaders—had to do with loyalty to a country or cause.

Outside an airplane hangar in Dover, Delaware, soldiers in white gloves grip the copper-toned handles of a casket draped in an American flag. In Mashhad, Iran, a white shroud with a body wrapped inside is held above a cluster of heads chanting in Farsi. Beneath the ceremony, in the quiet of their minds, they do not really know what to say about death.

I wondered whether Iranians still felt that they were in a state of war—whether animosity, coming from both within and without, made it necessary to think of love and loyalty in all kinds of dishonest and tortured ways.

ON THE TEHRAN Metro the businessman was staring up at me skeptically. My smile was melting off my face like a waitress with her back to a table of diners. He was being a good host, but like being asked whether you're having a good time at a party, his demand that I smile filled me with doubt.

There were many seats open now but I stayed standing, squeezing the handrails above my head. The two soldiers were talking excitedly. Sanjar said they were villagers doing their military service. One reached out a moist, meaty hand to shake mine. In his ragged, ill-fitting national uniform he seemed goofy, like his little sister had asked him to play dress-up.

Their stop neared and they edged towards the door. It was a slum of South Tehran. He insisted that I come to have lunch at his aunt's house. I thanked him for his offer. He lumbered off the train with his quiet friend.

Sanjar laughed and raised an eyebrow. "Oh, they *liked* you. He told his friend, 'You know, he looks much better when he smiles.'"

THE YOUNG COLUMBIAN ran out of English verbs and nouns and was waving his arms around wildly in a dingy bar in San José, Costa Rica. Marie and I had taken our young family to the Latin American paradise to live well, like Canadian drug dealers who had cashed out.

"I love Guns N' Roses. In Bogota concert they start playing the song 'November Rain.' There was a cloud and a storm and then rain was coming into the stadium. The people, the people, the stadium ..."

He lost contact with English again and was pulling his cheeks and hair.

"Him, he, crazy." Juan, the other Columbian, was pointing at his friend.

Juan had moved into the extra room in the apartment we were renting the day I met him. Two days later I took an overnight bus to the coastal city of Nicoya to check on a job. I trusted him enough to leave him with my young family. Looking back, I try to figure out why I trusted him. Traveling sometimes makes the mind work faster.

When I talk to Marie about this episode, she shakes her head.

When I was in Nicoya, Khalil, a toddler at the time, locked himself in the bedroom and couldn't get out. Marie tried everything to get through the door. She could go down to the busy street but would have to try explaining the odd situation in piece-meal Spanish. Costa Rica is a very safe place. The country abol-ished its military a half century ago, but at the time we were living there the gentle Costa Ricans (or *Ticos*, as they call themselves) had been alarmed by a recent surge in violent robberies and drug smuggling.

It was night, and if something happened down there, Khalil would remain locked in the room. Then Juan arrived home from work. He first tried to pick the lock. Then he removed the door-frame to release a red, sweaty toddler. Juan and Marie got out their English-Spanish dictionaries to tell the story to each other and joke about it.

When I remind Marie of this she says, "Was I supposed to feel better that Juan knew exactly how to pick a lock?"

I got home late from Nicoya unaware of the minor calamity that had taken place. As I was walking from the bus stop, I noticed three men in black coveralls and combat boots eyeing me from the other side of the street. When I looked ahead there were two more in front of me. I was surrounded. The recently re-armed police took me aside, searched my backpack, examined my documents, and questioned me about my trip.

Thinking back on the faces and hands of those Costa Rican police officers, it's clear they were country boys, like the conscripts I met on the Tehran Metro. The uniforms were nicer but hung just as awkwardly from their innocent frames.

Chapter Fifteen

IN MY NOTEBOOK I did not write about what happened one night at Bame Tehran. In fact, I didn't write about much at all.

What prevented me was a waking nightmare about a security agent reading through my pages on my way out of Iran. In it, I am in a room at the airport with an agent. He looks down at my notebook with a frown and scratches his stubbly chin. He holds it out to another agent, and they say something in Farsi. They tear a sheet out and lift it to the light like a counterfeit bill.

They leave with the page, to search for an interpretation that matches my guilt. I try to accommodate myself to the idea of small rooms like this, a prison sentence. I flinch. There is a man across the table whom I hadn't noticed before.

Looking more carefully I see his beard growing longer before my very eyes, like pasta out of Strega Nona's magic pot.

The meaning of what I had written begins to transform. My scribbled notes alchemize under the interrogators' gazes into a subversive and poisonous tract against Islam and the Iranian state. The doors fly open and guards appear. They take me away.

I am led to my cell and pass some prisoners who are clean-shaven. I know they are writers. Pushed into a dark room beneath a mountain, I laugh and weep hysterically about the power of the pen. How patterns of thin ink shapes on paper can spook grown men.

As the door to my cell slams shut, I think: if nothing else, writers get a twisted respect in Iran. Censorship confirms that words are the building blocks of new worlds, and new worlds might have new masters.

SANJAR LIVED on a quiet block in Minneapolis. His redbrick apartment building was a block from a co-op and a couple of small cafés. It was a year after the invasion of Afghanistan, and a meanness hung in the air, smoggy and acidic, backlit by a glow of fickle patriotism.

"They are bugging my phone," Sanjar said with certainty.

"How do you know?"

We were standing in an alley behind a car wash. I looked at the apartment building on the other side of the alley. A curtain was half-drawn. Through it I saw a bike propped against the wall. A pudgy torso drifted into view holding an unpeeled banana. The idea of agents slinking through the neighborhood was far-fetched.

"I just know. There are noises, clicks, and this and that. Plus, some things were different in my room."

"Are you sure?"

"You know, big deal. Man, I don't really care. What am I saying anyway? They can listen all they want. If they're educated, pretty soon they will see that I am the biggest wimp and wouldn't do anything. But the problem comes when an uneducated redneck gets excited about some words he hears."

"Iran? Tehran? Kebab?" I fished for the fatal words.

"Anything political. He'll think, 'Oh my god!' It's not his fault. He just doesn't know. For example, if I say that the US Army has old Soviet maps showing over one trillion dollars' worth of minerals and metals in Afghanistan, the guy listening in is going to jump. But what have I done?"

I shrugged.

"They'll get bored with me eventually."

"Unless you're talking to your sweetheart," I added.

"That's right. You know, we have a saying in the Middle East: 'Talk to people in accordance to their understanding.' I try to do that. But how can I, if someone is eavesdropping and I don't know what they do or don't understand?!"

I DID NOT WRITE about what happened at Bame Tehran in my notebook, but it turned out that my backpack was not even opened at the airport. My words were not read. I began to understand the larger goal of censorship: getting people's own minds to do the work of the police.

Still, I waited until the plane was thirty thousand feet above Iran on the way to Dubai before I opened my notebook to see if I had written anything. It was around the time women on the flight started loosening their headscarves. Inside the notebook there was a backgammon board sketched in black pen, sentences in German about having a *Flugticket*, and a green sticker from Emirates Airlines with a picture of a plate and fork that says, "Wake me up for."

Then, a line written in English: "If I shot a wolf up here, I would get a medal."

They were the words of a skinny young *Artesh* at the mountain police post on Bame Tehran. The *Artesh* is the regular army, made up of twenty-month draftees. I saw them in various states of boredom all around the city. It appeared this one had some ambition. He had said the words to Sanjar in Farsi, but these weren't his exact words. In one of the few instances in which Sanjar translated something for me in a timely manner, I heard the one and only line that I didn't want to hear in Iran.

"If I shot an American up here ... I would get a medal."

THERE ARE OTHER reasons I didn't write in my notebook. I did not set out to write a book. I set out to see a friend. My notes from the trip add up to fifteen small journal pages of notes and a few drawings.

I am amazed at what came back to me. Episodes from Iran kept breaching out of the muddied waters of my forgetful mind.

Stories I hadn't thought about in years rose, until the calm surface of the present was roiling. Thoughts and tales were communicating in kinship like great whales that had been sounding off to each other in the depths all along.

MY COUSIN SAM is like an African griot, except he is white and grew up Catholic in Iowa. A memory like his is really an oddity in the West. He remembers all the lore of a tribe: his own. The stories migrating in the ocean of his subconscious make mine look like a group of minnows in a puddle.

In his early twenties he became the bearer of his family lore.

His mother was killed in a car accident, and the very next year, his father died of a brain tumor. He and his sister Melanie were left with a big house, a pool, and a modest life insurance payout in a town (Cedar Rapids) that grew smaller and stranger for both of them as time went on.

During the years of Taliban hysteria, he moved to Minneapolis, where he haunted the posh neighborhood of Linden Hills with a monumental beard. He is a tall man, so when you talk to him, finding his face through the whiskers is like looking up from the foot of a majestic willow tree.

Soon after my son was born, Sam took on the name "Uncle Hawowshi." Hawowshi is a sandwich made by filling pita bread with spicy meat and baking it in the oven. My father would make the Egyptian street food every year for a Super Bowl party.

Uncle Hawowshi's size and kindness towards my son turned him into a legend. When Khalil was five, he made some calculations: "Uncle Hawowshi was born when the Indians were born, and now the Indians are dead and Uncle Hawowshi is still alive."

"But Khalil, Indian people are still alive," I told him.

"Wow! That means they are as old as Uncle Hawowshi!"

My father has an interest in people and their histories, so Uncle Hawowshi appreciated him. My cousin's knack for storytelling would have made him at home in my father's village in the Nile Delta, on a bench with the elders. Once in a while I would meet my cousin by chance at a tame neighborhood café. One morning I saw a beard fill the doorway—it was Uncle Hawowshi. He sat down at my table.

"You want to hear something funny that happened at work?" He pushed his coffee aside.

"Yeah. What was it?" I lifted my paper cup to my mouth and found that I had used too much honey.

"I was at the register when a customer came up and asked who the author of a book was. I told them, 'Oh yeah, that's Isherwood. It's over there in fiction.' Then a coworker came back from her break and I went to shelve books. The whole time I was shelving books, I was thinking of this memory I have of watching a movie about the Revolutionary War starring Al Pacino. I'm sitting on the couch with my dad and it's the last scene of the movie. Pacino's character has finally found his son, who was conscripted into the war by a villainous British Sergeant Major. The father and son are on the Atlantic shore, and Pacino has his musket pointed at the Major, but he doesn't pull the trigger. Then my dad turns to me and says, 'I sure would.'"

THE WORDS SPOKEN by the young police officer at Bame Tehran were not about an animal and not about me. They were for Roy, Sanjar's friend. In my cautious attempt to not write anything that would catch the attention of security officers at the airport, I had chosen the word "wolf" to replace "American."

Roy spent a lot of time hunting in the Alborz mountains as a child. It was his explanation for why his face was like it was: friendly and red, but also tired and hangdog. He was just getting older. He ate fruit for breakfast and was a fast walker. All of which kept him vital and trim, so he could always be on the lookout for more "POW-sy." In Roy's abbreviated taxonomy of life on Earth there remained two categories: "nice, fresh, POW-sy," and the "expired ones."

Before I came to Tehran, Sanjar had not been out with Roy for a year. "Man, I can't keep up with him." Each time I heard a story about the two of them, I had to remind myself about the discreet color palette of bachelorhood.

One time they picked up a woman who was a black belt in karate. As Sanjar says, the black belts in Iran are earned.

"She could have easily taken care of both of us. And ten more men," Sanjar boasted.

Arriving at Roy's apartment, she offered them each a breast. Claiming them like twins, the three of them laughed together in vaudevillian camaraderie.

I thought Roy had dyed his hair, but he was naturally reddish-blond. This helped with his ruse: that he was a Spanish-American from California doing business for a couple of months in Tehran. He told women he "imported and exported raw materials" for a company called RAF RAF. The innuendo was lost on them, while Sanjar and I giggled like teenagers.

Roy knew the streets and was a skilled driver in a city full of grandmasters. Finding threads of space in the gridlock before they appeared, like timing a shift in tectonic plates, he brought us through Tehran traffic to his new hunting grounds: the parks and malls of Tehran. Pulling the car over, Roy jumped out and aimed for the nearest group of females. If a woman was unpleasant, he would make accommodations; if the woman decided he was a jerk, he would make more, never giving up.

THE FIRST TIME I met Roy was in the lobby of the Hotel Enghelab. The conference was still on and all the participants had gone to the revolving restaurant on the top floor. Sanjar had departed earlier, while we were still in Parviz's writing workshop at the National Library, to attend the funeral of a family friend. The plan was to meet up at the hotel.

When Sanjar left the seminar it was the first time I was alone in Tehran. Even though most of the other participants were foreigners, I had not gotten to know any of them besides Andrew. Not being plugged into the group, I missed little pieces of information and was unsure of our departure time. I stayed talking to Parviz after the class ended.

When I walked out of the workshop at the National Library, no one was around. A fountain trickled in an empty courtyard. I had missed the bus to the hotel. I picked through the pockets of my cargo pants and pulled out photocopies of my passport, but not one dollar or *rial*.

I wondered if I could even find my way out of the library complex. One by one, sensible thoughts deserted my brain, until I was a frazzled top spinning along the marble walkways of the library.

Suddenly a small brown figure appeared to my left. It was Masud, a Bangladeshi man who had been at the workshop. I had noticed him in the larger conference room. He had walked up to a panel of mullahs in mid-discussion, raised his camera, snapped a picture, and sauntered away.

"Do you think the bus has left?" I said, shoddily concealing my anxiety.

"Might have," he replied. I felt he was a little amused at my state.

In the workshop he had come off as abrupt, the way South Asians can to Westerners due to a clipped rhythm of speech. Then he had flattered me about my writing a few times in the workshop. I was at his mercy. We started walking together.

He charged ahead through a dark passageway. I doubted that it led to the exit. The white and black tiles cooled in the shadows. The mason work under our steps was solid. I trailed a few feet behind in the delirious calculation that if we were treading somewhere we shouldn't, I would be a few feet less guilty. He was walking faster now. I didn't want to totally lose him either, so I scooted along.

"Do you know where you're going?" I called out.

"This is the other way," he said, as he reached a terrace where he was caught in a honey-colored tractor beam of light.

Faith is the bird that feels the light and sings when the dawn is still dark.

IT WAS NOWHERE near dawn, but my thoughts did not care. The words of Rabindranath Tagore, one of Masud's countrymen, detached themselves from the postcard my sister had sent them on a decade before and recited themselves in my mind as I stepped onto the terrace. The bluish-purple shapes of the mountains fizzed behind layers of smog in the distance.

"I think the bus has left," Masud said as he looked down the steps to the road.

IT TOOK A FEW seconds to realize my name was being called.

"Kareem?"

I was sitting in the large old lobby of Hotel Enghelab. The room was dimly lit and all around were plush velvet chairs clumped in threes and fours. An eight-foot chandelier hung near a large spiral staircase—a frozen waterfall emitting off white light.

The glowing crystal soon resembled the icy tears of the Shah of Iran's second wife, Soraya, abandoned because of her infertility. "I Cry Like Soraya," went the French song written at the time. Like every place and person in Iran, the Hotel Enghelab, literally "Revolution Hotel," had its own tales of transformation. Its name had been changed after 1979. Rebranding in Iran was ideological, spiritual, and historical before being commercial.

The Hotel Enghelab was once known as the Royal Gardens, a five-star hotel owned by a Jewish family. After the Revolution armed thugs overran the hotel, blindfolded the last family member who had stayed in Iran, and took him away. His friends risked their names to remove his body from the Evin Prison morgue. I wondered if any employees from that time still worked there.

Recalling that story had chilled me, so I dug for a different layer of history as I sat waiting for Sanjar. In the late 1950s, Iran and the Royal Gardens had been in the cozy bosom of Cold War cooperation with the United States. In the lobby there would have been signs of the Shahs hankering for anything Western.

Businessmen from America would have been seated on those red velvet chairs chatting up Iranian clients: "Hey big spender! Naugahyde chairs are in!" or "Sir, I want you to picture a Coke machine in your office. Cold drinks at the push of a button!"

Iran was flooded with business in those days. There are legends about Tehran's popularity. Take the two American businessmen who staggered into a hospital with stomach pains. They spent the night in comfort, and the next morning, their symptoms having cleared, they left for their business conference. It was their way of finding a place to sleep for the night in a Tehran that was four thousand hotel rooms short.

Hospitals began to view foreigners with suspicion, especially if they were middle-aged white men.

It's possible the multimillionaire German playboy Gunter Sachs got his first glimpse of the Iranian Princess Soraya in the lobby of a hotel like the Royal Gardens. After her divorce from the Shah, she had fled to Germany, and I imagined Gunter remembering her from his visit to Tehran. Being chivalrous in the way playboys could be in the glory days of Serge Gainsbourg and Leonard Cohen, he offers her a gilded refuge in Berlin.

YEARS BEFORE GOING to Iran I was sitting in my apartment in front of a computer. A half glass of cold tea sat next to a sugar dispenser. On the screen the cursor was flashing. I looked out the window and saw the crown of Target Corporate Headquarters change from purple to red, red to yellow.

The Minneapolis skyline lights up at night as a sort of Midwestern illusion: what you see is a *real* city. Few are in the buildings and nightlife is sparse on the streets below. The cursor flashed again like car hazards. I had no idea what I was going to teach the next day, my first day as a student teacher at a junior high.

On my desk, next to the glass of cold tea, was a book, *The Wrath of Nations*, by William Pfaff. I picked up the book, got up, and took a few steps on the Berber rug I'd brought back from Morocco, before dropping onto the couch. Written on the first page was the epigraph "*Les morts gouvernent les vivants.*"

I walked into the kitchen, poured out the cold tea, and put the kettle on to boil.

The assignment I settled on involved students interviewing a few adults and asking them if they agreed that "the dead govern the living." After the lesson the girls in class talked about how rules were passed from their grandmothers to their mothers, which meant they had to act a certain way. They guessed that their great-grandmothers, now dead, probably were to thank or blame. One student with a thoughtful, shadowy face told me his dad "didn't like the question" because it belonged in a "philosophy, not American history, class."

A WAITER STROLLED soundlessly over the carpets of the lobby, an empty tray swinging at his side. Taking in the faded opulence of the Hotel Enghelab with my eyes, my mind was revisiting the feeling I had in the boarding area at Dubai International. The room was about a third full, a few men in suits smoking here and there. I tried to take on the disinterested air of a rich inheritor. Then I switched demeanor to the harmless wilt of a jet-lagged tourist. It was a fair question for an American in the Middle East those days:

who was I and what was I doing there?

As I fidgeted, my eyes caught those of a man who had been reading a newspaper. He looked away. I looked down. The conversations around the lobby slowed to a quiet patter, my discomfort powering the flywheel of a conspiracy.

I sat still, monitoring my composure. Across my face nonchalance and tension twitched off and on. Stronger than any layer of history was imagination. Imagination shifted the geology within me so that experiences could never harden into a bedrock of facts, certainty, confidence. The foundation of normal life that would allow me to sit in a lobby in Tehran, or on a bus bench in the Midwest, like I belonged to this world.

"Kareem?"

I didn't understand the sound. It took a few seconds to decide whether I should respond. I looked up and saw a man dressed in white with a cell phone to his ear.

"Kareem? I'm Roy. Sanjar's friend." He reached out a hand, and spoke into the phone, "Yeah, I found him."

ON THE TERRACE of the National Library, Masud and I watched as Tehran's sprawl was reined in by the setting sun. The poorer neighborhoods in the south became a few specks of orange light.

The largest of cities is still humbled by the coming of night, and even the wealthier parts of Tehran switched footing.

We looked out at the settling metropolis. Panic fluttered quietly inside me. Masud and I left the terrace and wound our way down and around the walkways of the National Library. He was casually smoking, and his pace had slowed. I had given up my weaselly ploy of letting him walk point.

"We'll get to take the metro back to the hotel," Masud volunteered cheerily.

"Yeah, the metro."

I didn't want to admit that I didn't have any money, any knowledge of where a metro stop was, any desire to stumble around Tehran at night.

"Well, maybe the bus is just parked a little way downhill," I said.

I felt the pride I had had when I left Andrew at the airport with the conference representative trickle away. The pretense of careless movement around Tehran with a local friend only worked if I was with that friend. At the time, I would have gladly accepted a chartered and government-sanctioned bus ride to the hotel.

As Masud lit another cigarette we spotted the bus down the hill, hidden behind some walnut trees. On the ride to Hotel Enghelab he spoke of his plans to "pop over" to visit Mashhad, a few miles from the border with Afghanistan. Mashhad, one of the holiest cities in the Shia world, translates into "The Place of Martyrdom."

Early on the rhythm of the trip had asserted itself: stops and starts of fear and revelation.

Chapter Sixteen

A WITCH DOCTOR peeking out of a brick hut, was my first impression. The woolly head, with an unshaven face below it, was halfway out of the ancient doorframe. Ted Storm and I were standing on a medieval cobblestone street, with a convent at our backs, and one hundred feet separating us from the Cathedral of St. James, in Spain. We had left college and gone on a pilgrimage to Santiago de Compostela to become better soccer players, and we were looking for a room to rent.

The rest of the body attached to the woolly head fully emerged into the sun. To speak, a week's worth of black stubble was parted by some lips.

"You should know that I'm a writer," he said abruptly, as if warning us that he was a different species. Adding, "If you don't mind the tapping of a typewriter after midnight you should be okay."

"That's awesome," Ted enthused, looking at me. "I think we're cool with that."

"Do you read any?" the writer asked.

"I just started *Siddhartha*," Ted replied, straightforward as always.

The black mass of hair shook up and down, slowly.

The last thing I had read was Chapter 24 in Steinbeck's *East of Eden* on the plane ride. Ted had passed me the book over the middle of the Atlantic, with the chapter marked like it was a secret Bible verse. I somehow thought Rumi might help us pass this interview.

"I don't know. I've been reading a little Rumi."

"Rumi, yeah, he was kind of the cherry on top," the man knowingly replied.

Ted and I squinted in the sun and waited as the woolly head enumerated the "house rules." We agreed to the price and to help exchange the propane tank for the stove and shower once a month.

"Well, okay. Come back later with your bags." The head plunged back inside the door to reclaim some deranged literary solitude.

When we returned no one was home. We knocked harder and the girl upstairs let us in. She had a black tooth that was on life support. Her large breasts swayed under a thin white tank top. Later, David, the writer, told us that he had to stop giving her English lessons because she "screwed like a rabbit." I can't go beyond this caricature because that was the last time we saw her.

Ted and I settled into an ancient back room, where I did spend many sleepless nights straining to hear rabbit feet hopping along upstairs.

There were other inhabitants. A Mexican named Miguel, who lived in the room next to ours, was writing a book on the Zapatista movement. David dismissed the work as a "scrapbook." David was happy to give us the room next to Miguel's because Miguel didn't take off his big ring when his girlfriend Mariola visited, and it would slam against the wall, keeping him awake.

In another room was a kind, middle-aged Spanish woman enduring the austerity and chastity of a convent without the free housing. Next to her was an Armenian with a precise beard, apparently no possessions, and a nine-year-old daughter somewhere. David was in the smallest room. His pregnant girlfriend, Shawnee, a street artist, had gone back to Malaysia to have their baby.

David and I got along, mostly because we were usually the only two people in the apartment. He had lots of books. After training with the Compostela soccer team in the mornings I would grab one and read, while Ted went out to learn Spanish, explore the city, and find a girlfriend.

~

SOON DAVID and I were passing our thoughts back and forth on a wad of folded up paper. Like monks in a monastery with a code of silence, we tiptoed through the dank hall and slid the wad through the yawning cracks under each other's bedroom doors. I only remember one note written on that wad. It was accompanied by a drawing of a circle with a dot inside it. It was a quote by an American Protestant preacher named Ralph W. Sockman:

The greater the island of knowledge
the longer the shoreline of wonder.

David had a few of those spiritual formulas on hand. He was convinced, though, that he had to spend time in an Islamic country. I had just finished reading *The Alchemist* by Paulo Coelho, so my head was filled with desert journeys, treasure, and destiny. I egged him on to go to North Africa.

One night, Ted and I ran into David at a café. We sat down and spoke for a while. David delved into his personal life in a way he didn't in the ancient apartment. He had been traveling ever since he was offered a scholarship to college.

"It was like they were offering me a pile of shit on a silver platter."

"How long ago was that?" Ted asked.

"Eighteen years."

From the café speakers an old Dire Straits song began. It was "The Sultans of Swing." David stopped talking for a few minutes, sideswiped by a melody from high school.

Late that night I saw David standing alone on some stairs that led to a square facing the cathedral. The wet cobblestone all around was skimmed with lamplight. On the ground in a heap was his Guatemalan ikat backpack. It held his passport and manuscript. All he ever "needed," he had said.

I snuck up and dragged it behind a pillar.

I peeked to see if what he had said about the bag was true. It was one long minute of watching my friend smoke alone. The orange glowing tip traveling the arc from his lips to his hip three times.

David had spent the same amount of time abroad as he had in America. After one last drag he dropped the cigarette and ground it into the medieval stone. When he saw no bag next to his feet his head slowly rose, and he stared at the cathedral or something beyond it. I thought I saw him 'shiver in the dark.' I stepped out from the pillar.

"You *little* fucker."

On the walk back to the apartment he invited me to cross the Sahara with him, to Egypt, where he wanted to live. I offered my aunt's apartment without a second thought. Miles of golden yellow sand whooshed by until the Great Pyramids appeared on the horizon line. Foreshortening was truly the mystic magic of travel planning.

My own feet were below me moving along the ancient streets of Santiago de Compostela. Past the yellow haze coming from old black iron streetlights there was a starry sky. We were at the door to the apartment. David stepped in and disappeared into his writer's cell. I looked at my worn sneakers on top of the blue-gray cobblestone. The specific gravity of stone was pushing back beneath me, heavier than the substance of my dreams.

WHAT GOT MY ATTENTION was not the repetition of my own name, but the words "I'm Roy." Sanjar's stories filled in the outlines of the figure standing in front of me at the Hotel Enghelab. I stood up and shook his hand.

When you venture towards the tip of an extremity, the weight of a thought or a single situation can bend the continuum until you are standing at the opposite extremity. A circle is formed, a snake munching on its tail. The rebel superiority I felt ditching the conference itinerary was shaken by the helpless feeling of thinking I had been left behind at the National Library.

Now I was ready to savor the certainty of the conference, the chartered bus, the guides, the dinner reservations. Then Roy showed up, and I accepted his invitation to go out that night. It would take me out of the safe fold of the conference for good. Just like that I was headed to the other extreme again, at the mercy of the lusty whims of two bachelors.

Andrew and the other conference attendees were at the revolving restaurant on the top floor, spinning while images of Tehran came in and out of focus like jewelry in a locked display.

I followed Roy as he swaggered ahead in the wrong direction, straight into the doorless corner of the lobby. We circled back in front of the undercover agents smoking in the red chairs like it was a Cold War fashion show and then out the hotel doors.

"Agent": I use the word casually, but my imagination was competing with the geopolitical reality of Iran. I felt like a bumbling double agent myself, not knowing up from down. But I was moving again, and my sneakers pressed back against the ground as I strode forward.

TO CROSS THE STREET I took my position at Roy's side. One of us had to be the human shield. In the middle of the street drivers nudged their cars a few centimeters to the left or right to spare us. A side mirror clipped my arm, and maniacal laughter spilled from a speeding Peugeot. I consoled myself. Getting run over in Tehran would at least have been death by natural causes.

While leaving his parking space, Roy knocked over a motorcycle. A small pool of liquid formed under it. A cop and an armed soldier emerged from under a store awning. They both used the gesture—an upturned hand—internationally known as the opening statement of any street-side court hearing. First, the hand reaches out until someone starts to explain. It hangs on the first few syllables before sweeping back and forth over the entire site of the injustice to make clear that no matter what anyone says, there is a mess—and money to be made. It is the sign language of third-world hustles and entrepreneurship.

Roy got out and fought back with two upturned hands, adding an extended shoulder shrug. He told me to stay in the car and struggled to lift the motorcycle back up. Some combination of the words "foreigner," "guest," "hotel pickup," and "no fucking place to park" did the trick. The cop and the soldier smiled and stepped back into the shadows of the store awning. We sped away to a small shopping mall to meet Sanjar.

AT THE PLAZA outside the mall entrance I witnessed Roy's approach to meeting women. Taking a seat on a bench next to two young women, Roy began a series of mundane questions that served no purpose but to establish that he spoke English. I recoiled, checking the lines of sight surrounding the bench. The plaza was sunk below street level, with rows of benches, and small trees and bushes in raised cement boxes. There was a dry fountain in the center. On the street level there was a secondary mall made up of tents and vendors with wares spread on blankets.

I heard Roy ask, "It's okay to talk to you, right? No policeman is coming to punch us?"

The women looked at each other and shook their heads.

Then, from across the square, a voice screamed out. A primal sound that hushed the relaxed evening chatter. Around the square people sat up straight, eyes wide, tuning their bodies for drama. Everyone disengaged with their frontal lobes. Remaining in the square were creatures, instincts poised on a razor's edge of fight or flight.

I concluded that the scream had come from the mother of one of the young women with whom Roy and I were sitting. I've been guilty of tolerating jokes about rape before. At a thrift store with my Zimbabwean college roommate, I tried on a really tight jacket. The sleeves were riding my arms up to the elbow. My friend turned to me, looked over his shoulder, and said shyly, "In Zimbabwe we say, 'He is raping the jacket.'"

When I heard the scream, I instantly convicted myself of being a violator. In high-strung, conservative Iran, flush with a pantomime of purity, I questioned whether I had somehow deflowered a woman with my breath from four feet away.

I braced for a baton blow across the back of my head.

Roy put the phone to his ear and waved. Sanjar had shown up with his cousin. A few moments passed and I saw a woman hugging a crying toddler. He had been lost. Fear worked its way out of her frazzled body to the ground like a lightning bolt.

WE ROAMED AROUND the mall with other groups of men and women who were cruising. The restrictions in Iran turn adults into teenagers. Always worried about getting in trouble, always wanting to get into it. Most of the adults in Iran—which has one of the youngest populations in the world—are indeed teenagers. In public places, a form of speed flirting ensued, punctuated by the quick exchange of numbers.

Roy had zoomed around the corner of a shoe store in pursuit. When we saw him next, he was standing next to three sisters who were each a foot taller than him. The last black roots of their hair had been expunged by industrial bleach. Long nails clutched purses, and pouty mouths were covered with lipstick applied with a putty knife.

Their male counterparts were at the mall too: muscles vacuum-packed in close fitting T-shirts and jeans, gelled hair, jewelry, and an air of insouciance and crudity.

An argument made by those who wear traditional robes is that tight blue jeans suffocate some of a man's vital components. Looking at the painfully form-fitting pants of the guys, I thought there were elements of the Islamic Revolution's platform that I could relate to.

I found myself getting less flippant about the ills of Iran as time passed. Words are not automatically wrong just because they are spoken by a mullah. In a conversation with the American scholar Geoffrey Wawro, a mullah in Kashan replied to a question about the banning of Western media, films, music, literature, and so on: "If it is sunny and you pull a shade across the window, is that bad? Westernization is like a plague of flies, and we are trying to put screens on our windows. Is that bad?"

According to Professor Wawro, his article, "Letter from Iran," in the *Naval War College Review*, became required reading for all Marines by the commandant at the time.

Anyone who has felt a gnawing sensation in their chest as they pass a strip mall, or who has seen the blanched face of their child after watching a loud and vacuous Hollywood movie, or who has miserably (out of convenience) sunk their teeth into a burger designed in a laboratory, will have unwittingly embodied the concern of that particular turbaned mullah.

Tahir Shah, the British writer who moved his family to Morocco, wrote in his book *In Arabian Nights* that he was afraid that Western tourists and influence would destroy the soul of the place. Soon he realized that they bring wealth and change, but their effect does not penetrate. Westernization passes lightly over a place with such deep cultural roots, the equivalent of a tourist stopping to take a photo.

Some Iranians would argue, at great risk, that it is the same with Islamization in the former Persian Empire. That there is a deeper culture that has accommodated Islam but has not been fundamentally altered by it.

WITH A FEW STROKES, ROY had gotten the sisters' numbers. Weeks later he claimed that they had called, wanting us to share a vacation house with them in Shiraz. That night at the mall we were content eating fried chicken and french fries at a fast food joint, sipping colas and joking. Enjoying the perks of Westernization.

Chapter Seventeen

SEPEHR WAS UP from a nap and at his table working. I never saw crumpled papers—the tumble weeds of writer's block and wobbly diction—lying around. A steady, almost flawless pace was what made a man think in terms of volumes for a writing project. He was on Volume III. A Koranic commentary from the fourteenth century was splayed open, next to a stack of books a foot and a half tall.

Filling the huge flat screen was Polish MTV. The volume was low. Lady Gaga was ordering around an army of oiled men in a dark warehouse. (They had been locked in there since Madonna made her last music video.) I could barely make out the lyrics until she yelled and a word became audible: "Alejandro!"

I made little circles with my hand so I could feel the weight of my teacup. A few drops of tea rolled around the gooey sugar crystals on the bottom of the glass.

Sanjar came out of his room with his phone in his hand.

"Hey man, let's do it. Roy is here."

We said goodbye to Sepehr, leaving him alone with the tiny voice of Lady Gaga tinkling from the flat screen. The elevator opened and we saw Roy in his small white Peugeot on the street. The windows were down, and through the glass of the apartment lobby I could hear his car stereo pumping.

Sanjar pushed the door open and one of the voices of the era came back to life in full volume. Roy made sure to hit the gas before we were buckled in. The last line of the chorus of "Poker

Face" landing on a cool, understated 'E' note. We sailed into the Tehran nightscape on a synth-pop high.

THAT NIGHT, Sanjar, Roy, and I were sitting with a group of young Iranians at a fancy place called Cinema Café that Sepehr had recommended. It was next to the gardens of the Cinema Museum of Iran known as Bagh-e Ferdows. They were studying for an immigration interview at the Canadian Embassy in Turkey. Each had a flavored concoction many generations removed from a basic cup of café au lait. They planned to go to Quebec and the interviews would be in French.

The most forceful one there was a journalist. She worked for a government publication requiring her to wear the more traditional black chador hair covering. We eyed each other and she guessed that I probably did not trust her because of her profession. It was clear she had gotten a nose job. Sanjar whispered to me that she had gone too far trying to make it perfect. He was turned off by the attention she wanted for her investment.

When I told them I was American they thought it was strange that I spoke a little French. The American reputation for worldly disinterest existed alongside beliefs in America's omniscience.

"Uh … can I ask why you know French?" one of the men ventured to ask.

"I'm with the CIA," I responded.

Sanjar shook his head in a quick but unmistakable rebuke. Joking about the CIA in Iran is like making a "bomb" joke at an airport. I hadn't just put my foot in my mouth; I had thrown my whole body into my mouth. And, terrifyingly, the would-be Canadian believed me.

CANADA AND IRAN had not been getting along. I was surprised this was the exit route the young Iranians chose. When I looked up the Iranian Embassy in Ottawa to get a visa, it was clear that a diplomatic freeze was on. There had been ambassadors pulled, and United Nations condemnations. Relations had been good until a Canadian photographer was arrested for taking photos of family members protesting outside of Evin Prison. She died while in custody.

When I found this out, I thought of my own photo of Evin. Inside my camera was an image that was now one among many: the photo of the jagged wall rising near Darakeh.

I didn't plan on making any human-rights posters with it. I wanted to establish for myself that Evin was a place on Earth. A place with physical limitations, and walls with specific measurements end to end. Dimensions of an endless hell for some, to be sure, but subject to the laws of history. It was a place that would close one day and transform beyond recognition. A place that would become a museum in time, then a dusty tomb where teenagers scratched graffiti.

Only caves large enough to have their own pressure systems have wind. They call it 'cave breathing.' This would be Evin. It would become another handful of rocky caverns at the foot of the mountains where wind would pass blankly in and out of a collapsed entrance. It will be haunted but it will be cool and quiet, and empty.

Sanjar told me it was okay to keep the photo. I would like to say that what goes on behind the jagged wall has troubled me like a cursed ring signaling from the bowels of the mountain, but it hasn't. It hasn't any more than a picture of a maximum-security prison in America.

IN MINNEAPOLIS I was washing dishes at the kitchen sink. A ragtag spattering of instant oatmeal had spent the day drying on a bowl Khalil had left out. I dropped the sponge and engaged in hand to hand combat, leaving DNA samples on the plastered grains as my fingernails scraped and chiseled.

A half-year had gone by since I had been in Iran. Life was pretty easy. From time to time I thought about what it would have been like to be held up at the airport and whisked behind that jagged wall into Evin.

The nearly exposed bone of my finger was jabbing at one last cemented grain. A National Public Radio program was on in the background. It was an episode called, 'Tossing Away the Keys,' by Sound Portraits Productions. Wilbert Rideau, a prison journalist, had interviewed prisoners serving 'natural life' sentences inside Angola Prison in Louisiana—which is life without the possibility of parole. I gave up, sunk the bowl in a pan of hot water, and listened to the thick Southern accent of the first interviewee:

> My name is Moreese Bickham, my number is 75251, and I'm seventy-two years old. I've been in prison ever since 1958. My crime is murder of two white deputies in a small town called Mandeville. They was dragons of the Ku Klux Klan and I was a black man living in a white neighborhood and they came to my house to kill me, and they shot me with my hands up and I fell and loaded my gun and I shot 'em. So here I am, 31 years later and I'm still locked up.

> Since I been locked up, I lost all my family mostly. I can see losing my mother and father, but all my sisters and brothers? All my aunts and uncles? God bless me now. The judge is dead, the DA's dead. The lawyer's dead. Everybody's passed on but me. And when I look at it I say, "Lord, why am I still here?" It makes you wonder.

DURING THE COLD WAR, whenever challenged on human rights, it was a cherished rebuttal of the Soviet Union to point out America's treatment of Native Americans and black people. Each time Iran was up for a beating on the international stage, I waited to see how the condemnation would be tempered.

Iran, like the Soviet Union, has volleyed back each accusation, UN resolution, and human rights report with reports of abuses by America's own government. Evin becomes Abu Ghraib. A Canadian journalist killed in Tehran becomes an Iranian boy shot in Vancouver by police. Instead of trading knowledge and goods we exchange descriptions of each other's finest turds, ignoring the ones filling our own pants.

It reminded me of a Mullah Nasruddin story Sanjar told me at the Stinky Café one winter night.

Mullah Nasruddin had many years of success as a smuggler. He would arrive at the mountain pass on his donkey and greet the guard charged with inspecting goods. His bags would be searched and sometimes confiscated. For years this official knew that Nasruddin was moving contraband but could never figure out what it was.

Time passed and the official retired. One day at a beach far from the mountains Nasruddin came upon this very official, who recognized him immediately and came running over.

"Nasruddin, all those years I could never catch you. It has always bothered me. Please tell me just what it was that you were smuggling."

"Donkeys."

THE CINEMA CAFÉ AT BAGH-E FERDOWS was not the first time that I was associated with spy work in Iran. Amateurs like myself just like the charge of saying the letters: CIA. I couldn't hold it against the young Iranian at the café for wanting to believe me. It's a plausible, almost casual label if you are American. Fruit of the Loom, Michael Jackson, Doritos, Cadillac, CIA.

One day Sanjar, Roy, and I went to the Jamshidieh Stone Garden. Jamshidieh used to be the private orchard of a Qajar prince and engineer. He designed an elevated pond with a waterfall to channel water to lower areas of the garden. Citizens of Tehran have picnicked there with a vengeance ever since it became public.

The weekly picnic was orchestrated with the seriousness, romance, and elegance of the Victorian Era—a European era that had itself mimicked the styles of the East. It was the era when Richard Francis Burton's translation of *Arabian Nights* became very popular.

At the gates of the park, I saw the white hair of a small man floating in a sea of headscarves: wife, daughters, and granddaughter. It was another example of an average Iranian family, to add to my list of mundane sights that I had begun to catalogue on the drive from Imam Khomeini International Airport my first night in Iran.

I asked Sanjar to request permission to photograph them: a quiet family in the sun at the gates of a garden, each with ten fingers and ten toes. They made a formal line, brushed their hands over their clothes once, then twice, and I snapped the picture.

Stepping through the park gates were other families with neatly-packed bags filled with pistachios, various Iranian foods such as *paneer sabzi* and kebab, rugs, and samovars to make tea. They padded along the dark green stone of the serpentine pathways in orderly packs, like the cleanly-spaced leaves on the Acacia branches above them. Mature elms, ash, and plane trees added shade to their search for the perfect spot.

Each group found a pocket of solitude amongst the terraced rocks—places still fragrant with the grateful energy of others who had spent time there together. I imagined people chewing down the bitter trials of the week in Tehran, and once fermented and a bit sweeter, releasing them into the ears of family and friends in the form of entertaining stories.

Those worn picnic spots became wineries, where each day someone new performed the miracle of turning the sour grapes of contemporary Iranian life into wine.

I looked for the family I had photographed but couldn't find them. Being so normal, so polite, they were camouflaged in the quiet and civility of Jamshidieh.

WE PLUNGED DEEPER into the stone garden. I saw groups of young women huddling tightly around the shining dare of a dream, juggling an ember of gossip, or dipping naked feet in the cool streams trickling down from the pond.

My attention focused on cuddling men resting their heads on each other's torsos. I looked down on a larger group whose lounging, intertwined bodies formed the curves and perpendiculars of secret letters. Built in flesh was the affectionate creed of an ancient brotherhood, the same creed that is turned on its head during times of war.

Persian picnics: grand, ornate, even superstitious. For example, staying inside is deemed bad luck during *Nowroz*, the Persian New Year. A darker undercurrent ran through these outings too. From the path, I watched a group walking gracefully to a spot in the dirt. They seemed to be anticipating the picnic like inmates approaching recreation hour at a penitentiary—with dignified resignation, gratefulness, and fatalism.

I thought again of Moreese Bickham at Angola Prison, in Louisiana. Commencing the fourth decade of his sentence he was irritatingly humble and good-natured. He described a rose bush in the yard that he cared for: "See if it wasn't for these bushes, I wouldn't have nothing to do. So these bushes have come to be close—very close to me."

THE SCENT OF FOREIGNERS must have carried over to them. It was Maryam and her friends. Roy had noticed them grooming themselves while we were talking to another group of women. One had promised to be my guide if I made it to Esfahan. Roy got a couple of numbers and we walked over and joined Maryam's Jamshidieh picnic.

"Are you getting ready for us?" Roy asked when we got close.

"Yes." Maryam, the prettiest of the three, spoke the best English, and went along with Roy's game.

They were in the shade of an enormous boulder, and we gathered around. The boulder was taller than our heads and was not moving anywhere. Even Sisyphus temporized, yielding to Roy's unrelenting sense of arousal.

Maryam was a PhD student in psychology, a few months away from taking over her own class. We sat down and talked about our identities as Americans and Iranians, and how the "producers" in our respective medias would demand rewrites that turned smiles into devouring jaws.

Observed from afar, our national stories, even the continuous reign of Persian civilization, ended up a chicken scratch on the heritage of humankind. Technology, by which I include writing and recorded history, makes us bigger than we are in space and time. That little chicken scratch is magnified, broadcast, until we think our nations are something lasting and important.

In the view of the human species, our mutual hostility amounted to this: a brief family squabble, akin to a sister and brother poking each other in the back seat of a car.

I felt cavalier for thinking these thoughts, for launching myself a thousand miles high and looking down. After all, the pain of sanctions was immediate, the proxy wars in the Middle East devastating to millions.

I could only blame my heroes. Doris Lessing writes in *Shikasta*: "This is a catastrophic universe, always; and subject to sudden reversals, upheavals, changes, cataclysms, with joy never anything but the song of substance under pressure forced into new forms and shapes."

The time-scales she deploys in the book are something only rocks can endure. Millennia and eons mercilessly dissolve our current concerns. It's discouraging and refreshing, and yet there remains a small individual voice in her story that we can always hear.

WHEN I WAS BACK in the US I didn't remember what else we talked about by that big boulder, so I asked Sanjar for Maryam's email. They had become friends.

She wrote back, "We talked about Muslims and our religion. You talked a little but Sanjar talked a lot. You said Iranian men are too bad but Iranian women are very good!"

Her message sparked my memory. Sanjar had decided to challenge them that afternoon with the subject of the afterlife.

"Excuse me, what is there for women in Paradise?" he asked them.

"What do you mean?" Maryam adjusted her headscarf.

"It sounds a lot better for guys!"

Non-Muslims like to joke about the rewards of paradise in Islam. An American actor, George Clooney, breezily concluded, "I'd rather have one pro than seventy-two virgins."

That well-known promise of virgins is modest compared to an 800-year-old tract by a religious scholar that sweetens the deal for men. He wrote that in paradise each believer gets 374 castles. In every castle there are 374 rooms, and in every room a virgin. As a man visits the rooms it becomes time-consuming because he possesses the forty-kilometer-long endowment that has been promised him.

Our understanding of physics has improved since the thirteenth century. It was clear even then, however, that the benefits of another dimension were needed to convince people to behave in this world. I have never heard any Muslim reference this Playboy Mansion in the sky, but it drives home the impression that paradise appears to be better equipped for the pleasure of men than for that of women.

SANJAR TOLD ME a story about an anthropologist who went into the bush of Central Africa to study a tribe. An old grandmother told her about a time when the men were so blessed that they had to tie it around their waist. Twice.

At the end of the interview the ancient woman turned to the anthropologist and said, "Ahh, the good ol' days." It was this last line that made Sanjar have to chew down his laughter in the café in order to keep from falling out of his chair.

Still, it is hard to see how a forty-kilometer-long penis can amount to any sort of paradise-like situation for women. There is little, if any, mention in the religious and scholarly material of what actually is in it for them.

SANJAR WAS MAKING trouble with his startling question. I chalked it up to the influence of our Syrian friend, Ferris, back in Minneapolis, who liked to pronounce, "Huh! If you see no trouble, make some!"

Of the three women, Maryam did not flinch. As her clash with Sanjar began I lost track of whether there really was an answer to the challenge. Maryam made a stand, then we moved on to another topic. Her friends, who were cued into the topic by Maryam's translations, began to sour. Unaware that Sanjar and

Roy knew Farsi, they bandied around indictments found daily in government newspapers and speeches.

"They're probably spies sent to change our minds," said one.

"He looks Iranian, why does he know English so well?" said the other.

"They want to take Islam away from us," warned the first.

I thought about how nice it would be to replace the word "Islam" with "Christianity," and put the two of them in touch with their spiritual and patriotic counterparts in the United States.

Maryam was devout, educated, and confident enough to bring her beliefs into contact with the wider world of ideas. She unwittingly caused her friends to wither before our eyes. The religious classes that had bored her through grammar school all the way up to her doctorate studies had not desiccated her own faith. Where intellect often destroys faith, Maryam used it to shield her own against the morbid charade by the authorities to make it compulsory.

An honest, intellectual Muslim woman in other words.

Meanwhile, the big Persian eyes of her two friends had shrunk to pinholes of jealousy. It was time to go.

Maryam. In another life it would be a name worth etching into that huge boulder. It rolls up and then back down the hill. Belief and unbelief taking turns as forces worth yielding to and resisting, like gravity and mystery.

I thought of Maryam's friends, black robes wound around dry stalks of piety. They had refused to sit when we joined them. They stood wearily outside the shade of the boulder, old scarecrows tilting in the sun. I can respect customs, but I wondered if you had to settle for husks to be a believer: a long wait in a fallow field, imagining that life is so far removed in time from a world where the Divine is expanding and revealing itself to humanity with each breath.

Maryam was green. Not the green of reformists and revolutionaries, or of naiveté. She was alive, cultivating herself. My government (through sanctions), as much as Iran's, would present to her the proposed limits of her growth. Inside, the eye of her heart was looking upon a lush orchard, listening to the voice of the *Simurgh* of Persian lore—the mythical bird strong enough to carry off an elephant, old enough to have seen the destruction of the world three times, mediating between sky and earth with the knowledge of the ages.

BEFORE GOING TO BED, I roamed around my house in Minneapolis, wondering which lights should be left on and which turned off to save the world. Sleep was a gift. If I stayed awake though, maybe I'd learn a little more—harvest the exclusive melody of an idea from the air long after the neighborhood had gone silent.

In the kitchen I pulled my son's bowl out of the pot of water. The last oat flew into the sink with a flick of the finger. I held the blue Fiestaware and considered giving it a final scrub, but then dropped it back in the soapy pot. The radio was off, but looking at it brought me back to the last segment of the Angola Prison story.

On his final night in prison, one minute separated the life Moreese Bickham had lived behind bars for thirty-seven years from the one in which he would be free. A life in which, he said, he "could turn the lights on and off" as he pleased. The governor had been merciful, and his life term, commuted, would end at midnight. At 12:01 he walked through the gate, kneeled, and kissed the dirt.

Chapter Eighteen

THE FACT THAT ROY wanted to sleep with as many women as he could was not a mystery. His beeping phone, and endless commentary on "POW-sy," solved that one.

Where he got his energy was a mystery.

Despite his agenda, or because of it, Roy invariably treated women well. He would offer courtesy even to women who pissed Sanjar off with unearned hostility. One woman, an English teacher who had ditched her beefy boyfriend at Bame Tehran, let out a continuous hiss about Iranian men the entire descent down the mountain. She was given a ride home by Roy, himself an Iranian man, to the other side of the city. (Granted, he was in his perennial disguise as an American.) It was a three-hour ordeal. Sanjar scolded him the next day for being the biggest dog.

Roy would set up two or three dates a day. The world was his dating site. He called numbers and followed leads. He juggled four cell phones. Three were for different sets of women, the fourth for his mother. He couldn't read the numbers on the phones unless he slid reading glasses onto his head. Roy managed this while turning the volume up and down on Enrique Iglesias and driving through Tehran at top speed.

He lived in an apartment on his own, in a newer building in central Tehran. It was a clean place with souvenirs around that established a previous life in America. There was a picture of him and Elvis in Las Vegas, where he had been a card dealer. This was before owning a pizza shop in Inglewood, California. I did not know when he had left the US or how long he had stayed; these are some of the details men can live without when dealing with each other.

When I first walked into his apartment, I saw to my left a dried iguana in an aquarium. He had found it on a desert road, brought it home, stuffed it with salt, and put it under the sun. Straight ahead there were two bedrooms, with a kitchen and couch in between them.

Roy entered, walked to another aquarium (this one filled with water), leaned over, and waited for his two goldfish to rise to the surface, where he met them each with a kiss. This was his homecoming ritual. I saw him alter it only once when I was there.

Her name was Ida.

SANJAR WAS MEETING his girlfriend in the family garden and I was hanging out with Roy. We were driving to nowhere in particular. Twilight is a time when many Iranians stand along the roadsides calling out place names to marked and unmarked taxis: "Tajrish?" "Valiasr?" "Darakeh?"

This unofficial transportation economy hung on trust. Out of necessity it is used by ordinary people, at times by sociopaths, and at others by prostitutes—the age-old mediums that link the two. Men, women, families make swift judgments by squinting through the car interior at the driver. Sometimes a woman would jump in the backseat of an unofficial taxi and be driven into the darkness. The brute would rely on social embarrassment to keep her silent, and sometimes he would make horrible guarantees.

One day Sanjar and I were stuffed in the backseat of one of these unmarked taxis with a completely veiled woman. We were speaking in English for some time. Sanjar remarked that her veil worked well to block the sun angling down into her window. Suddenly, the lady opened a broad and bitter attack on the government, fed from a sulfuric pool of remorse resting just behind the watchful eyes of many Iranians. Even more surprising was the perfect American accent she did it in. She was "green," as they say, a reformist, and could not forgive the waste of able-minded

Iranians. Her voice and demeanor reminded me of a robbery victim I had once seen talking to a cop in America.

Sanjar and I used these unofficial taxis to get around, but when we were with Roy, we were the ones picking people up. His technique was to drive by slowly and ask in English, "Do you need a ride?" or "How do you get to Darband?" It worked when Ida, a skinny twenty-one-year-old returning home from her job as a secretary, scanned the car and got in. The first thrill was that a stranger got into the car. The second vicarious thrill was that Roy persuaded her to go to his apartment.

During the fifteen-minute drive I was puzzled. It happened too fast. My list of the attributes that made up her true identity would not shorten: she was a prostitute, an agent, a prostitute who was an agent, a woman who needed a ride home from work.

Halfway to the apartment she made a call and an obligation materialized. I wondered which part of the act I was witnessing. Since her English was not good, and Roy refused to reveal he knew Farsi to negotiate with her, he called an Iranian friend who translated his case to her. Doubting that his translator was sensing his urgency, he accused him of trying to "ruin his party," hung up, and switched to his emergency plan: sheer momentum.

Glancing back at Ida, I noticed she had a large camera in her lap. Her face was calm, and she was smiling as she tried to talk to Roy. She could be an artist-secretary looking for new experiences. I was uneasy. This was another Iranian social dance that I didn't know the steps to.

ARRIVING AT ROY'S apartment, the car passed through the garage gates and tilted down, sliding under a bulky white building. Like a mobster's girlfriend, I became blank, letting the situation move me passively like debris caught in wind, withholding judgment.

I drifted. I would base my claim to innocence on incomprehension when the Morality Police came crashing through the doors. This was not an impossible outcome. Roy had been bothered before by neighbors who saw women come and go from his place. A man complained that his family should not have to witness such immorality. As usual, the reality was that this man wanted to destroy what he could not have for himself.

We entered Roy's apartment. I crouched to untie my shoes and collect my thoughts. I had promises to keep and I intended to keep them, but I was willing to see where Roy was taking this.

Looking up again I saw that Ida had taken her *manteaux* and scarf off, and was sitting on the couch with her big camera. Roy was cutting some fruit in the kitchen. I walked over to the couch and sat down, making sure I could fit a piece of *sangak* bread between me and Ida.

A bowl of cold green melon was passed around. When each of us had taken a ceremonial chunk, the bowl was set on the glass coffee table, making a sharp tap as it hit.

I took a bite out of the melon chunk in my hand. I should have put the whole thing in my mouth because the juice was now running down my fingers and covering my knuckles.

The ease of Ida's transition—from pious citizen to European art adventurer—paralyzed me. My nose felt greasy like I was in junior high. Roy turned on Polish MTV and I focused on it like a laser. An Australian dance club hit, "We No Speak Americano," by Yolanda Be Cool and DCUP, was playing. The song samples an Italian song from sixty years ago, "Tu Vuò Fà L'American" (You Want to Be American). The lyrics describe the folly of an Italian taking up the habits of an American: smoking Camels, listening to rock 'n roll, drinking whiskey and soda. The singer, Renato Carosone, wonders how a lover can be understood, under the moonlight, if they are speaking 'half-American.'

AFTER A NERVOUS trip to Roy's bathroom, where my pee came out like a sidewinder snake all over the rim, I was relieved to find that Ida and Roy had gone behind a closed door.

I sat still, converting Roy's living room into an erotic bomb shelter.

I saw a shadow flash under the crack of the bedroom door, but there were no noises. The air swelled with a balmy magnetism.

Ida came out of the room twenty minutes later, hair tussled and fully clothed. There are time frames in Iran. Time frames that speed up the normal processes of courtship and reorder its stages. Girls will give guys their numbers immediately when it's requested. Sanjar told me that he had asked a girl about this.

She replied, "Do you want to have a long conversation out in the open? Would you like to explain to the Morality Police what you're doing? First the number, so we can talk safely on the phone, and then let's decide whether to meet up."

Quickies, a sexual novelty in America, became, in Iran, the stolen moments away from custom by which a relationship was coordinated. Sanjar's and Roy's girlfriends could not see them at night. They had two hours between the end of work and the time their mothers and fathers expected them home. During this time, it was okay to do the following things: "buy clothes," "have tea," "meet friends."

Sanjar would also meet his girlfriends in the morning, in the window it takes to give a good "English lesson," "French lesson," "German lesson." It was often just time for less *on*, period.

It wasn't so simple, though. Sanjar was not the image of a heartless player, but (dare I say) more of a Casanova. Sanjar was straightforward, never promising marriage, fidelity, or profound transformations in character for their sake. Many of his girlfriends were extremely bright (geniuses, according to him), top students in the university or accomplished lawyers or engineers. Many were also very lonely, hamstrung by custom, and despairing of finding suitable companionship, wary as they were of the death spiral often awaiting women in traditional marriages.

Unattached but not uncaring, he was something rare and necessary: a lover.

BEING A FOREIGNER in Iran, I assumed women were falling in "love" with me at first sight because of what I represented: travel documents and a green card. I did not think they could be attracted because they did not have to marry me. Ida wanted an experience, a taste of intimacy, without the mechanisms of custom. Once set in motion, such a moment of exploration in Iran could be used to tie her to the man for the rest of her life.

Like Sanjar, Roy bypassed custom, and in a way was safer than most guys for Ida.

In Tehran, when you are a young woman standing on the side of a polluted road and dreaming of what love might be, dreaming of how a life you could love might be, you sometimes jump in.

"You see, nothing happened, nobody got hurt. We are friends." Roy was putting his shoes on by the door.

Ida was smiling, putting on her headscarf. They made plans to spend Friday together, with Roy's "translator." I wondered what else needed to be said or done between them. It was a back-to-front way to start a relationship, and I couldn't pin down where they were in its trajectory.

When we got near her home Ida insisted on being dropped off a few blocks from her apartment. It was in the south of Tehran and the chance that neighborhood guys would want a chance to defend her honor was high. It was understood. She gave us each a quick kiss on the cheek and jumped back onto the side of the road. I do not wonder where she is and what she is doing. She's in Iran. Where could she go and what could she do? It is possible, though, to wonder how she is doing.

In Iran there was a balance between what people were willing to do and the lengths people were willing to go to stop it.

Walking among a crowd of young and fit Iranians one night, Sanjar conceded as much: if the cultural constraints on sexuality were lifted, people would go absolutely crazy for a few years— something witnessed in the underground parties of Tehran. A bad state of affairs, in Sanjar's opinion. The restricted youths engorged themselves on drugs and casual sex, damaging their capacity for subtler sensations and normal relationships.

There was no chance for the carnal increments by which boys and girls come to know each other in America: holding hands in fifth grade, a first kiss, a pair of legs thrown over a lap at a junior high party, giggles, false starts. Then, weeks or months later, a short prayer preceding the hand sneaking out of childhood to finally test the curve of a breast under cotton and a layer of Lycra.

ROY WAS FROM NEITHER the world of the wildly debauched, nor from that of the gently and romantically debauched. He moved swiftly and fearlessly between his fantasies, letting others join in with their own if they could match his timing. He was rarely checked, and frantically mined the seam of desire compressed beneath Tehran's buttoned up surface.

One day Roy, Sanjar, and I drove across Tehran to a restaurant to meet Roy's steady girlfriend, Parvin. The lighting was low and red rugs covered the floor and seating, which was made up of a number of giant wooden oxcarts and daises. It all tempted one to lie down. I didn't get this part. In a society so hung up on the relations between women and men, every café and restaurant looked like a love nest.

When Roy and his girlfriend sat too close to each other, it was a bit of a relief to hear the restaurant manager tell them to separate. At least it was confirmed: scenarios that to my mind were ordinary were managed by watchful eyes in Iran. Roy and Parvin scooched a few inches apart.

I remembered a dinner party in the US where two Christian men found themselves squeezed together on a bench. One warned the other that a piece of bread must be able to fit between two people for chastity to be safeguarded. The other corrected him, saying, "No, you must be able to fit a Bible." Roy and Parvin couldn't have had much more than a chapati or the first chapter of Genesis between them.

The manager, in a tight black vest, peeked from behind a pillar. He was beholden to two desires when he saw Roy and Parvin cuddling. Although some authority might walk in and give him trouble for allowing his customers to sit so close, young people looking for a signal that the place was "cool" might latch on to the sight of their intimacy. It could be good or bad for business.

Luckily the food showed up. I saw the manger's head disappear behind the pillar. The meal required some assembly. It was called *abgoost* and arrived in three clay pots. When I peered inside my own pot, I saw a stew of lamb shank, lamb rib, chickpeas, white beans, potato, onion, tomato, and spices.

I jammed my hand into the steamy pot with a piece of bread. Roy's hand had found its way onto Parvin's lap but he lifted it above the table to stop me. "No, no."

He was the one feeling up his girlfriend in public. I didn't know why I was now being scolded. "What? What did I do?"

"Like this." Roy carefully strained the broth from the pot into a soup bowl. While I followed Roy's demonstration, Sanjar dug into his kebab, ordered for the sole purpose of confirming that Anoush grilled a better kebab in the family garden.

"Now take the bread and rip it up." Roy was dropping pieces of barbary flatbread to soak in the broth. When he finished, he lifted the soup bowl to his mouth and started sipping. Parvin had already rolled her sleeves and was a few steps ahead of us, grinding up the drained meat, beans, and potatoes with a pestle. Bowls of fresh scallions, creamy yogurt, and pickled vegetables still sat untouched on the table. I kept an eye on Roy and Parvin for clues on when to reach for them.

With the broth gone, the shapes of lamb cuts and the fuzzy remains of potato chunks became visible inside my pot. I picked up my own pestle and smashed down into the pot. I looked up and Roy and Parvin were busy eating. My lesson was over. From that point on all was fair. Nearly all, because when I stopped to wipe my mouth, I saw a black vest dash around a corner.

ROY'S RENEGADE STYLE was once challenged more seriously by the authorities while I was there: the time of the "wolf" at Bame Tehran, the 'Roof of Tehran.' Located in the north of Tehran, Bame Tehran is a wide paved walkway that leads up to cafés and a lookout point. From there you could see the boundaries of the city as the light broke against the dark mass of mountains.

One anomaly was a cluster of lights, higher up the side of a mountain, that was connected to Tehran by a single chain of lights marking out a road. It was a group of houses and apartments built high up the face of the mountain.

This was a *Sepah* development. Sepah is a group led by veterans from the Iran-Iraq War and the revolutionary struggle. They are the Islamic Revolutionary Guard Corp. They were on the ascendant, and of all the power centers in Iran, they were the one that could evoke the most genuine fear. Apprehension to talk openly about the mullahs or other religious authorities had its degrees. When people said "Sepah," others actually looked to see who was around.

A week later I was on Sanjar's balcony. I saw buildings reaching up a mountain and asked if that was the Sepah neighborhood I saw from Bame Tehran. My relatively carefree friend told me to "be careful talking about them" in the open air.

Nobody seemed to know how powerful Sepah was, and I could *live* without ever really knowing, unlike the average Iranian. They were allied with "so and so," doing "such and such." Political gossip was entertainment in America but a means of survival in Iran. I tried to remember this as Sanjar and our cab driver tossed around the question of the likely aspirations of Sepah. Sepah fueled itself on feelings of entitlement and righteousness, as any group of self-described guardians would. Unlike the conscripted Artesh, it was made up of volunteers. Young men who chose to serve two years with Sepah distinguished themselves with nicer uniforms, more extensive facial hair, and better training.

I was reminded more than once that it was Sepah who was in charge of the Mountain Police Station at Bame Tehran.

AFTER SUNSET the foot traffic at Bame Tehran began to pick up. The steady incline up the road was attacked with pace and frantic joy. New trainers with fresh white laces snapped forward in the dark under pumping limbs. The rush peaked an hour before midnight.

We left some nights at 12:30 a.m. and there were couples, gangs of friends, and families just entering the gate. It was another one of Tehran's casual zones like Darakeh. Those with means made their way to Bame Tehran in a pilgrimage mirroring those being made to shrines by the underclass. The thin air, darkness, and critical mass generated a sort of liberal social preserve.

Before the night of the "wolf," I had only seen a police officer talk to someone at Bame Tehran once, when he told a girl to button her manteau as she passed through the gate. Her compliance was performed in stride with a pantomimed buttoning of her manteau. A hundred yards past the gate, she dropped the act and it flung open again, as she kept pace with her speed-walking friends.

Sanjar and I broke into a jog as Roy swerved ahead like a heat-seeking missile. We reached the parking lot for the ski lift. Tents were set up on one side. Sanjar began bargaining for some candles in one of them. A scrappy teenager, seemingly straight out of a comic strip, slouched by with a worn-out "Got Jesus?" T-shirt.

Roy was gone and Sanjar had a cardboard box packed with bird-shaped candles. He took a long look up at the stream of twenty-something women heading into the dark upper reaches of Bame Tehran, took out his phone, and gave Roy a call.

THE SKI LIFT PARKING LOT spread flat and wide, surprising for the side of a mountain. Under yellow streetlights dozens of shuttlecocks drifted in slow arcs. Before hitting the ground, they were swatted back up again. As couples swooshed their rackets through the cool air, I thought of Farid ud-Din Attar's poem "A Conference of the Birds":

> It was in China, late one moonless night,
> The Simorgh first appeared to mortal sight— He let a feather
> float down through the air, And rumors of its fame spread
> everywhere.

We crossed the blacktop. A few groups hit a volleyball around, but badminton was the sport of choice. For one, it was cheap. There was no need for a court or net. There was also something about the discipline of the shuttlecock. The shuttlecock would not roll around and out of control. When it hit the ground, the players knew exactly where it was. People just returned well-behaved birdies to others they knew or hoped to know. Badminton gave a girl and a guy on a date a chance to show off their bodies to each other at a safe distance of ten feet.

Sanjar and I continued on our way up a small hill that led to a lookout. A couple hundred meters past the badminton players, on the benches lining the dark edge of the mountain, daring couples would come the closest they could to "parking."

LOOKING OUT from the Roof of Tehran brought comfort in different forms.

I stepped in front of the benches to the edge so that there were no people in front of me. My eyes softened. Emitting from apartments and streets were uneven splotches of white-orange light. The Milad Tower of Tehran presented itself many stories above anything else in the city. I did not feel anchored until I had swept the skyline and found it. Its space-needle shape gave it a gaudy touch of modernity. I called it the "phallus" of Tehran and thought of Saleh in Granada, Spain, and his album full of handsome men from the Islamic world. I found out that *milad* means "birth."

Sanjar tapped my arm and we started walking again.

The famous hospitality of Easterners—of Bedouins and desert people—does not grow solely out of altruism. The traveler has information from the outside to transmit. It is for this reason that he finds himself with bread and dates in front of him and some straw to sleep on. According to tradition, travelers may also be angels in disguise, sealing the importance of taking in a stranger.

Along the lookout, on benches and blankets, late-night picnics were in progress. The ease with which people let us enter their groups betrayed how desperately people wanted contact with the outside. I had to remind myself of the selflessness *and* self-interest of Eastern traditions as each new group accepted our company. Whatever the motives, eating fruit at midnight with strangers was an unexpected pleasure. An act of trust and fellowship surpassing that of a shared goblet in a cathedral. Sitting on a vacated corner of blanket and biting into a plum, I felt profoundly welcomed. The old ways were still maintained by Iranian youth.

When people find some space to be more fully human, they also, oddly, become more like animals. What were Roy, Sanjar, and I, and our smaller, less hairy counterparts on the mountain, but beasts—smelling, looking, touching (in Roy's case), and moving on? Bame Tehran was a place to meet up with other members of your species, and "fart around," as Kurt Vonnegut instructed.

WHILE WE FLITTED from picnic to picnic, loneliness, righteousness, and jealousy churned within an old lady who was spying on us from afar.

She resolved to single-handedly defend the honor of Iranian women by notifying the police that an Iranian man was going around speaking English to girls, and claiming he was American. She had a mission—the opposite of "farting around."

The old lady's complaint fell on enthusiastic ears. A Mountain Police pickup sped through the crowd walking up the mountain, headlights on full blaze. When it came to where Roy and Sanjar were sitting, it braked so hard that the truck rocked back and forth a few times on its locked wheels. Roy and Sanjar had been sharing some bread with two women. All four of them stood with pieces of torn bread in their hands as the pickup doors opened.

A few feet away, I was sitting on a stone wall between three sisters and one swim instructor, looking out at the haphazard light garden of Tehran. They thought I was a famous American actor. I thanked them for their misunderstanding and basked in the attention. When the pickup jolted to a stop behind us, my clout was subsumed by the headlights aimed at our backs.

I could not bring myself to turn around.

I tried to nestle deeper into the cracks between the rocks like a scorpion, to blend and vanish in the half-blind shiver of darkness and headlights. I squeezed my eyes shut. When I opened them I was looking straight into the cityscape of Tehran. Lights rose up and closed in like fireflies, their glow unblinking and unnatural. My vision blurred.

They say you have to face your fears, but I was happy to show them just my profile. I played dumb with one of the girls, quietly asking why she was suddenly silent, stuck in her own more practiced mold of invisibility.

She mouthed back, "p-o-l-i-c-e."

Again, I waited for a blow across the back of my head, the heavy paw of ignorance. It did not come. The pickup spun away, at a pace clearly meant to send a message about swift justice. When I finally turned around there was an empty spot where Roy had been.

"They took him." These were the first words from Sanjar. "I can't believe they took him." These were the second.

We all knew it could happen. Preparing to deal with it ourselves required uttering these words out loud.

I turned to Sanjar. "What will happen to Roy?"

A FEW DAYS earlier, outside the Milad-e-Noor Shopping Center, Sanjar, Roy, and I had witnessed a scene that, in hindsight, enabled us to evaluate the possibilities of what could happen to Roy. The police were talking to a young man who had badmouthed a family. The young man, whose black shiny hair reached his chin, was not cooperating with whatever request the authorities were making. He was a big guy, in a thin purple shirt that hugged his muscles. He jerked away from the cop who was corralling him. Two others quickly overpowered him, and he was stuffed inside a white police car. It was the kind of nervous escalation that black people face in America when a police officer feels a twitch of disobedience.

The white police car aggressively peeled around the corner. I turned to Sanjar and asked, "What are they going to do with him?"

Roy offered his theory first, "Probably they'll take him to another street to talk. They won't beat him up. They just want to scare him and maybe get a few dollars out of him. They'll reach an understanding with his family that their name is on the line now."

Sanjar shook his head, "Nah, nah, they may give him a good roughing up to make *sure* he understands."

Later, Sanjar's uncle, the geologist who was at the apartment from time to time, offered a third theory. I didn't know whether to take him more or less seriously because he claimed that when he was in the mountains a US Special Forces helicopter locked on him with a spotlight. At any rate, his guess at the outcome for the man in the purple shirt, included a beating, and a confession, and ended with a signature and a new file at the intelligence office.

There were other fates too. We were all happy to be spit-balling about the fortunes of someone else.

WHAT CAN A MAN rely on once he is in the back seat of a police car in Tehran? He has entered an evolving labyrinth of paperwork, bribes, and humiliation. He'd better have connections to find his way out.

Precious front-end crowd support at the scene of the crime would dissolve in the rearview mirror—but in the beginning it *was* there. A feeling of solidarity emerged to support the rude man in the purple shirt, whether deserved or not. The bulk of people gathered outside Milad-e-Noor, including us, rooted for him— there were calls for mercy, appeals to consider his family, excuses of misunderstandings. Even the family he had insulted pleaded for leniency in the end.

The multiple voices in the crowd made its power anonymous. But prolonged and individual advocacy for the man in purple would bring consequences. Activism needed to wither at the end of the show, with the decisive peel-out of the police car. There's nothing left to see here, folks.

For governments around the world this is the fulcrum of chaos and order: the same bulge of anonymous social power that frees people to loot and rampage, or demand justice, must also be used to smother and bore individuals into a shared submission.

SANJAR, JAVID, AND I witnessed this crowd theater another night at Bame Tehran, long before the night of the "wolf." The nightly cooldown of the desert had leveled over Tehran. Friends and families strolled about in the dark, unwinding from the busy day. We were sitting on a bench near a young man who was playing guitar. He was talented. I noticed tentative steps in his direction. The gentle songs were slowly attracting a larger group of admirers.

As they inched closer to him, they were making it harder for the Mountain Police to ignore him. I wondered if this was a ritual sacrifice, agreed upon by the guitarist and audience. Playing Western music was an act of trespass and corruption.

It was a form of movement that authorities, from parents to government, had a hard time preventing. Car keys can be taken away, exit visas can be denied. A melody only needs the breath, then people slip into a land of irreverence, open roads, shooting stars. A place where feelings gather like phantoms on the blank plateau at the end of the dictionary, before being possessed with a harmonic spell of moans and howls, and set loose in our hearts. Time warps, dust settles, and Clint Eastwood eats key lime pie in a diner. Each song is a journey, taking a girl or boy farther from the message of the state.

I knew that the bench where the man was sitting could soon be swirling with a fresh emptiness.

I saw some heads turn before hearing the lurch of a police vehicle. It was not long before the headlights were fixed on the singer. A crowd gathered around the pickup and a rehearsed confrontation ensued. Both sides spoke: the crowd negotiating the release of their star, and the police offering an explanation on why he was not harmless. For the police it was at the far end of successful public relations but not brutal indifference.

I sensed the dark secret of the crowd—this confrontation too was entertainment.

The folk hero of the night would pay an unknown price. The crowd relented. The pickup disappeared back down the mountain. Its cargo: a singer and his guitar.

The Greek chorus of Persia drifted apart again, separated by silence.

LOUD MUSIC MAY get you a ticket for being a public nuisance in America. It would take quite a concert to get you taken away in a police car. Jim Morrison of The Doors had to drop his pants to pull it off. I wondered if the insistent appeals from the crowd in Iran would be tolerated in America, where people have succumbed to a system that eats people up more efficiently. The image of unchallenged law enforcement contrasted with the messy exchanges I saw in Iran. America's authorities have delegated more of the violence and messiness to its citizens: beat and shoot each other and we will come investigate.

I like law and order, but it has its discontents. In San Francisco, pushing Khalil in a stroller, we started to cross a street on a red light. I heard shouting. Startled, and now standing in the middle of the street with a stroller, I turned around and saw a cop. When I tried to say the street was blocked off for a festival, she ordered me back to one side of the street and commanded: "Have a nice day!" I knew what that meant.

It was nearly imperceptible in the grand scheme of things, but the command signaled the more insidious expectation of control and perfection that haunts American life.

It has many manifestations: the false bonhomie of customer service; fine-tuned images of the good life promoted by marketers; the search for relationships designed through a collage of magazine articles, romantic comedies, and apps; edged lawns; spiritual quests that correlate attainment with ambition and dollars spent; and, most potently, the stringent enforcement of traffic laws.

Between our dreams and actions there is the world Bruce Springsteen reminds us in his song "Dead Man Walking." When reality does not meet expectations in America, look out: meltdowns in grocery checkout lines delayed two minutes by a grandma digging for coupons or a mother tending to a sniffling toddler; mayors who feel disgraced when a city isn't snowplowed by dawn; swells of rage when a fat-free latte is made with two-percent milk. Most dangerous for us all was the shock of learning that the senseless destruction that other parts of the world, from Europe to Asia to Africa, have experienced can also be known by us.

September 11 was a tragedy for Americans, but it was also a betrayal.

For Iranians, who might never get their day in court, scenes on the street, like those with the man in the purple shirt and the folk singer, become impromptu trials. The public takes what it can get. The expectation that life will be anything but perfect often guides the Eastern mind into an admirable, frustrating submission to the contradictions and reversals of life. There may yet be perfection in the world but it arises on its own terms. It's an orientation at once more humble, expansive, and ancient than that of the West.

Perfection is a return to a preconceived notion. In the East life is about perfectibility. The handling of the human psyche is not reliant on the latest pharmaceutical offering that promises a return to the known, it depends on following a path laid out hundreds if not thousands of years ago, into the unknowable.

WHEN THE FOLK SINGER was taken away in the police truck, the crowd quickly disassembled. We took a seat on a nearby bench. Sanjar turned to Javid and said to him, "Get strong, my friend, they may back down now, but one day ..."

"Get strong for what?" Javid replied, glancing down the mountain at the city, and back up at Sanjar.

"For whatever comes next!" Sanjar jeered.

It was true. No one knew what was likely to happen to Iran over time. From "hardliners" to "green movement" members, the one thing they had in common was a sense of Iran's uncertain future. Sanjar's uncle, the geologist visited by the Special Forces UFO in the mountains, had told a story at a garden party that entered my mind as we sat in a row on the bench.

Once upon a time there was a weak and clumsy girl who was abandoned at an orphanage by her father. A man who worked as a gardener in the castle passed the orphanage each day on his way to collect materials from the forest. He noticed the pathetic girl and took pity on her. He brought her to work in the castle garden and soon found out she was very capable.

Many years later, the King was out hunting on horseback when he found the girl, now a young woman, walking up the mountain path carrying a grown cow on her shoulders. He stopped for a moment to watch the young woman carrying the enormous beast.

"How is it that you can walk this steep path with such a heavy burden?"

"When I was a girl, I saw a calf with an injured leg. She was not going to reach the high pasture on her own. Since then I have carried her up on my back. As she has grown in size, I have grown in strength."

Chapter Nineteen

SANJAR'S MIND WAS RACING. He summed up his state: "I feel like shit."

We were walking away from the wall where we had been sitting when the police took Roy. It was not clear whether we were going to leave the mountain and hide or track down Roy. I wanted to get out of there. I thought we should just stay out of it, and prepared to make myself invisible as we passed the Mountain Police Station. We could wait for Roy at the bottom of the mountain, call him, or, if need be, send him letters in prison.

I was a little disgusted with my reaction. Shamed by the way fear was making me move. After all, I was in the best position to inquire about Roy. The complaint by the old lady was that an Iranian was pretending to be American and speaking English. I *was* American, and the only thing I was concealing was that I was scared to death.

When we reached the police station it was Sanjar who walked up to it. I stood twenty feet away eyeing the assault rifles that hung heavily on the skinny soldiers. I expected the barrels, pointed at the ground, to swing up as young limbs filled with blood at the slightest provocation.

Sanjar greeted them and peeked into the doorway, calling out to Roy, "Are you okay man?"

"Yeah, man." Roy's voice was shaky.

What followed was a long and persuasive plea by Sanjar on Roy's behalf. Sanjar's decision to intervene was triggered by his own maxim: you never know who you can trust until you need them the most. What he hoped was that they would tell Roy what he did wrong so that he would not do it again. Sanjar spoke with them for several minutes, planting doubt into the potential success of their prosecution, by alluding to the social status of his father without using his name.

"Well, everyone has a father," the lead officer sniffed.

Sanjar continued, this time indulging the officer: "I know you can hurt him. I know you can do much more, *much* more ... but don't."

Meanwhile, I stood at the far side of the path. I focused and refocused on my shoes, my hands, the silhouette of the trees in front of the Tehran skyline. When my former admirers, the four girls from the wall, passed by warily, I managed a cocky smile, returned discretely by only one of them.

As they disappeared down the mountain, the romance that propels so much of the energy of revolutions filled my chest with heat, and the faint taste of aluminum seeped from my gums.

The numbers descending the mountain swelled. To my spinning mind it resembled an unspoken, self-organized evacuation. A bizarre wave of panic hit, placing me and my two friends at the center of an impending security sweep that Iranians were anticipating with a sixth sense.

JACK CARSON, OR JEAN-PAUL, or Juan (depending on where he was in the world, he liked to say), had a greying black afro that was blown back at a crooked angle. Years ago, at the University of Wisconsin, I proposed to Jack Carson, my math tutor, that black people in America were better than whites at reading body language and situations, and had empathy with each other that bordered on telepathy. Organs of perception that had evolved to deal with a hostile world.

Jack Carson had large, thick glasses, and when he took them off, his face didn't look right, by his own admission. He nudged his glasses onto his forehead and rubbed his eyes with the backs of his chalky hands.

"What, you mean black people are special?" he finally said.

I backpedaled a little: "No, just a group that hasn't been able to say and write whatever they wanted over time. If people have to hide their personalities in front of …"

"Bullshit. Now if you want to check up on something like that, you can go study the Greeks or Egyptians and see if there are stories of telepathy going on among the slaves all of them years."

I DROPPED IT. Jack Carson won, but I had another case on my mind: that of some island tribes in the Indian Ocean who had survived a tsunami by climbing to the hills long before it slammed into their tiny islands. Observant in ways different from modern man, they had seen the water recede, and marked changes in the songs of birds and the swimming patterns of marine life. Inherited knowledge, passed on through stories, advised them on how to act in the present, and they moved away from the shore.

Imagining the power of the security apparatus in Iran, I felt my thinking turn magical outside the Mountain Police Station. I believed a message of warning, detectable through years of paying close attention to the group mood, had networked its way through the Iranians walking down the mountain.

Standing alone on the mountain, I felt like a kid again, at the mercy of stronger adults.

When I was ten years old there were reports of a kidnapper in our neighborhood. It was summer, and my sister and I were at a playground when a van whipped around the corner. We waited for it to circle back, but the only thing that returned was fear—each time we saw vans for the rest of July.

On the mountain road in Iran I found myself scanning for fast-approaching vans. Having yanked an image from Hollywood's stock of evil Middle Easterners, I was poised to see the white van and bazooka that had terrorized Doc and Marty in *Back to the Future*.

I TRIED TO SEE myself through the eyes of the poor young Artesh from the countryside, deputized by the regime and now standing guard outside the station. I appreciated why he might be receptive to the crazy lady's accusation of Roy. Loitering around in olive drab, he was on the lookout for some way to make himself useful. He would have seen Roy chatting the girls up with a breezy, fraternal ease that was impossible for him, because of a lack of experience and the constraints of his culture.

Girls were listening to Roy because English words were falling like blocks in the yellow brick road—a fantastical route out of Iran. The young Artesh may or may not have known about that dynamic. He would have seen lines being crossed, and girlish giggles that dangled like unreachable trinkets in the night air.

On Bame Tehran, the young Artesh was like King Tantalus of Greek mythology, doomed to standing in water up to his neck that recedes as he tries to drink it, beneath a fruit tree that is just beyond his grasp. The beautiful girls parading by would never stop for him—at least until he had a job and his own apartment. Given the state of Iran's economy, it would be a long wait for a horny young man.

Roy was Alexander the Great, waving a sword above the Gordian Knot, doing a hack job on the intricacies of Eastern courtship. All he was doing was flirting—but to the young Artesh it may have looked like Roy was conquering all of Asia.

SANJAR JOINED ME at the far side of the road. He had finished his first appeal. I was in awe of, and reassured by, what he was risking for his friend. The first problem was that they had taken Roy; now we wondered whether they would keep him. Sanjar hoped that all they wanted was to "scare him real bad." He paced around. Put his hands on his hips.

He had come over to think. I resisted begging him to leave.

Sanjar went back over to the station. A light illuminated a row of motorbikes parked along the wall, where he stopped to talk to an officer. This time the skinny Artesh with a semiautomatic walked over too.

"What did he do wrong?" Sanjar repeated.

"He lied to us," said the senior officer.

"Okay. Just tell him what he did wrong, so he won't do it again."

"Why was he saying that he was American when he is Iranian?" the officer barked. "And why did he speak English when we started talking to him?"

"Is it a crime to speak English?" This was the answer Sanjar said out loud to me later on. At the station Sanjar had agreed with the police: Roy should not have spoken to them in English. What Sanjar could not explain to them was the suicidal commitment Roy had to his American persona in front of pretty girls.

"Our chief is not in tonight," the officer confessed. "It's better for you that he isn't. He's tougher than we are."

"Trust me, you're tough enough!" Sanjar replied. Later Sanjar admitted that the officer was right. We were lucky that the chief, who was Sepah, wasn't there.

"By the way, who are you?" the officer casually asked.

"Let's not go there." Sanjar was shaking his head and smiling while his hands crisscrossed in front of him.

The young Artesh stepped forward, wanting to join in the conversation. He adjusted the strap on his assault rifle and said, "You know, if I shot an American up here, I'd get a medal."

Sanjar walked back across the road toward me. I was in the middle of draining the last tablespoon of blood from my body with a vision of perpetual incarceration in Evin.

"Man. Let's go." He looked more troubled than I had ever seen him. Rocking forward, with his hands on his hips, he stared past me, "I can't believe what that soldier said."

Then he told me.

We were walking back up the mountain towards the bathrooms. Not the direction I wanted to go. After rinsing my hands, I looked in the mirror, half expecting to see a skinny figure in olive drabs behind me. I shook the water off into the sink and ran a damp hand over my face.

WE LEFT THE BATHROOM area, paced and circled, then headed back down the mountain. A shuttle bus pulled to a stop ahead of us and we jumped on. There were two seats open in different rows. After a minute or two I felt a light brush against my hair, then a little tug. I connected them with the buffoonish snickers I had been hearing behind me.

Sanjar was sitting in front of me busy thinking about Roy.

I felt another inspection of my hair. It was the Persian jocks again. They were squeezing the last fun out of the night and my cooperation was needed.

Sanjar once described some workers at an office in Tehran dragging a metal cabinet across a fine marble floor. "Savages!" he had said then. He used the word again in Minneapolis after some rich, white, elderly women left garbage on a table at a bakery. When my eyebrows scrunched, he added, "You don't have to kill thousands to be brutal—you just need to pinch someone." Nyasha, my Zimbabwean roommate in college, had said the same thing: "One who has pinched has fought."

I couldn't tell what had done more damage that night: the old woman with her gossip, the soldier with the machine gun, or the fingertips of the jokers on the bus.

THE YOUNG ARTESH didn't know the extent to which his comment raised alarm in Sanjar. When we got off the bus, I slowly raised a finger towards him: "So, did you say anything to the soldier when he said that?"

Sanjar pushed up his glasses. "I told him, yes, you may feel like a hero, but do you have *any* idea what you would do to your country?"

"You did?"

"No, man."

"What did you say?'

"Nothing. You see ..." Sanjar trailed off, something he rarely does. "He has *no* idea the problems he would bring to Iran if he did that."

My own indignation became muted. I began to equate this young soldier with some of my junior high students back home, who casually call Muslims "terrorists" and fantasize about how they would "just shoot them if they tried anything." It was a concordance: the infantile glory of minds keyed to a narrow spectrum of thought; youthful bravery and ignorance ready to be levied for use by the powers that be.

Part of a legacy of careless comments, laughed off until they swarm through civilization like locusts.

We passed through the gate and out into the quiet streets of North Tehran. Sanjar had five messages from Roy on his phone. They had released him. Unable to reach us, he thought we had left and gone home. He had orders to report to the Central Police Station the next day. They had checked out his information and called his family's number. They got his elderly mother on the phone. Roy later said she was physically sick for two days.

With Roy safe, Sanjar refused to nurse the trauma. "Things have gotten a lot better, a *lot* better. A few years ago, we might have all gotten twenty or thirty lashes!"

NYASHA WAS FROM the Shona tribe in Zimbabwe. I never got used to walking in on him crying and singing gospel at the top of his lungs in our dorm room in Iowa. The day I walked in on him browsing porn sites I did some rejoicing myself.

I was more interested in stories from his village from the time before he converted to the Broadway musical of Pentecostalism.

Nyasha was in grade school when his country won its independence from Britain. He was seven or eight. One day a rebel soldier back from the war took a seat in his class. He was twenty-two years old and wore huge combat boots with his school uniform. He'd been fighting his whole life. All the kids would say, "Hey, there goes James and his big boots."

Another story from Nyasha's childhood that has stuck with me was about a man returning late one night from a journey. The way led through a huge grove of jacaranda trees. The man had never liked this stretch of road, but it was the quickest route back home. He continued through the hopscotch of moonlight and shadows. Suddenly he heard footsteps. Before long there was a man walking beside him.

He tried to ease his fears by striking up a conversation with the stranger: "You know, taking this path by night always scares me for some reason."

When the stranger smiled and showed understanding he felt better.

"Yes, I know what you mean. When I was alive this road used to frighten me as well."

Upon hearing this the traveler took to a full sprint, running so fast that his own heel swung back, hitting his head and knocking him out cold.

Chapter Twenty

ONE OF THE FIRST THINGS I remember Sanjar telling me about growing up in Tehran was that he was not allowed to speak about politics outside the house. Not much had changed since then.

I was told that if I saw one street in Tehran that was dirty, and one that was clean, it was politics. The speed or delay of transactions at a bank or government office reminded people that everything was political—you just weren't supposed to mention it in public.

The air you breathe in Tehran is political. Economic sanctions have forced Iran to process oil in outdated factories, producing low-quality fuel that contributes to the yellow smog that envelops the city. When I became short of breath I was reminded of Iran's geopolitical situation.

Politics worked its way into everything, including childhood memories.

When Sanjar was studying in a French grammar school with the sons and daughters of the Iranian elite, he had a playground scuffle with the Shah's nephew. The kid, who was bigger than Sanjar, would not leave him alone. So one day Sanjar grabbed his wrists tightly and shoved him away. Thinking back on it now, he becomes more worried than he was at the time. Was that guy in a strong position in the government now, and did he hold a grudge? Unlikely, since anyone associated with the former king fell out of favor after 1979.

On the surface, days in Tehran seemed to be built upon the apolitical background of life—the toil of average people making ends meet. I witnessed only one self-conscious political street scene while I was there: a small clump of men, dressed in black, outside the Hotel Enghelab, chanting a generic blend of slogans. I finally saw the mob of bearded men that had a starring role in any news report from Iran. They were actors whether they liked it or not, their narrative created in the editing booths of media outlets.

IN SPORTS, POLITICS lurks around uncomfortably. National pride hinges on actual merit on a playing field. A competition threatens to unleash predictable emotions that lead to unpredictable outcomes. Even if you pay the referees, a victory or loss begets mayhem that is hard to control.

When Iran beat the US soccer team at the 1998 World Cup, it was time to celebrate. People had cover to take to the streets. There was public intoxication and dancing; women tossed off their headscarves. No one in power in Iran, or anywhere, wants masses in the streets unless they are orchestrated with clear constraints. Iranians insist the team has since been systematically weakened to prevent any future errant euphoria.

At the start of a more recent World Cup qualifier, some players wore black armbands in solidarity with the "Green" reform movement. After halftime the armbands were gone. After the game some of the players were gone too.

The theory of a deliberately weakened national team conflicted with the desires of the President of Iran, a player and fan. Even the US State Department felt compelled to comment on soccer drama in a classified diplomatic cable entitled "Iran's First Fan: Dissatisfaction with Ahmadinejad May Extend from the Soccer Pitch to the Ballot Box." He had associated himself with the beloved national team, but after showing up at a World Cup qualifier against Saudi Arabia, won by the Saudis on a last-second goal, he was accused by "soccer-crazed Iranians" of "jinxing" the team. The cable noted with glee that a loss in a qualifier against Iran's economic rival, the United Arab Emirates, to be held a few days before national elections, could further "damage his image."

Politics enters the picture in a local derby as well. In Iran, two soccer teams, Esteghlal and Persepolis, represent opposing sides in the minds of Tehran's fans, even though both are government owned. Traditionally the Shah and other institutional elites had supported a team called Taj FC, 'the Crown'. It was the royal team. After the Islamic Revolution its name was changed to Esteghlal, 'Independence'.

In Tehran's poor neighborhoods, loosely-organized groups of men would act as guardians of property and decency. The chivalry of this "neighborhood watch" expressed itself in the fact that they did not worry about getting paid. Instead they settled for the poor man's cultural capital: being on the side of athletic champions.

These neighborhood clubs got behind a common man's team called Shahin FC, 'the Falcon'. The club was established by a teacher, who, legend has it, opened up a book of fourteenth-century poetry and saw these words:

In the air, you will circle a few times with glory;
Oh pigeon, be worried, Falcon is on its way.

Eventually Shahin FC took its star players and re-formed into Persepolis FC. In 1986, while the war with Iraq was raging, the team was taken over by the Oppressed and Veterans Foundation and renamed Azadi, 'Freedom'. Players said they would not play if the name was changed. A year later, when the Foundation gave the club to the Physical Education Department of Iran, the players agreed to a third rebranding—the team would be called Piroozi, 'Victory'. All the while on the street, its working-class fans still called it Persepolis.

I could barely keep track of the name changes. In Iran, names are changed to suit the political market. In America team names were chosen to fit the commercial market, except in the backwards cases of teams like the Cleveland Indians, who should have changed to match the political climate but haven't yet because of commercial pressure. I wondered what names would be on jerseys if the Republican and Democratic parties, or the National Rifle

Association, or Black Lives Matter, had such a role in naming NFL or NBA teams.

When the poor man's team (Persepolis) and the rich man's team (Esteghlal) played, it was preferable to the powers that be to have the game end in a tie. A win for either team sent the wrong message.

After the contested summer elections of 2009, a poll showed that 64 percent of Iranians supported Persepolis over Esteghlal. Game day approached. Some of the players joked, in private, that they should take the day off and just call it a draw. Suspicions among fans and players of referees being bribed led sports officials to hire foreign referees for the derby.

Keeping an eye on deviancy in Iran: The International Atomic Energy Agency and a soccer referee from Switzerland.

Political statements are made by the color of the jersey you wear, but other styles of dress tell stories and betray opinions as well. Resistance is measured in centimeters as women push back their headscarves to reveal a bit more hair. Another tactic is to wear detachable sleeves. Then, according to the liberality of their surroundings, they can take them off to reveal their forearms.

I learned that boys have their own style benchmarks. If the morality police suspect that a shirt is too tight or small, you can be asked to lift your arms. If your belly shows, you fail the test. It gives new meaning to the command, "Hands up!"

THE NORTH AND SOUTH of Tehran are linked by Valiasr Street. It is known as the longest street in Iran. Recently the flow of traffic was reversed on one side. After observing the movement of people during the 2009 post-election protests, the authorities made the adjustment. The Cinema Café was located along Valiasr Street. The café seemed modeled after the owner's memory of some place in Beverly Hills, and it glowed with torches and pretty rich girls. Despite its chic spotlessness and a cappuccino costing five dollars, it resembled dusty Darakeh in one respect: its casual atmosphere.

Roy, Sanjar, and I went there again one night. In the car I had gingerly asked Roy about his visit to the Central Police Station. Roy was unbowed. He said something quick about gold coins, turned up Enrique Iglesias on the radio, and sped into traffic.

My impression of Cinema Café was that it was reserved for a sort of secular Iranian elite. I also I counted the most foreigners—nine in one night—that I had seen since the conference. A group of Eastern European businessmen showed up. They were large, ex-military types, confident and a bit oily; even so, they kept their voices down in the Islamic Republic.

The other foreigners were Vietnamese. There was one businessman, his visiting friend, and two women who were studying Persian literature on scholarship at a university. We were interested to know how the two young women had chosen to study in Tehran. Young Iranians, walled off from the West, were heading to Southeast Asia to study, get degrees, and even work. Malaysia, a Muslim country, was the most popular. The exchange was apparently going both ways.

Roy was offering his car and knowledge of the streets to the visitors. He also made his apartment available in a nonchalant gesture of hospitality. Roy would try to help people visualize the path from introduction, to car ride, to involvement with his crotch.

Roy was at it, and I tried to stay out of the way, looking at the long rectangular fountain and the lit-up trees and not saying much.

Hanh, the taller student, upbraided me for not looking interested in the conversation. I liked learning their stories, but I picked up on a gray vibe going through Hanh. When she gave me her e-mail address, it was a hybrid of the words "loneliness" and "stupidity." She said if I came to Vietnam, she would put me on the back of a scooter and take care of the rest.

Meanwhile Roy tried out his Vietnamese, and Sanjar told the story of his friend Tranh, the valedictorian at his high school in Minnesota. Sanjar always wanted Tranh to prove he knew martial arts. Tranh would just shake his head. Sanjar would then grab

Tranh's wrists with all his might and Tranh would gently slip away, all the while saying, "I don't know anything."

The group was loosening up and the women were not shy about showing off the Farsi they knew.

"Your Farsi is good. Better than mine," Roy said.

"Man, they have to be good if they're studying Persian literature," Sanjar added.

A smile passed between the two women.

Hanh put her palm over her warm drink and said, "We're actually studying political science."

"Aha." Sanjar said the word in a slow knowing way.

It didn't really matter to Roy, he just wanted to keep the ball rolling. He asked, "So how did you end up here for that?"

Serious and poised, I saw a little pride flash across Hanh's face before she said, "The Iranian government is sponsoring us. They're taking care of the entire course of study."

Their story changed because of who they thought we were and found out we were not, or vice versa. Politics again, altering what the truth was from one hour to the next at a random café table.

AFTER HEARING AGAIN and again how everything was political, I decided to give my Iranian friends a test. I made a plan. During dinner, when mouths were full of rice and lamb, and heads of forgetfulness, I would see if this was really true.

I waited for my moment. It was Ramadan, which had started a few weeks after I arrived. Anoush, Neda's husband, was a devout Muslim. He was also the best at grilling kebab. The meal would be served during the afternoon, well before sunset. This meant Anoush would be in front of a smoky grill, at the hottest time of day, fasting.

The meal had been in the works since the previous afternoon. Ground meat, from the "best" butcher in North Tehran, was mixed and wrapped around long metal kebab sticks. The gravity of the event made me wonder if my visa had been extended by an officer from the Ministry of Culture for this specific meal.

Back in Minnesota, Sanjar would take a bite out of an Egg McMuffin or pizza slice and say, "If you come to Iran you will have real food—the kebab there is something you have not seen before."

Sanjar and I walked with Anoush's two sons, Javid and Maziar, to the walled garden, while the supplies and the rest of the group were ferried over in a black Peugeot. There was a new warning out in Iran this Ramadan: get caught eating in your car and the authorities would take it from you, both the car and the food. The walk to the garden took us through streets near Sanjar's apartment that were becoming familiar to me.

In spots there were trees growing in the middle of the street, with the blacktop laid snugly around their trunks. Trees also grew through the middle of concrete walls, the masons carefully leaving foot-wide cracks to accommodate growth.

Their immunity to urbanization came from a thousand-dollar fine given to anyone who laid a finger on them. Burn marks blackened the bases of many neighborhood trees, traces of covert attempts by residents to slowly kill off some annoying survivors.

Most large trees in Tehran are remnants of Reza Shah's program of beautifying the city. During his charge into modernity he smashed down old buildings and widened streets. Sending his soldiers out with poplar seedlings and watering cans, he warned them, "If the trees die, you die."

An old man was washing an ancient red Paykan, the first car made in Iran, and known as the Iranian chariot. Water dripped off the car's body and ran down the alleyway. We stepped over the stream and passed Khalid Al-Islambouli Street, a short, forgettable road, named after the assassin who shot the Egyptian President Anwar Sadat in 1981. Egypt has repeatedly asked that the name be changed, and it is a sore spot between the two countries. I looked up at the Farsi written on the small rectangle of metal. A few letters spelled out 'Al-Islambouli,' but nationality and ideology would determine whether you saw the name of a murderer or hero.

Part of the alley leading to the garden was lined by walls made of mud and straw. The millionaire who lived in a mansion on the other side of the walls had succumbed to village nostalgia. On the earthy walls there were some slogans in Farsi denouncing the government. Farther on I recognized graffiti that championed the American hip-hop artist Tupac Shakur.

On one wall I saw "3 Pac" touchingly scrawled in blue. A red "X" had been sprayed over it. On another wall someone had made the correction in white: "2 Pac."

As we walked Javid told me about a family friend's pretty daughter who showed up at these parties. Sanjar and Javid giggled, but Maziar kept a straight face. They joked that she would definitely be there to see the American.

We stood at the thick iron gate of the garden. It was still not possible to tell that anything was going on inside: there were no sounds, no music. After a moment, the Afghan gardener swung the gate open.

Inside, a stream ran along the wall, and to our right a small group of family and friends waited at two long tables, including the daughter. I did my best to take a well-rounded view of people, but when I saw her, I instantly knew why Maziar—the guy in our group who was fasting and denying his carnal appetites—had had to discipline himself when her name was brought up on the walk.

As for me, a decade of satellite television can be blamed for her mild disappointment when she did not see a muscular, blonde, blue-eyed dude. After introductions she would turn away to her laptop where she plaintively studied the website for the Pritzker Architecture Prize.

Huge sycamore trees enlarged the space around us, pinning the greenery up against the sky like tent poles. Under this canopy refined personalities, normally bound up in the city, opened up a little. Voices got louder. Inside the garden walls there was good air, quiet, and space for not being quiet. In Tehran this garden was a treasure, earning the hype Sanjar had given it back in the US. It felt like the safest place in Iran.

We all sat around being friendly until I was called over to watch Anoush grilling on the other side of the garden house. He was wearing a blue surgical mask because he was worried the kebab smoke would invalidate his fast. Ten kebab skewers sizzled toward perfection. The stream moved serenely behind us, under the wall, and into the next garden.

I headed back to the tables, my eyes stinging from the smoke.

"How old are you?" It was Sanjar's uncle, the geologist.

"I thought I might be interrogated in Iran, but not in my friend's garden," I joked.

"Sixteen, but you only count the nights, right?"

"Right."

I could never keep up with this type of wit, so I smothered the conversation with a long, silent, toothless smile. The empty plate next to the grill began to pile up with kebab. Due to sanctions Iran could not get parts to fix bicycles, let alone build nuclear bombs, but for high-quality kebab meat, arrangements were made.

SANJAR ORDERED me to return to the grill and stand with Anoush. I was to take a bite of meat the minute it was taken off the grill. Anoush held out a long fork. A sizzling strip of meat dangled from its end. The honor of enjoying his work would have to outstrip the guilt of eating it in front of him.

Above his mask creases formed at the corners of his eyes as I held up one finger. Anoush selected another sample with his fork. I juggled a bite of the meat in my mouth until it cooled, swallowed it down, and cleaned my hands on a towel Anoush was holding out for me. Some juice hit the coals and smoke spiraled towards the sycamores. The flavored steam did seem capable of breaking Anoush's fast.

Back at the table kebab was piled high on two plates. I turned to Sanjar. Surely this moment was out of the reach of politics. I licked my lips.

"So … is the *kebab* political?" I folded my arms in triumph. A fly landed on my plate. I waved some fingers at it and leaned way back in my chair.

"Yes," Sanjar said. He put two swords of meat on his plate and smiled.

"What?"

"Yup," Sanjar repeated. "If someone decides to stop by the garden and accuse us of eating during daylight hours, my father has prepared an answer. We have guests with medical conditions that make it necessary to eat regularly."

"Seriously?" I unfolded my arms.

"Man, I love him, he's always ready!" Sanjar nodded to the head of the table where Sepehr was holding court.

The fly hopped around on the tablecloth next to my plate, stopped to wash its legs and took off.

SANJAR HAD A KNACK for leaving parties before they turned too sticky with gossip. The lethargic intimacies that get revealed as a party drags on weren't for him, and things were slowing down. Anoush put a plate with two fresh kebabs in front of Sanjar and me. The only available space left in my body was my mouth, so I rolled around a hunk of lamb with my tongue. Watermelon and sweet green melon tumbled from enormous platters. After sampling the fruit, Sanjar, Javid (Anoush's oldest son), and I got ready to go to Darakeh before the sun went down. Maziar, the younger brother, was fasting, and stayed to rest.

The gardener closed the heavy green gate behind us. Parties like this one formed a private network of speakeasies for those who could afford it. I dragged myself, and the two pounds of lamb inside me, towards the mountains, grateful that we had known the password.

UNCLE HAWOWSHI and I were at the used bookstore he worked at in Dinkytown, Minneapolis. He was behind the counter and I was holding an old biography of Lou Andreas-Salomé, the Russian psychoanalyst who had toyed with Rilke's heart and Nietzsche's head. Uncle Hawowshi had always enjoyed the strange poems I wrote in college, and asked if there were any more.

During his last few years in Iowa, when it was just him and his sister in their parent's house, he had conjured a drifter named Vercingetorix who would roam around the country composing "Verce." My sister and I would get single sheets or whole booklets of "Verce" in the mail, describing his adventures and composing odes to America like a grunge rock version of Walt Whitman.

"Have you done any writing lately?" he asked, taking a look at the bewitching portrait of Salomé staring out from the book cover.

"I don't have anything to say," I answered bluntly, pushing the spine of the Andreas-Salomé biography until the book locked in its slot on the shelf.

Uncle Hawowshi went on to bemoan the vagrants who collected around bookstores and libraries. He spent entire evenings chasing them around the store. I empathized with him and them. Bookstores and libraries were the last places in America besides bathrooms where I could spend time without buying anything and reflect on life. It was close to impossible to avoid the pressure to consume in America. Years later I found out that it was impossible to escape the pressure to interpret things politically in Iran.

The next day I was inside a pristine bathroom in a museum. I entered the stainless-steel compartment and sat down. On the indestructible partition someone had labored to scratch the words "God is not what you think." Bathrooms were indeed among the last spiritual places left in America. I began to meditate, only to be interrupted by a staccato burst of diarrhea in the stall next to me.

Sounds of fellow animals could be embraced, accepted as part of nature. I remembered that a few days earlier I had been standing at a urinal in a restaurant bathroom. A tall man walked up to the urinal next to mine. Immediately my shy bladder syndrome kicked in. I tried to picture us as guileless, naked beasts—two cows pissing in a field. When he left, I looked up hoping to clear my mind, and saw a flashing screen in front of me advertising beer, and then breakfast sausages. I zipped up and saw the screen change again: a blonde and a brunette were yelling and grabbing the arms of an ordinary guy at a blackjack table.

"There's nothing as underrated as a good piss, and nothing as overrated as a good fuck." My dad said that when I was around twelve. I remember it was the first time I heard him swear. It was a line he probably learned at the factory he worked at when he just got to the United States. It rang in my ear as I dried my hands and left still feeling like I needed to pee.

After leaving the restaurant I was sitting at a Dunn Brothers café in downtown Minneapolis. I overheard a business meeting at a large table next to me. A sales manager was talking to his team about who had what "territory" covered. A homeless man arrived and sat down at the piano. After roaming over the keys his fingers found the tune to the Genesis song "Against All Odds." When the chorus came around the second time, he called out to two women who were coming to terms with the end of their conversation.

"Come on, everybody!"

Chapter Twenty-One

DEAD PEOPLE IN AMERICA do not stay around long. The process of hiding the dead starts while we are still living. We begin by avoiding telling our children about death, and end by shuffling off our aging parents to nursing homes so that none of us have to confront its inevitability. The only dead people we talk about are supposed to be still alive: Elvis, Tupac Shakur, Jesus, Michael Jackson.

In Iran the dead are painted on the walls.

Martyrs from history as well as martyrs from recent conflicts fill entire sides of buildings in full color. Iranians live with three-story-high portraits of earnest, whiskered, deceased soldiers staring down the triviality of their daily bustle. My eye was drawn to the words on some murals: "They are gone. What have you done?" Initially this message is inspiring, but I imagine that over time it begins to taunt a person preoccupied with getting a license to open a shop, finding a job, or even connecting to Wi-Fi.

Iranians pass murals on the way to the bakery to buy *lavash*. They see them on the building across the street while waiting in line for the bus. Out the windows of their apartments. In time the remembrance of death becomes part of everyday life—ignored wallpaper, but still the color of the room.

Sameer, my friend from the deadly serious no-man's-land of tribal Pakistan, and I were at the Stinky Café. He made a face after looking around and said, "Sometimes in America I feel like I'm living in a sitcom."

The martyrs on the walls represent something unintended: the hope for those left behind to have lives that are valued. In Black and Latino neighborhoods in the US that are suffocated by economic, police, and gang violence, buildings have become canvasses for similar rituals of hope and irredeemable waste.

ROOSEVELT GREEN had done some hard living. He said so himself. He knew he was in his last days. I met him during my final year at university. I was at his hospital bed with a few friends from the mosque. Roosevelt was thin, just some bones inside a light blue gown. His skin was taut and dry. The whites of his eyes had turned dark yellow. We were able to look hard at each other as I held his hand before leaving.

I squeezed his hand tighter and his eyes got bigger. He told me this: "All God wants is for you to find a woman and get a little house."

I'm married to a good woman and have two children. And, goddamn, our house is little. Harmony has a dark side: boredom. When it gets too quiet and peaceful in our home, I remember Roosevelt's words. I wonder if the creator of all the worlds has a desire for the created that dovetails with the American dream of the mid-twentieth century—but life is good.

THE SUICIDE SQUADS of news headlines have done a disservice to the fine Islamic tradition of contemplating death. Life has been repurposed as an opportunity for dying by the clever manipulators of desperate people; these manipulators have hijacked some parts of Islam. There is another tradition of thinking about death within Islam, one with a better pedigree.

Contemplating death used to be a handy corrective for ordinary life. The prophet of Islam, Muhammad, recommended that you "die before you die"—embrace the reality of death so completely that you experience the benefits of the deathbed perspective, not in a fleeting way during your last breath, but in a way that sustains your life. The eleventh-century Muslim scholar Al-Ghazali, who was born in Persia, heeded the message and put the world in its place: "You possess only what will not be lost in a shipwreck." In college I wondered about the mystical payload behind these words but I'm growing to see brutal practicality in them.

"YOU WILL DIE if you stay," Sepehr's closest friends told him. Sepehr, who had sent his children to America a few years before the revolution, stayed.

Sepehr had mastered living in Iran before, during, and after the revolution.

One day Sanjar and I were getting a ride from Anoush. He was taking Sepehr to be dropped off at his office. Anoush and Sanjar were trying to persuade him to let them circle around the block so that he would not have to cross the busy central Tehran street. He refused. Soon I was watching an eighty-three-year-old plot his way, in slow motion, across streets that I refused to cross without an Iranian holding my hand.

It made me think of Mark Twain's tales of riverboat piloting in *Life on the Mississippi*. Twain memorized the deadly snags and sandbars en route from St. Louis to New Orleans. Over time the dangers shifted, bringing destruction to those who did not revise their routes. Delivering valuable cargo depended upon knowledge of broken tree limbs submerged under volumes of muddy water stretching hundreds of miles. Farmers plowing in the Mississippi floodplain still find paddle wheelers buried in their fields—boats piloted by men who were inflexible or just unlucky.

Sepehr did not end up buried in the mud. Having studied Islamic law with the mullahs, and having served as a judge and justice department leader, he had just as nimbly navigated the Islamic Revolution and its aftermath. For example, one of his old friends had become prominent in the new government. Sepehr invited him for tea. When he opened the door a group of men holding machine guns rushed in. His friend followed. He liked his friend, and they had tea, but he politely skirted that scene as best he could.

For thirty years he had quietly struggled in the courts to take back the family's land from post-revolutionary opportunists. The garden was one of those jewels, as was a plot in the neighborhood.

Immediately after the Shah was deposed in 1979 a sort of finders-keepers mentality took over previously disenfranchised people. The assets abandoned by Iranians who had fled the country were taken up by a set of squatters ordained by the clerics. Apartments, gardens, country houses, and shops shuttered in haste were opened by people who, with clean consciences, had forged backgrounds of humble poverty into battering rams of avarice.

One man who had worked in Sepehr's garden laid claim to the place after a few years. He was "sitting there," as they say in Iran. Over time he planted ten trees in the garden and was therefore sheltered under the Islamic law called "right of roots." In return for leaving, he wanted an apartment, and eventually sued for $150,000. Not being a violent man, it took Sepehr some work and a lot of money to dislodge the guy.

What helped Sepehr in those grim years was a long history of generosity. His deeds, like comets, took long elliptical paths around the social system, returning to Sepehr's horizon ten, twenty, thirty, even forty years later.

REVOLUTIONS NEED to feed themselves, and this one came to swallow Sepehr for good one day. In the post-Shah chaos Sepehr was taken to prison. Many people did not return from such trips. As he was being led to his cell the head of the prison stepped in front of him.

"Hello, Doctor," the man said.

Sepehr did not recognize him.

The prison boss introduced himself. "Hello, Doctor," he repeated, "I know you. I had a legal problem. I came to your office. Your worker was not there. You brought me tea. You helped me with the problem that I had."

Sepehr had the respect of the warden the first day he entered prison. They kept him for fewer than ten days. While he was in prison, the guards and prisoners came to him for legal advice. He helped people he did not know during a time when the best of friends were hurting each other and turning each other in.

WE HAD FALLEN behind our parents on a hike at Minnehaha Falls in Minneapolis. My sister and I were very young. Black trees jutted out of the white snow all around like giant arrows that had pierced a battlefield. We could hear the creek next to the path still moving under its frozen surface.

I see a man in a puffy light-blue ski jacket slipping down the side of the ravine. He starts to walk towards us. His head is a white bulb with a few wisps of brown on the sides. A pleading, high-pitched whine comes out of his mouth.

"Please, can you help me?"

My sister tugs my shoulder. We both know instantly that the man is not right. She walks me backwards. We are in the wilderness. At the top of the ravine city life carries on, but below, we are alone.

"Please, *please*, can you help me take this rubber-band off my penis?"

My sister grips my arm and says, "Don't stop walking."

The puffy blue jacket gets closer.

Suddenly he darts off the path and starts scrambling back up the ravine, sliding back a few steps in the snow. We cannot see him anymore. A woman is walking in the opposite direction of our parents on the other side of the creek. We jog parallel to her until we reach the steps leading up to the parking lot. They are covered in packed snow. My sister turns around to look. My moon boots lunge ahead of me up five flights of pure ice.

In the parking lot we wait in the warm station wagon of a young couple.

When my parents eventually find us, I'm glad, because my mother isn't adding to my fear by being hysterical. She has an appreciation for adventure and danger, one my father lacks, and is curious about what happened. My sister, having carried the responsibility of our escape, tells her: "A man with his penis out."

We had survived, and if my mother is guilt-ridden, she quietly hides it for our sake. She bundles us into our own car.

I remember looking out of the frosted window of our old maroon Volvo on the ride home.

"Dad, who was that?" I ask.

"He was just a man. He was born, grew up in a house, in a neighborhood. He might have a sister." I can see my mom turning toward him as he answers me.

What could have become the menace of the world in my mind became an acceptance of its strange, broken inhabitants. This memory has been a touchstone for me my whole life.

MEETING SEPEHR and thinking about my own father and mother made me reflect on what we leave behind for our children. Sanjar was frustrated with his father because he was writing a series of very complicated books. Sanjar wanted him to write down the stories of his life. The stories he and his sister and brother had been raised on.

Sanjar would gently imitate him, puffing his chest out and pursing his lips. Then in a deep voice he would say, "This book is a technical book—*only* for professors." Then Sanjar would tell him, "*Baba joon*, no one is going to read it."

PASHA WAS AN INDIAN man who came to America long ago as a Fulbright Scholar. He then became a visiting professor at the University of Wisconsin. I met him in the mosque in Madison when I was a student. I saw a small man sitting cross-legged in the prayer hall having a discussion with an American convert. It looked lively so I walked over in my socks and lowered myself to the carpet near them. They let me into their tiny circle.

The American wore a brown kufi and had a thick, dark-red goatee anchored between rosy cheeks. The texture of the goatee was powerful, and with just the memory of it, I could polish my dress shoes. Abdul-Samad had taught himself Urdu and was now learning Arabic. He leaned in close to Pasha.

"There was darkness," Pasha continued. "There were bodies without heads writhing all around in the darkness. In the black there was a circle of people. They were passing around a lamp, and this lamp was Muhammad."

When there was a pause in their dialogue, I shyly mentioned a dream that had troubled me.

"I was in a mosque. It might have been this one. Everyone is facing Mecca and praying. There is a problem: I am facing the other way."

I saw Abdul-Samad absorbing it into his intellect, but Pasha tossed out an idea using the fast-twitch muscles of intuition: "There was a terrible stampede in Mecca the other day—maybe it is related to your dream."

I learned that Pasha was a man who said exactly what he wanted to say.

He communicated in a clear, non-patronizing way. We went to a Taco John's one time, and when he said his name to the cashier, she froze.

"Yes, my name is *Pasha*."

"Pa ..." The young girl's tongue bumped up awkwardly against the unfamiliar name.

"PA-SHA. Try it."

"Pasha," she said with a giggle.

"See, you can do it."

PASHA KNEW ROOSEVELT GREEN and mentioned to Abdul-Samad and I that he was ill at the hospital. We went that night. The next afternoon I stopped by the mosque to see if Pasha was there. It was filled with all kinds of people from the world of Islam, studying in Wisconsin. There was a bit of excitement in the air. I worked my way through the doors and into the carpeted hall. Everyone was standing.

A harsh, tangy odor filled the room. It arrived suddenly as if it was coming from my own body—hitting the back of my nostrils before I even took a breath.

I now know it as the smell of death.

A body wrapped in a white sheet was being carried to the front of the mosque on the shoulders of four men. When it arrived it was set on a raised stretcher. There was some loud chanting, followed by a very short prayer. Someone got up and asked that we remember "our brother, a fellow Muslim" who had died early that morning.

Abruptly the body was back on the shoulders of the four men and headed out the door.

The loud chanting began again.

I was in a sort of trance, a bit woozy from the smell and loud voices. The body wobbled underneath the sheet as the men bounced past me in their bare feet. Through the din I heard a lone voice from the corner of the mosque. It was drowned out by the shouting.

"His name, what was his *name?*"

It was Pasha.

Chapter Twenty-Two

NO BIG PRAYER, no whispered grace, no hemming and hawing as others came late and filled their plates. The unceremonious start to meals in Iran startled me.

The main concern was to eat while the food was hot. God, people, and etiquette played their part, but at the critical moment, it was food being honored. I began to understand Sanjar's ashen face when we were at restaurants in the US and food arrived lukewarm.

Once, at lunchtime, we paid our respects to a stew. Sepehr had fallen silent after the last spoonful. Satisfaction had immobilized us. It was time for a siesta.

Sepehr got up and walked slowly to his bedroom. He had spent the morning writing in his pajama bottoms, so he was prepared for his bed. His slippers scraped across the marble floor. From the hallway I heard him muttering in Farsi. Finally, I pried loose a translation from Sanjar.

"He's saying, 'I've been shot.'"

Sanjar and I tried to get up from the table but failed. It was a multiple homicide. There was only one suspect: Neda.

Neda was the cook for Sanjar and his father. She had worked for the family for over thirty years. Her parents had lived in the feudal village of Sanjar's grandfather. When they first brought her to work for the family, she was eight years old. Sanjar's grandfather said she was too young, so she returned the next year and began working for the family. I held back a middle-class American reflex to question the arrangement.

When Sanjar and his brother and sisters were in America, Sepehr's wife passed away. During that time Neda was a companion for their father. They both loved to talk. This was a relief for Sanjar who tired easily of chitchat.

In the kitchen Sanjar pointed at a Tupperware container. It could have fit an artisan loaf of bread. Inside were the medications Neda needed to manage her health.

"Look at all those pills. She is sick and in a lot of pain all the time. But she's always smiling. She's a good woman, a very good woman."

While telling me this, Sanjar lowered his voice. He was thinking about the years she'd spent making life better for his father. Most of the time, she would cook at her apartment in South Tehran, and her husband would bring the hot food to Sepehr in his office or apartment. Other times she would help manage the house: cleaning, decorating, making decisions that Sepehr did not want to be bothered with, niggling with him over the details of those he did.

Since Neda was from a village, she was the person who most reminded me of my father and his family in Egypt. After leaving their village, my father's family had maintained an earthy touch and an ancient reflex for hospitality. Neda would constantly ask Sanjar if I liked the food, not out of insecurity but as a prod to eat more. She had a loving but heartsick weight to her—encompassing, smothering, like my aunt in Cairo.

THE BASS ON THE END of my father's line is so big it looks like a cartoon. It is a humid afternoon and I am a small boy. Our close friends, an Egyptian musician and his son, are there. We are all catching fish at the lagoon that connects Lake of the Isles and Cedar Lake in Minneapolis. The sky is darkening. After the bass is hauled in, the water calms. I can see the seaweed and the light, sandy bottom again. The shapes of army-green fish cross over it. A fin punctures the surface and disappears in a panic, creating a tiny whirlpool.

In the distance we hear one loud crack of thunder.

A thunderstorm can quickly push away ornamental clouds with a wall of black and grey in a Minnesota summer. Within minutes it's pouring. I'm running to the car, dragging a stringer heavy with fish across the thick July grass. The wind is throwing the rain sideways and it's like we're walking through a car wash. We get in the car and roll slowly through the plumes of water.

The windshield wipers swish at high speed. In the half second of visibility I see a pathetic figure standing in the rain.

It's a man in a rainbow-colored, ragtag clown costume. In his arms is a poodle, soaked and exhausted looking from the pounding drops. My father pulls over and invites the man into the car. He opens his mouth to say thanks. As I peer inside, his teeth remind me of the randomly strewn beads of an old abacus at my elementary school.

My father brings him to our house and sits him dripping wet on our living room couch. He gets him a towel and some clothes. Then he disappears into the kitchen to prepare a meal for him. I'm sitting there looking at this strange man. His puppy is on his lap and he's talking to it while he dries it off. He puts the sweatpants and sweatshirt to the side.

I can't make sense of him. There is a smudgy chaos surrounding him: it is mental illness. I withhold judgment because I don't know I am supposed to make one. We sit together in the scattered alphabet of innocence that is his mind.

My father reappears with a tray of food. The man, who is still wearing a soaked beanie hat over bushy hair, looks down at the steaming plate of eggs. He looks back up at my father. I don't know if he is grateful or doesn't like eggs, or both.

The storm passes. My father and the Egyptian musician drive the man home. I step out into the charged air with my sister and my friend. We walk around the neighborhood, stepping over smaller branches ripped from larger ones.

JAVID AND MAZIAR had been taught very, very well by Anoush and Neda. They were in their early twenties and had grown up with Sanjar's family. Sepehr had helped the family get a nice apartment and stay healthy. He had also sent the boys through private school. The easiest way to tell the brothers apart on paper was that Maziar was religious and Javid was not. Sanjar promotes his friends with enthusiasm so we got reports about each other. The stories Sanjar repeated on either side of the six months he spent in Iran or America became groundwork, and we were all ready to like each other when I arrived.

Javid and Maziar knew about Ferris, the ferocious Syrian who lived in Minneapolis. He had been banned from the Stinky Café after punching a hole in the wall during a chess game. Sanjar was fond of saying, "So, you say you don't *like* civilization? Let me introduce you to my friend Ferris!"

To them Ferris was a full-fledged character constructed out of one-liners. His art was the curt statement declaimed in a low growl. Something good was "highly awesome" or "good a lot." While you were stupidly describing the gentle affection you were beginning to feel for a woman, Ferris would interrupt you: "Yes, but is she BANG-able?"

After a forceful chess move, Ferris would hold out his hand and say, "Each finger is like a hammer." If Ferris had you stumped in a game of speed chess, with your time ticking away, he would grunt, "Move it man. I'm not here for cosmetic purposes."

At the apartment, Javid, Maziar, Sanjar, and I were playing the game Blokus. Afternoon had turned to evening. I moved a red game piece into an advantageous position, picked up my tea glass, and declared, "Let me sip on my martini."

Javid and Maziar laughed and at the same time said, "Ferris!"

The four of us were sitting in Sanjar's room. The balcony doors opened wide to the lights of Tehran, its skyline only broken up by the top branches of a couple of sycamore trees. The board was on a small table. Sanjar was sitting on his bed, and the three of us on chairs. A bookshelf filled one wall. In it were journals, language books, and Will Durant's *History of Civilization*. Volumes bought over time for a dollar apiece at the Friends of the Library bookstore in downtown Minneapolis. I remembered packing them up to ship to Iran by boat when Sanjar moved.

The other feature of the room was a large Persian rug. The giant rectangle was a tribal circuit board, signals of enduring meaning and complexity flowing through its silken patterns.

A cool breeze blew in through the balcony doors. It smelled clean and fresh, a stream of air purified by desert and mountain. Under a starry sky, it linked Iran to Iraq and the rest of the beleaguered Middle East, and cradled them in precious indifference.

LIFE HAD NOT always been tinctured with luxury for Sanjar. When I knew him in America, his material comfort level was debatable. We walked or bussed most of the time, searching for dollar burgers and discounted pizza slices during happy hour around the city. His apartment was a small box in an old redbrick.

I worked at a bakery called Turtle Bread and was slow to the game of bringing home free food. I told Sanjar, "I feel bad taking expensive cake."

"You should feel bad about not bringing a piece for your friend!" He replied. Then he pinched his fingers together making the sign for an infinitesimal speck, a moral misjudgment collapsing on itself. "This is the size of the wrong you would be doing."

It was not long before I was leaving the bakery at night with grocery bags packed with tomato-basil soup, quiche lorraine, and chocolate cake. Uschi, the petite German manager, with a washcloth in her hand, just smiled and carried on closing down the bakery with lighthearted industriousness. Sanjar and I would have gourmet picnics by Lake Bde Maka Ska, taking breaks to practice our roundhouse kicks against juvenile ash trees.

IN SANJAR'S ROOM we did nothing except apply our brains to a child's game and talk. In Iran, the oral tradition was still alive. There was a chance that something culturally valuable might be passed along.

"I'm going to bang the hell out of you if you move your piece there!" Sanjar was threatening Javid.

"You want to bang me?"

"I do but I'm afraid you might *like* it!"

I decided to join in. "Hey now, wait. That's impossible in Iran."

"What?" They both said.

"I learned from your own president that there are no homosexuals in Iran."

"Shit. He's right. It's impossible, our president said it. I'm still going to rough you up." Sanjar carried on with his threat, and Javid dropped a yellow zigzag-shaped piece into Sanjar's territory.

"You little bitch!"

Maziar was smiling in his chair. Not always being able to keep up with the English, he was able to concentrate on his next move. He won the game while the rest of us found inconsistencies in each other's manhood.

HAMID, THE AFGHAN who took care of the garden, also worked at the apartment. He appeared at the door of the bedroom with a tray of fresh tea.

He was a soft-spoken man. His shoulders were square—he didn't have the tell-tale dip in one of them from carrying a Kalashnikov since boyhood, as some Afghan men do. He had just an afternoon's worth of beard growth. I went into the laundry room one afternoon and saw Hamid standing with an iron in his hand and my flattened underpants in front of him. It brought mixed emotions.

I had met Hamid at the garden. There was a small cottage there, and in it Hamid supposedly had a wife and child. After a few weeks, I finally saw a tiny boy with jet black hair kicking through the leaves along the path. I never saw his wife. This was normal but, alas, experienced as abnormal by me.

After I returned to America, I heard that Hamid and his family had gone back to Afghanistan. In Iran he had saved for years to afford his wife's dowry, had gone back to collect her from their village, and started a life in Tehran. Sepehr would have looked after the schooling of Hamid's son, but his wife's isolation became too much for her. Their departure was a source of sadness for Sanjar.

In the Afghan village Hamid's family would help educate the boy. Listening to ancient stories he would get a sure sense of himself. He could perhaps live in more dignity than he would in Iran. If history would just leave his country alone.

I noticed that Sanjar took care to call Neda, Hamid, Anoush, and the others *workers* instead of *servants*. Still, I felt uncomfortable being served tea and fruit by Hamid. There was no shame in the work he was doing, but I could not close the place where it festered in my mind. It was the conditioning I had as a middle-class American: you could go out anywhere and get served hand and foot, but to have someone serving you in your own home was both economically and culturally questionable.

Hamid walked forward from the doorway in his slippers. A glass of tea was put in front of each of us. I told him, "*Merci.*" I had heard Iranians saying "thank you" in French.

With a timid smile Hamid took the sugar bowl from the tray, caught my eye, and set it down.

MY OBSESSION with the hand-cut sugar chunks was noticed and eventually drew out a story from Sanjar.

I wondered why I saw Iranians dipping their sugar cubes in their tea. Sanjar told me that sometime in the colonial past the British wanted to import sugar cubes to Persia. A mullah wanted a share of the profits but the British refused. In response the mullah told a crowd that the sugar was made white by the bone of dogs. Sugar sales went down the very next day. With profits plunging the British ran to the mullah and said, "What did you tell them?"

After receiving guarantees that a share of profits would go to him, the mullah set about reviving people's taste for sugar. He told them that the way to clean the bone from the sugar was to dip it in the tea until it was light brown, and then put it quickly in your mouth.

A BOWL OF NUTS was towering before me. I was sitting on the couch in Sepehr's living room.

Almonds, cashews, pistachios, hazelnuts: I cracked a few and chewed them down. My throat became dry and I eyed the kitchen doorway, hoping for the figure of Hamid to appear with a glass of tea.

Across the room Sepehr's writing table and the television playing Polish MTV were a lot farther away. The room had grown three times in size. A move to a new apartment had been completed.

It was done a week earlier with the help of two burly Iraqis. They fulfilled stereotypes as each had arabesques of chest hair emerging from unbuttoned shirts, and black mustaches as thick as beaver pelts.

One of them heaved a refrigerator onto his back, secured it with a fraying strip of cloth, and walked down three flights of stairs.

I had been told that as a guest I could not help. When the Iraqi arrived at the bottom, I was standing in the street looking at the tan dust covering my shoes from the last time we did *kuh raftan*, going to the mountain. He looked both ways and said something quick in Farsi.

I looked both ways and said something in English.

Both of us frowned. His partner showed up. They nodded at me and said something else much richer in Arabic. Sanjar appeared at the doors of the new apartment next door and held it open for the Iraqi.

"What did he say?" I asked, embarrassed that the US had invaded his country and bombed it for twenty years, and now I couldn't tell him which direction to go when he had a refrigerator on his back.

"Oh, he just told his partner, 'That guy doesn't even speak Farsi!'"

A COUPLE DAYS later I was back sitting on the couch with the glass coffee table in front of me. On the table was a bowl of shelled walnuts soaking in water. Next to them was an empty bowl for their casings.

On the streets of Tehran and on the mountain paths near the city, large jars of what look like tiny raven brains in water sit on flimsy card tables. Some of the vendors peel off the black-brown casing, creating jars of bleach-white raven brains that fetch a higher price. Sepehr bought them with the skin on—a case of wanting to "fart around" with something. I dug out the casing from the wrinkles of the little brain and bit into the squeaky, delicious, nutmeat.

Sepehr and some guests were speaking in Farsi and I disappeared into a daze of incomprehension and walnuts. I imagined a distant ancestor in Egypt preparing a raven corpse for mummification as I picked my way through the nut casing. Sanjar had left the room to take a call.

"You know Iran is not really like this?" I heard a voice, then realized it was English.

"Pardon?"

"What you see, what Sanjar is showing you, is not the real Iran. It's a privileged world." It was the voice of a man who had come to ask Sepehr for some legal help.

"Oh?"

"Iran is poor and people are miserable. If you just leave North Tehran you will see."

I thought of the goofy soldier on the metro, with his thick, moist hand, and said, "I know Sanjar is not showing me some places."

"You see."

"But …" I politely protested.

"But what?"

"But I don't *want* him to."

I saw Sanjar with his phone to his ear standing in his bedroom doorway. He was looking out warily.

"After the election, everyone was in the streets to protest. Poor and rich," he continued.

"Everyone?" I picked a scrap of casing from a fingernail.

The man pressed his agenda. "Yes. The city was taken over, that's how people really feel."

Sepehr's household did have to work to maintain equanimity in the face of unrest. Sanjar had told me once that he was against a new revolution, he was for evolution. Revolution had ripped his society apart once already. He advised Javid and Maziar to avoid crowds.

"Really? So the protests were that big?" I gave a small concession, hoping to get the man to back off. I had heard differently; many parents refused to let their kids go to the streets during anti-government protests, and whole sections of the city functioned normally throughout the demonstrations.

"Young, old, parents and their kids were all there. Sanjar doesn't know the real situation. Has he taken you *anywhere?*" The man nodded to the bedroom, seemingly unconcerned if Sanjar heard him.

"Lot of places." I wanted to stick up for Sanjar but it would mean possibly offending a guest of Sepehr's. I had no idea who this person was. I checked the weight of my tea glass with one hand and then the other.

I stared at my pile of little bird brains. They were ready to eat.

THAT NIGHT I LAY down on cool sheets and listened for a lone dog bark or car horn. It was very quiet and peaceful in rich North Tehran. I saw my hand reaching out to the soldier's beefy paw on the metro and then my despicable recoil. I considered the slim chances that a poor young man in America would offer his hand and his lunch to an Iranian traveler he met on a city bus.

In the shadowy room, my mind strayed, and commandeered memories to use for a midnight philosophical quest.

In my travels I have been invited over to eat by people who sheltered under the standard corrugated steel roofs of the third world poor. People who worked hard hours to secure what they offered me lightheartedly—a meal. My father's stories of the village in Egypt ensured that I never romanticized poverty. One look at the teeth of my Egyptian uncles exposed an ongoing dental pogrom due to the simple lack of fluoride in the village water supply.

Still, I could not figure out how poor people kept discontent and anger at the elite consistently in check. Humility and grace must be the orphaned offspring of the powerful, adopted and cared for by the powerless.

I have always noticed a flickering of honor in the poor people of Africa and the Middle East that is harder to find in America. This is a mystery to me. Something rich and deep seems to sustain the poor in older societies. Is it fatalism or wisdom to know who you are, and where you belong? The people there walk on something more solid as they carry on in their dusty villages or flimsy, polluted shantytowns.

In America, the poor are adrift in a wasteland.

Replace each promise America has made for the good life with a mistake; someone who accumulates these mistakes is poor. Their squalor has been earned. It is a choice they made. When that is the story eating away at people, facing the day with dignity becomes exhausting.

The balcony doors to my bedroom were open. I heard Sepehr's slippers brushing the marble floor at the far end of the hall. A door closed, and the apartment went silent. Under me the sheets had become warm and I rolled to one side.

I looked out towards the yellow lights of South Tehran and closed my eyes. A little movie played across my lids. I saw the weary face of one of my middle school student's grandmothers.

Pulling into the disability parking space, a thick, elderly woman watches the blue placard with the wheelchair swinging from her mirror. Sighing and resting in her seat she looks out the car window, hesitant to get out, crippled by poorly managed diabetes and arthritis. She lights a cigarette.

She turns off the ignition, dabs out her cigarette, and savors one of the few privileges of her life: a good parking spot and a short walk.

She raised her daughter and her daughter's daughter. Did most things better the second time, by her own account. Her apartment is still not empty, and she likes to keep the multiplying kids happy with pop and chips.

As the years pass the old woman reaches an elemental parity with the wealthy when illness finally overtakes her. In the hospital the differences between rich and poor expand in some ways but diminish in others.

In hospital beds, all talk turns to food, no matter what walk of life people come from—so I have been told by Marie, who is a nurse.

In what may be her last days, the old woman will get to pick from the room-service menu: turkey and gravy or Salisbury steak. After a light tap on the door an orderly will enter. Hot under the plastic plate cover will be some food—one of the choices she had.

FOR POOR IRANIANS, privileges have come later than a last meal at a hospital. For martyrs of the Iran-Iraq War, glory, by definition, would come after the fact: wall-sized murals adorned with their faces, songs and movies starring their sacrifice, and careful, government-subsidized management of their legacy. It was a celebrated fate in a world that had been indifferent to their existence. Compensation and assistance continue to trickle to their families years after they were gassed by Saddam or eaten up by minefields.

Many of the properties and assets seized after the 1979 Revolution were handled by charitable trusts like the Foundation of Martyrs and Veteran Affairs. Loved ones survive on the privilege of being connected to death.

My eyes were wide open now. Sanjar was asleep. I even heard Sepehr, the nighthawk, shuffle to the bathroom for one last visit and then to his room. Tehran gently hummed outside the balcony window. From below the window, I heard a single bark.

Here it was, that place between A and B. Nothing but fleeting thoughts, a few billion neurons firing blanks off into the night.

One thought hovered a bit longer than the others: my memory of the guest who had advised me to seek out the real Iran. Even though I never saw him again, I kept trying to ignore him.

EIGHTY STUDENTS training to be teachers packed the lecture hall. I was finishing my license in Minneapolis. It was midsummer. I had arrived late and looked up into the seats to see an uneven checkerboard of bare arms, legs, and colored cloth.

One older student had a distinctive bald head, the size of a medium-sized tortoise shell. He sat in the front row and had just been coolly reprimanded by the professor for eating during class. He put away his Tupperware container of pasta and sat dutifully for the rest of class.

When I walked into class the next day, the bald man had his big high-tops swung atop his desk. In his hands was an enormous submarine sandwich stuffed with a piece of lettuce that, now that I think about it, was the size of a piece of *sangak*. It drooped over the perimeter of the bread as he took monstrous bites.

During the class period we talked about testing in schools. People went on about how to prepare students for tests and this and that. Feeling my heart beating fast, I raised my hand.

"You know, we get students so worried about these standardized tests that they won't recognize a real one when it shows up in their lives."

The professor and the bald man were nodding their heads up and down. When I spoke, I was thinking of Mulla Do-Piyaza, the adviser to the Mughal emperor Akbar. His definition stated: "A test is an unexpected hardship." I was also thinking about Saleh deep in the Albaicín of Granada.

Chapter Twenty-Three

WEEKS, THEN A MONTH had gone by without my getting arrested or killed. I calculated the number of days left on my visa, stamping them off in my head like a free-drink card at a café. I caught myself leaning towards the day when the card would be complete.

During a game of Blokus one night I had one of my waking nightmares. It had been awhile. This one slid into my mind smoothly, and left the same way.

The balcony was open and the breeze was coming in, but going out the same way were our voices. I was telling Sanjar, Maziar, and Javid how nice it was to be hanging out with a bunch of guys so late at night. Where I grew up, the only places I saw men together at night, I said, were a club called the Gay 90s and the Global Corner Café. The café was where a full tribal council of Somali cab drivers was raging at all hours over bad coffee—only interrupted by games of chess and foosball or a dispatch.

I follow the sound of our voices out of the balcony and see them drifting into the headset of a security agent in the apartment next to us. There is a large Persian rug beneath him but no other furniture. He stares deeply into the rug's interlocking shapes as he listens before turning to his notebook. A case is being put together out of the bits and pieces of our conversation. As with the shredded top secret documents of the besieged US Embassy in 1979, a weaver would connect the little parts into a condemning work of art. Circled in his notebook are flagged English words: "boobs," "freedom," "America," "green," "war."

The agent shuts the notebook and deftly slides it into a backpack. He wraps the cord of his headphones around his hand and secures them in a side pocket.

Before leaving he opens the shades, turns on the lights, and recedes into my subconsciousness.

THE FIRST NIGHT I met Sanjar he said he was from Persia.

I struggled to picture where that was. Across a vague expanse of Asia, a giant Persian amoeba expanded and contracted, slid a little west, then a little east. Sanjar tried to explain why the map of his country had changed over the years. Eventually I was able to pin the wavering borders down. Then replace the name Persia with Iran.

Another night, early in our friendship, I met Sanjar inside the Stinky Café. The place was filled with twenty-somethings, people between school and career. The kind of people you find at cafés at night. The spirits of hundreds of incinerated cigarettes began to possess my clothes.

We went outside and picked a table. Sanjar grabbed the ashtray from the middle of it and dumped the butts in the garbage. Across the street the Super America gas station lit up the corner. Pieces of a crazy man's mind zipped around in front of him as he sat wedged between the sidewalk and the wall of the liquor store next to the café.

"It would be so exciting if you could see Iran someday."

I didn't respond. The crazy man yelped something, and I glanced over.

"You would see things you never saw before. Hear things you never heard before."

Reaching for the handiest excuse, I said, "I don't know any Persian."

"We call it Farsi. But man, you'll learn. It's not a hard language."

"Man ... I don't know."

Sanjar wanted to check on a friend at another café a couple blocks away. I got up and decided to go along. I collected my coffee cup and plate. Sanjar was already crossing the street.

As I turned from the table a brown sugar packet fell off my plate. The words on it read: "IN THE RAW."

BECAUSE THE PERMISSION to go to Iran came so suddenly from the Foreign Ministry, it was too late to study Farsi. I sent my passport to Washington, DC, for the visa and bought my plane ticket. After years of hearing Sanjar's stories of the dark-eyed beauties of Iran I grew impatient. In phone calls to me he would passionately describe women he was seeing. It was like he was describing *houris*, virgin companions of the faithful in Paradise. I planned to keep my promises to Marie, but I had a scholarly interest in examining Sanjar's claims.

I purified and validated his exaggerations about his sexy girlfriends in the strength of my own desire, eventually settling for vicariously enjoying the tumult and excitement of his relationships.

As I looked at my young family before my departure I came back to the real world with a vengeance. I felt guilty stowing little private fantasies about the trip and superstitiously thought this would end up cursing me.

The eve of my flight I ran my fingers through Khalil's hair. He has light hair. When the two of us were out together people sometimes looked at my Mediterranean complexion and then very slowly back down at the little blonde boy next to me.

As my hand rested on his head, I thought of the strange emotional world he would live in with a father locked up somewhere in Iran. His feelings would play wonky like an accordion on a fading radio station—his heart a squeezebox itself.

From the outside things have always looked scary to me. Biking around Minneapolis I would see an intense pickup soccer game. Players were fast and aggressive. I'd think, man those guys look good. I'd linger on the sidelines until someone invited me in. When the ball rolled to my feet, I instinctively dribbled around people like they were potted plants. Once inside I was the master.

IT TURNED OUT that the first words I learned in Farsi were suffi-
cient to answer questions about the mysteries of the world, the
future, and what sauces I'd like for a late-night snack of kebab in
Iran.

Nemi-doonam. I don't know.

The second words I learned, however, were fitting for questions
about what I wanted to do in Iran: *kuh raftan,* go to the mountain. For my young friends in Iran the answer would often be *kuh
raftan* as well. There weren't many other choices.

Maziar had a university break and Javid was off work, so we
could spend time together in the last portion of my trip. Some
nights Neda, Anoush, and the boys would lay mats over the huge
Persian rug in the living room of Sepehr's apartment and have a
sleepover. The ride home to South Tehran could take them three
or four hours. They could leave at midnight and still get caught
in a traffic jam.

One night, Sepehr sent Anoush out at one in the morning
to get kebab. We all gathered around the kitchen table. When
he returned, we ripped into the tinfoil and jumped on piles of
steaming roasted lamb and chicken.

Then, at two thirty in the morning, as we sat in Sanjar's room
playing Blokus, Hamid showed up in the doorway smiling.
Incredibly, at waist level, a tray was in his hand, with four glasses
of hot tea on it.

MAZIAR, THE YOUNGER brother, was taller and darker, and had
a pharaonic face. A black goatee was securely fastened beneath a
wide smile.

He was submerged in the focused slipstream of mid-college
ambition, and rarely reflected on the general discontent of his
peers. He had been the top student in his high school and was
now studying engineering. He had the seriousness of a man with
a hand on the next rung, fueled by desperation and optimism.

Javid, a couple of years older, with a small, indestructible body, was more restless. Facing the post-college wilderness of so many Middle Eastern youth, he daily found his reach outrunning the limits of Iran's economy. Javid's feelings about the future had not become bitter, but his venting was more potent than Maziar's.

Both were doing all they could to improve themselves. They were taking English classes a few nights a week and would bring their books for me to look over. Javid was more impatient. He tried to say all that was on his mind, whether he had the words or not. He deployed words he did not quite know how to use, and words that even I didn't understand. One day, like a man pulling out a pocket watch to check the time, he dropped the word "troth."

Javid reminded me of Juan, the Colombian, who carried around a dictionary. I called it *la Biblia*. Juan would lift arcane words from its pages and hurl them into conversations. One day he called me a "milksop." Another day he was picking on his girlfriend, Marsella, and as she approached him with a hand wound back for a slap, he cried out that "the great *hen-witch*" was coming.

Sanjar liked to brag about how much the boys would study. High achievement was one way to show gratefulness to Sepehr's funding of their education. In reality, there was nothing else to do.

I asked Javid about his free time when he had been at university. He said they would try to hang out in a park or square but would soon be visited by the police.

"What are you guys doing? Why are you hanging around here?" the police would bark. They dispersed and went back to the books.

Javid said it was even worse in the winter. "Parks are cold, and you'll be frozen. If you survive the cold weather you will be sitting next to a police officer anyway."

I knew students were the most dangerous demographic—time on their hands and full of ideas. I didn't know a few buddies having a cigarette in the park in broad daylight could raise such alarm.

WHEN MAZIAR TRIED to handle his boredom at University one day through official channels he was rewarded with an illustrative gem. He went to the "entertainment center" at his college to find out what he could do with his free time.

"I asked the people there what was going on today. They gave me a form to fill out and said to come back Thursday."

IF A YOUNG PERSON had money there were cafés to go to. On the calendar there would be occasional weddings in soundproof rooms so that illicit music and dancing could take place. Those who were up for the risk could go to underground parties. These parties were warped mirrors of what young Iranians thought Americans were doing every night: orgies, drugs, alcoholic barf games—a syllabus of debauchery.

They didn't know the Uncle Hawowshis of America, with *Brothers Karamazov* cracked open; the Mormon youth groups camping together; the mousy couples cooking Thai food and playing Jenga in their apartments.

I asked Javid and Maziar what they would want to do if they could. I racked my own brain for the apparently endless itinerary of fun in America. There was a pause as they got over the fact that I would not understand their plight. Then named a very short list.

Javid answered first: "Discos."

"Yes?"

Maziar answered second: "Bars."

"You don't even drink, man," I said, which was not fair, as I had gone to bars my whole life without drinking. "Okay. Yes, and?"

"Yeah, bars and discos." They both shook their heads.

It did not impress me as a catalogue of deprivations. What I learned was that they desired to do ordinary things without being subjected to extraordinary attention. A generation of girls were learning to hate their country over the amount of hair they could show when they stepped outside to buy bread. The most natural activity of all—talking—had to be curbed. There was an eagerness to just talk and talk without having to look over your shoulder.

JAVID HAD STUDIED hard in school. Studying, and only studying, left no time to learn about life. On a societal level, this made for awkward young citizens: highly educated and highly inexperienced.

Every book has severe limits, despite our glorification of reading. We have an obsession with the types of information in books and, of course, on the Internet. It is the sensation of easy, productive accumulation that we are addicted to. Seeking information in books and on the Internet, we are less cued to symbols around us. The action densely packaged in a book, or the hum of web surfing, make the real world feel flat and subdued, a badly paced video game. We become heedless of teachers—ordinary moments and people—out there in the inconsequential bumbling of everyday life. We ignore their messages because they come from a discredited source: a human voice on the street.

We say, "Talk is cheap," "He's all talk," and "Put it in writing."

It *is* cheap. It is valued in the West only when we are paying a psychologist to be a friend—someone who knows how to listen, tell stories about what is happening in the mind, and pay attention to signs indicating the real tests of one's life.

IMPORTANT INFORMATION is still entrusted to people in Iran. Knowledge continues to be passed along in old teaching stories. Through Neda, the oral tradition had taught Javid how to be a good person.

Javid had a blind spot, however, that stumped the wisdom of the old tales and all the book studying: girls.

There were problems with how young Iranian men and women were relating to each other. The basis of contact between them was limited to marriage prep, sordid wham-bam affairs, or wholesale ignorance and bamboozlement.

Javid would lament to me: "You know, girls are trouble and made me a wimp. I mean I can't handle them in the correct way. Exactly the time I wanna screw them something happens. They say it's my turn and I have to turn and be screwed."

"Oh boy."

"Believe it or not, here in Iran we got a problem with honesty, cognition, and troth."

"What?"

"Troth."

"Troth?"

"Yes, is it right?"

"I don't know man, but what are you saying?"

"Girls."

"What about them?"

"They come lovely, get close, abuse invisibly, go like killers, and leave you to bleed until nothing is left. I prefer to be alone and talk, go out walking, play, and even jerk off with myself. And the worst part of it—loneliness!"

"Sounds rough."

"Here in Iran you always think win, but suddenly everything is changed, and you lose!"

JAVID AND MAZIAR were fascinated to hear my opinions on girls. I leveraged my tiny fortune of American relationship and sexual experience and held court.

"Don't get deep with girls, stay shallow. Shallow is good. It's where the sunlight hits the ocean floor and more life flourishes. It's warmer. Think of the Great Barrier Reef, and zip back and forth like a colorful fish."

"You mean they like laughing." Maziar had understood.

"Yes," I said, warming to my role.

"But I like to tell them what I think," Javid protested.

Self-satisfied, I brushed some lint off my pants. "Don't worry. Listen a lot and don't think too much."

"But I want them to know me," Javid said meekly.

"You're not special. Remember, girls always have a few guys in mind, even when you're going out with them. They're better shoppers than we are! Just be cool." I realized then that I had been quoting Sanjar word for word.

IN AMERICA, I had rarely followed my own advice, or Sanjar's.

I would get intellectually serious on the dance floor. It was a fatal habit of expressing ideas between loud techno beats. Inevitably a more direct type would work his way between me and a girl, dry humping us both until we were pried loose from each other. At quiet cafés too, I would stumble, then lunge straight for the heart. While telling stories I fell in love with the words that kept coming. Though amused with the weird novelty of my shameless and poetic advances, most girls could only stay guarded. Flirtations never led to destinations. They amounted to precious nothing. Except for the singular nights that came to a close with each of us letting our guards down. The café would lock its doors, and we would be standing on the sidewalk under the giant elm tree outside the Stinky Café.

These moments were like Wild-West duels. We lined up back-to-back, while a primitive part of our brains measured how our naked bodies would match up. We would describe some private ways we saw the world. Then we would take our steps. Only we never turned in these duels, we just kept walking in opposite directions, shooting our rounds off into the night, letting love vanish into the sky like an echo.

A conclusion that Sanjar believed was beautiful when I confessed in the morning another failed attempt to get laid. He told me, "Imagination is better than reality."

JAVID CAME INTO my room one night while I was reading and sat down. It was two o'clock in the morning. I was falling asleep but perked up to resume my role as romantic charlatan.

"Don't fall in love in the beginning, fall in love at the end," I counseled.

"I don't want love, I just want …" Javid scrunched his eyebrows.

"Want what?"

"I want …"

"Companionship?"

"A … blow job!"

"Okay, okay. But the first one you get you'll *think* you're in love!" I reasoned.

Javid laughed, slipped his feet out of his slippers, before saying, "I just want to start somewhere."

"Hey man, I remember this writer who said that he'd be lucky to write ten good lines on his deathbed after a life ravaged ..."

"Ravaged?" Javid squinted hard.

"Torn apart. Yes, after a life torn apart by love." I had run out of personal examples the night before, so I had to grab at literary ones.

"Are you talking about relationships?"

"I have no idea what I'm talking about. *Nemi-doonam.*" We both fell silent, allowing the Farsi phrase to reset my foggy train of thought. "I don't think we understand. There's a beautiful girl I know who went to Africa. This is a good woman, one I trust."

Javid leaned in, slid his feet back into his slippers. "Where is she now?"

"She's my wife!"

"Man, you are lucky."

"Yup." I pushed the book I was reading to the side. "Anyway, she was in Africa standing in the hot sun. She was at a dusty bus stop with an old woman in a wheelchair next to her. This old man came and moved the wheelchair a few feet into the shade of a tree. The woman looked up at him. That was the first time this girl, my wife, had seen love."

"That's a good one," Javid said. His voice was distant. I thought, man, this is a guy who needed the songs of Bruce Springsteen growing up.

THE ONLY WAY I could hold my own in a conversation with an Iranian was if they were at the intermediate English level.

Iranians are master talkers. Javid had hundreds of glorious stories he could have told me if he were fluent. In America, my self-designated job in all situations was listener, so I started to take interest in the other side of storytelling. I was not totally unprepared for it, and had formed a small repertoire.

I collected one story during a break from university when I went home. An Egyptian friend of my father's was over for dinner. He was dying, and would soon go back to Cairo to coast into the hereafter. He walked around in a djellaba, an ankle-length robe, with a small white turban around his head. I liked him and wondered why he hadn't come over before.

After a lamb stew I was fading fast, conceding consciousness to my stomach for digestion. The old man began telling a tale to my father. I took a sip of water and adjusted my posture. When he finished, I felt a greedy eagerness to hear more, but at the same time I was worn out, as though the story had put me through a long race in the hot sun.

The old Egyptian looked at me and read my face. "Patience," he told me.

I left the table and went to take a nap next to our family cat, Pinwheel.

JAVID WAS PERCHED on an overturned laundry basket. He was not going anywhere. I sat up against the wall. Inside my chest, something was scratching to get out, like a trapped animal. It was the tale the dying Egyptian had told.

I looked at Javid and said, "Do you want to hear a story, man?"

"Yes, of course. Does it have tits in it?"

"Goddammit."

"Okay, I'll listen."

Pressing my spine back a little harder against the wall I felt more alert. I hadn't bothered to change into pajamas and a bulky square pressed into my leg. I pulled the folded copies of my passport and Mr. Mostafavi's letter out of my cargo pocket, both were beginning to fray at the corners.

"Once upon a time there was a king who had a failing heart. Messengers were sent across the land to find a volunteer who would give up his own heart so that the king might live.

"Since he was a generous and wise king, within days there was a large crowd of men, young and old, gathered beneath the castle's balcony. From inside the room they heard the sound of violent coughing. It frightened them. The future of the kingdom was at stake.

"The royal vizier appeared on the balcony and slowly stepped into the sunlight. He raised his long, skinny right hand in the air.

In it was a white feather from the breast of a falcon. The crowd pushed forward to get a better look, muttering and speculating in excited voices. The vizier lifted an equally long and skinny left hand. The crowd hushed down. He lowered both hands to his sides.

"After slowly scanning the earnest, rough-hewn subjects of the kingdom, he called out, 'Which of you is willing to give up his life so that our great king can regain his strength?'

"Instantly loud shouts went up all around. Young men jostled for pole position under the balcony; old men used cunning to beat them to it. The narrow palm of the vizier's left hand was again raised palm out. The crowd settled into a quiet crouch like a cat in the grass, focused but tense and jumpy, triggered by a hundred noises, a hundred undefined anxieties. They waited. The vizier lowered his hand.

"'If you are chosen, your name will live on in glory for a thousand years for preserving our kingdom.'

"Again, loud shouts went up from every man in the crowd, hands gestured wildly towards the vizier. He then slowly raised his right hand in the air. The men went quiet as they strained to see what it was the vizier was holding. Pinched between two long, stick-like fingers was the white falcon feather.

"'I will throw this feather into the air. The person on whose head it lands will have the privilege of being our king's savior.'

"Without warning the vizier gave one flick of his wrist and let the feather go.

"The men grew silent, dropped their arms, and turned their heads up towards the drifting feather. It wafted and spiraled through the air. As it came closer to the crowd, each man mumbled to himself short prayers so that the feather might come to rest on his head.

"A man whose eyes had been clenched shut peeked one eye open and saw the feather above him. He let out a quick puff of air, closed his eyes again, and carried on praying. The feather swirled up until it descended towards another man who, with one eye open, gave out a sharp breath of air. And so it was with the next man, and the next, and the next."

I held my tongue and the story was over. I remembered how agitated Khalil would get at the ending of 'The King with the Bad Heart.' "Baba, what happens next, what happens *next*!"

Javid wasn't complaining. Perhaps his Eastern mind was traveling the length of its loose ends—seeing what it could find.

"Talking," The word came from Javid's direction.

"Yes," I replied, and waited to see what I had agreed with.

"When you talk, it puts heat into the cheeks. It's a Persian expression. How do you say? Eh, talking makes the mouth warm."

We settled into a silence. I closed my eyes for a moment, ready to sleep. It was an elegant ending to the night. When I opened them, I saw Javid sitting on the laundry basket.

IT WAS THREE O'CLOCK in the morning. In the next room Sepehr and his brothers and sisters, all in their late seventies and eighties, were still playing backgammon.

The only part of me that could move was my dry mouth. There was no more tea. Hamid had gone home, and I had become co-dependent.

"Why does a tough Iranian guy like you want to talk about girls all the time?" I asked.

"Okay, I have a story about kung fu class." Javid rubbed his hand down his arm. I was relieved: the dojo had to be all male. No counterfeit advice about women would be required from me.

Javid scratched the top of his hand. "I had to fight—sparring—with my master. So we went together to start. We were kicking and moving. I moved, he kicked, then I kicked, and it was fine. Then he did a fast kick. I don't know what happened, but my hands were over my face. I moved my hands from my face and saw them filled with blood. My master ran to me. He took his thumbs and put them on my nose and was giving it a good massaging."

"Dang." I looked up and for the first time noticed a kink in Javid's nose.

"I said to my master, 'Can you make it a smaller?' All the students were laughing. Then I went to the bathroom, and I did not know what was going on, I did not feel, it was like a shock. I put my hands down and blood fell all over. I looked at my face in the mirror and saw the nose was somewhere different."

"Ugh."

"A few days later I went to the hospital and a man was sitting next to me. A very big, tough guy. He had a broken nose too. The doctor had a very long … what do you say?" Javid poked a finger into his leg.

"Syringe?"

"Yes, syringe. And when he pushed it up the guys nose, he was screaming. Very loud."

"Shit."

"I saw him crying and I thought, my god, I don't know, I'm going to get banged by this thing too. But the doctor put the needle down and said my nose was in the right place. The master had done a good job."

WHEN SANJAR AND I went to Darakeh, Javid would come if he was around. One day he put on his camouflage cargo pants, boots, and a black "Ninja Tehran" T-shirt. One of my joys in life is being inconspicuous. Now I was sandwiched between two examples of unflinching manliness: Sanjar marching with chest hair poking out of the top of his T-shirt, meeting everyone's eyes, and Javid in his assassin's uniform.

We stopped for tea at Hooshyar's. Javid took me outside to a two-by-two-foot square of level ground on the steep street and demonstrated his best flying kicks. He threw his foot way above his head and then brought the next foot right behind it, slapping both onto the jaw of an imaginary foe. Sanjar wanted us to spar, but I made excuses, having witnessed Javid's stamina as he spoke deep into the night. The angle of my nose did not need adjustment either.

Passing Evin Prison I asked Javid if he knew anyone who had ever been in there. In general, I had not looked for trouble. Suppose someone he knew had been locked up in there. Was I itching to indulge in a gory tale of injustice?

It turned out that he did have a friend from the university who had been picked up in post-election demonstrations. We scrambled up a small rocky turn in the path. A couple were sitting on a rock, both dressed sharply. The man was emptying some pebbles from his hiking boot.

We got a few yards from them and I asked Javid about his friend in the least bloodthirsty voice I could manage: "What did he say about it?"

"What?"

I looked back. The man was retying his boots, "Evin."

Javid replied without breaking his stride. "For forty-five days he was there. People didn't recognize him when he got home."

"Physically? Because he had a shaved head, bruises?"

"I don't know. Maybe he no longer had fear. He was a little dangerous maybe. We friends in university were looking at him. Some said this was a sickness, something that made him ready for anything, good or bad."

We stopped. Sanjar was greeting the owner of a café.

I tapped a rock to the side with my shoe. "What was it like in there?"

"He said in prison they would shine a light on him. They were always coming to interview him, ask questions, saying they would let him go after few days. They had one paper saying he had made a mistake about the demonstration, but he refused to sign it. That made them keep him there. We were all looking at him and trying to find out what happened. But now he really says, 'I am not scared of any shit they say now.' I don't know, maybe in a year we are going to see how he is doing."

We walked past displays of flattened mulberry paste, dark red, on wax paper. Javid jogged ahead to tell Sanjar something. I thought that if his friend was broken, he seemed to have cracked in the wrong direction, from the government's standpoint. He may have been at the demonstration for the excitement, or to check out girls. He may just have been horny and curious; now he was darkened and steely. The imprisonment refocused his friend's mind, bringing it closer to resolve. A lesson to be learned for the authorities.

Looking around, I witnessed the power of the status quo, the way one could get used to anything sooner or later. People were spread out on the mountain, keeping their dreams and disappointments to themselves, swallowing the impulse to rally for change one more time just to keep the day quiet.

Routine engenders passivity. The government keeps the price of bread down: an Iranian can get a piece of *sangak* the size of a tanned deer hide for twenty cents. After bread, they set off to deal with the Rubik's Cube of bureaucracy, where paperwork—and keeping their sanity—eat up their remaining attention. It is easy to forget your troubles when troubles are your life.

The wisp of fear among the young was that the world was leaving them behind: they didn't so much hate the government as fear their own stasis, a condition both self-inflicted and perpetrated by world powers. The Iranians had no choice but to own all of their history, including the Islamic Revolution, despite all the griping about foreign meddling.

They insisted that they were the only ones capable of unlocking the complexity of their nation. The tragedy and triumph of their story was their pride.

THE VOICE OF MOREESE in Angola Prison came to me again. It was like an absurd blues song crackling from a minaret and penetrating my thoughts about Iran.

On the day he was set to leave he attended the funeral of a fellow inmate. Looking down in the hole, as splashes of dirt landed on the grey coffin, he said, "I don't want to get buried in Angola graveyard because no one passes here. This is the end of the line, and if you're buried here, you're really forgotten."

When asked about his long, long stay behind bars, he replied, "I don't have one minute's regret. It was a glorious experience."

MY SENSES WERE NUMBED by sleepiness. Javid sat a few feet away, unfazed. With my last conscious breath, I took another swing at the Iranian enigma.

"What do people do, I mean, what do they think of all this?" I nodded out the balcony towards the lights of Tehran.

"So everybody is home and calling each other to pass time. And night is coming, so you're going to sleep to be well prepared for tomorrow to do the same activities."

Through blurry eyes I saw an expectant figure in a white Lacoste shirt and tight black jeans. I saw Javid's face lighten as he sat on top of the laundry basket.

"I'm kidding, man, here is not as bad as I say. You are here, you *see*, and there's no more lies I want to say."

Chapter Twenty-Four

IN THE MORNING I opened my eyes expecting to see Javid still sitting in my room. Instead I found Maziar sitting at the breakfast table. It was time to go to the mountain, kuh raftan, before it got too hot. We unfolded a piece of sangak (whereupon it became the size of a Delacroix tableau painted in wheat) and took turns ripping off pieces for breakfast.

Sanjar was in his bedroom rifling off saucy responses to a woman on his phone. She had spent the night researching romantic clichés to say in an English database, cutting and pasting, and filling his phone with unanswered texts. I paged through Maziar's dictionary to find the word for "female suitor."

Two sugar cubes disappeared in my tea. I held up a third and inspected it like a diamond before dropping it in. Then out the door we went onto the streets of North Tehran, heading for Darakeh.

Maziar, like his older brother, had put on his fatigues, boots, and ninja shirt. Concealed in a pocket of his cargo pants were two *shuriken*, ninja throwing stars. We were armed. My blue linen shirt was flapping open, while Sanjar strode forward in beige cargo pants, a Calvin Klein designer T-shirt, and a baseball cap that read "San Diego."

We passed the usual sights, including the bakery where *sangak* was made on a bed of small grey pebbles heated from below. Men in white aprons stood by the oven door with giant metal spatulas. A professor once told me that janitors run the university. I agreed. Here were the true keepers of peace in Iran: the bakers.

With fast food, no matter where you go, a standardized ball of grease will go down easy and fill you with remorse. At this bakery I saw consistency on an entirely different level. The two men with the spatulas were most likely the latest members of a family of bakers who had been flipping the same surfboard-sized pieces of *sangak* for a hundred years. It was relaxing to think of people doing the same thing for so long.

I started to get dreamy about the bakers' lives, steeped in tradition. Then I remembered my father's friend, who was a handyman. Imagining craftsmen's guilds and the dignified lineage of carpentry, I asked him what had led him to become a builder.

The old Peace Corps volunteer let out a quick laugh. "I needed a job, and it was easy."

WE ENTERED THE NARROW residential alleys en route to Darakeh. There was an ancient door with two knockers, one for male visitors and the other for female. A light blue Paykan, recently washed, sat in a curvy frame of asphalt darkened with water. A tiny stream branched off and trickled down the hill.

There were a couple of building sites along the way. Usually, through the unfinished opening of the third or fourth floor, you could see a lone Afghan hammering away at something. Many projects were in slow motion, constructed casually in the hope that the real estate market would change. If contractors were persistent, they might get permission to build higher. Then again, the higher they built, the more units might have to be given as "gifts" to the officials who had made it possible. In Iran, sometimes even buildings lay low to avoid attention from the authorities. Still, the value of the Iranian rial was so low that property was one of the only worthwhile investments.

We passed Sanjar's garden. An old man was sitting above his shack near a staircase to the next level of the mountain. He remembered a time when the area was far from Tehran.

The sun glared off his corrugated steel roof, which was held down by a few bricks near each corner. It was quiet here even though the old man's eyes could see an unbroken chain of new buildings tumbling haphazardly down the mountain.

Looking at him and thinking of the fourteen million inhabitants of Tehran, I thought that behind those eyes were the stories of a life that could fill ten volumes. It is likely that he only considered one book, the Qur'an, his entire life. Filling in the gaps, though, were the poetry and tales of the Persian masters. I wondered where the lines of those volumes of his life existed: in his head, on the tablets of angels, in the worn paths that were now boulevards snaking up the mountains.

"*Khoda Hafez*. God protect you."

He wished us well and we continued up the stone steps that buttressed a high, crumbling wall. We had outwalked most of North Tehran's wealth and entered a place of modest single-family structures sitting on land that was skyrocketing in value. Occasionally eight- or nine-story condominiums rose out of the two-story-high plateau like flags planted on newly conquered territory.

WE PASSED HOOSHYAR'S bookstore and he offered us tea. Sanjar sat down and Maziar and I arranged ourselves in the two cubits of space left for us. My nose was two inches away from the blue spine of a Saadi poetry collection when Hooshyar pulled out a crate of pirated DVDs. After selecting Ninja Assassin for our next sleepover we wished Hooshyar well, passed the rest of the buildings, and hit the dusty path.

After an hour of hiking we stopped and unpacked some fruit and water. When we opened the bag, we saw that the tiny, thin-skinned green grapes had rubbed open against each other, and a sticky film had covered the other fruit. We sat on a huge boulder by the side of the stream eating nectarines, apples, and cherries, each coated with a hint of sour green grape.

Washing my hands, I imagined the splintering of the stream as the water filtered down the mountain. The cafés had their take. Long black, plastic tubes were fastened into the stream so the water could be used to power fountains, cool drinks, water plants, and spray down dust.

The remaining water would hit the village where it trickled slowly through a half-wild, half-concrete-walled ravine. As it reached the houses and gardens of North Tehran it was redirected into private gardens. Then the slope of the land pulled it towards the impossible thirst of Central Tehran below, where I would sometimes find it flowing beneath me on streets like Valiasr as I leapt huge gutters that could swallow a child.

Standing on a boulder I looked up at the canyon rim in the direction of Evin Prison. Maziar had just shown me how to grip a *shuriken,* the throwing star. I noticed the metal was chipped up.

"Man, do you use this thing?" I asked.

He laughed. "My brother and me, we go to the alley behind the apartment and throw them at some wood."

"You can aim and hit something?"

"Yes."

He said that they were used to "clear the way" for an attack. The *shuriken* also could be thrown in such a way that it would cut the victim, and then fly undetected into the brush. Your opponent would be distracted with the thought that he was under attack by an invisible swordsman. The periodic and mysterious malfunctions at Iran's nuclear plants and missile launch sites came to mind.

JAVID, ALONG WITH his brother, were the young Iranians who were supposed to be the vanguard of discontent, but the prospects of their family were being lifted through hard work and loyalty to Sepehr.

Sepehr was arming them not for belligerence or revolution, but for the long and difficult path of self-cultivation. Sanjar had also told them to stay away from politics. This went for the exciting protests as well.

When Javid was in high school, young men were lashing themselves with chains in the streets to honor Imam Hussain. Sanjar advised him to go the other way whenever he saw a crowd. A crowd in Iran was political, whatever its initial charter.

The Islamic Revolution, supported and born out of Persian exceptionalism, was now like a sort of Frankenstein. A marathon of strained patriotic enthusiasm fueled by the passion of the disenfranchised, the loyal, and the uninformed. This force was met by the simmering aspirations of reformers and youth, and the affronted dignity and embarrassed remorse of Shah-era intellectuals. A funeral, a birthday, a holiday, a soccer match, a Tuesday afternoon, held within them the energy of this backstory.

Still, I sensed Iranians taking a belabored pride in the independence born of being ostracized. They embraced their situation, despite the jazzy "hand of the British," always twinkling behind events, and clumsy American bullying.

Iran was like a rebellious prisoner turning on the guards because he feels the rules "don't apply" to him. He insists he has the talent and history to make up his own rules, and, like Cool Hand Luke, ends up in solitary again and again.

EXCEPTIONALISM MEANS one thing in America. In Iran, whenever I ventured an opinion on something—pistachios, politics, paradise—an Iranian would take exception. That's Iranian exceptionalism.

The need to oppose: perhaps it came from the culture's creation of and immersion in Zoroastrianism, where natural decay opposes creation, chaos opposes order, lies oppose truth. Persia was the only place where that religion had ever flourished, after all.

I would deliver a hard-won insight about life, and the first words out of Sanjar's mouth were often "No, no. Look ..." French culture, with its elegant disagreeability, has been influential in Iran. I've theorized that during Sanjar's early years at a French private school he was exposed to Michel de Montaigne's essay "The Art of Conversation." In it, Montaigne boasts that "contradicting judgments neither offend me nor irritate me; they merely wake me up and provide me with exercise."

ON THE WAY down from our sticky picnic we stopped at a spring for a drink. I splashed some cold water on my face. This was the spot where the elderly singers had pissed off Sanjar. No one was around now. The stone ledge where they had sat cooked in the sun. I did not recognize the spot on our way up because the light had changed it, the shadows were different. While the sun moves across the sky it creates different worlds below, many seasons in a day.

I thought of their ancient poetry and whether or not I agreed with Sanjar that they should step aside and let new songs, or at least new singers, onto the stage, as it were.

Then I had it. A story. At that moment, waiting behind Sanjar for my second drink from the spring, it came into my head. That night I would be well armed for Javid's visit to my room. Uncle Hawowshi had given Khalil a book of Mullah Nasruddin tales for his birthday. It was called, *Watermelons, Walnuts, and the Wisdom of Allah*. In it was the story of "Nasruddin and the Candle."

THE DARAKEH RIVER pools up in a few spots along the path, and some are deep enough to swim in. We passed two young men who had stripped down to their underpants and were daring each other to leap from a high rock. I contemplated their tight briefs longer than I wanted to. I know the pious girls did too. It was nice to walk past this with my friends in silence, as we were all a little tired. We admired the good times and moved on.

We arrived at the new apartment with our shoes caked in dust. Maziar was back from an errand and we promptly took up our positions at the Blokus table. A pile of colorful incongruous shapes lay before each of us, and Hamid's slight figure soon filled the doorway with a tray of tea.

MAZIAR HAD NOT yet started his mandatory twenty months of military service. I tried to cut and paste his face onto all the uniformed young men stationed around Tehran. The ploy was not necessary, as the majority of the young soldiers were unfailingly polite. The biggest threat to them was boredom, posted as they were in the city facing regular people making ends meet.

Sanjar encouraged Maziar to "get in" with the government.

One night, during a game of Blokus, Sanjar pressed him. "I'm serious, you should join the air force, become a tough guy, a general, *way* up there."

"I don't know." Maziar was humble. But he was also thinking. This was against Sanjar's usual counsel to not get involved in politics.

"You *do* know," Sanjar continued. "Look, it always helps to have connections. It helps so much. And you are smart and have a good body. You're tall and handsome, you know martial arts … and you're religious, they'll like you!"

Sanjar was never committed to his advice and it changed from one moment to the next, depending on the situation. He fit Zoroaster's description of a man whose ideas did not accord with one another, but he admitted it. His willingness to change his mind was also a marker of humility.

"Um." Maziar could only mumble a response.

We all laughed. Maziar was outnumbered in our group and took it well. He really was a man of faith. He wanted to behave and be a good person, for this world and the next. It was not a game to him, so he did not pretend to be offended to inflate his piety.

I quickly pictured him and Maryam as a beautiful Muslim power couple.

"I don't know," Maziar repeated, smiling. I could tell he was tempted to switch to Farsi to flesh out his thoughts.

"Man, you see, then you can help your family," Sanjar said. Then he pointed to me: "You can even get Kareem a visa!"

We all laughed again. I felt selfish imagining how the trajectory of a man's life would end up benefiting me as a travel perk.

"I'm serious," Sanjar insisted. "You saw how the words of the vice president made so much happen. It was nothing—just a few words—and here we go. If you have power … if you're a big boy, you can really help. Then we wouldn't have to bug the vice president!"

Hamid stepped through the doorway with a second round of tea. I had to tamp down my Midwestern urge to ask him to sit with us, to confirm my status as a regular guy. After all, here I was sitting with the children of Sepehr's workers. Hamid received some instructions from Sanjar in Farsi, smiled and left the room.

We carried on with our Blokus game. Building out from the corners, yellow, red, green, and blue shapes were linked together until there was a many-headed snake tangled in the center of the board. Each player concentrated on finding room for his next move.

This is why I wanted come to Iran without a tour guide or minder. Having one would have allowed me to come years earlier, but then I would not have been able to sit with friends and do nothing—do nothing to see what happened.

KHALIL SCOOPED THREE pickles out of a jar and put them in a tiny dish. We were being abused by another winter and the snow had been falling for a whole day and night.

It was morning, and the snow was still falling.

At dawn, I got a call that school was canceled. Khalil took a bite out of the first pickle and was staring at his teeth marks in it.

"Baba, who taught me how to talk?"

"I don't know. Everyone I guess."

"Well, how did I learn?"

"You just listened really good."

"I think Uncle Hawowshi taught me how to talk because he taught me funny words."

"That's probably right."

He held out the remaining nub of a pickle. "Do you want one?"

"No, cutie. Can I tell you something I learned in Iran?"

"Sure!"

"There was a great king called Jamshid who lived back when there were still woolly mammoths around."

"Did he shoot them with arrows?"

"No, he didn't live close to them. King Jamshid had a different problem. There was a terrible winter where he was living, and every creature was going to die."

"What happened?" Khalil now had a pickle in each hand and was taking turns biting from each one.

"King Jamshid made a throne with lots of rubies and diamonds on it. He then had magical creatures lift him high above the earth and into the sky. He sat there like the sun, shining light and warmth down. All the creatures in the world came around to look at him and they threw jewels all around him. They called that day the New Day."

Khalil was dipping his finger in the leftover pickle juice in his dish.

"Baba?"

"Yes?"

"What's a throne?"

Khalil looked out the window at the gobs of snow dropping outside.

I thought of Sanjar sitting on the edge of his bed playing Blokus, Sepehr on his black writing chair, and Javid perched on an overturned laundry basket in my room in Iran, telling me that talking makes the mouth warm. Then of Khalil, who had come to sit on my lap.

"Wherever a king sits."

Chapter Twenty-Five

EVERY MINNESOTAN KNOWS that in the hidden coil of their frigid fate is a pair of golden Californian flip-flops.

The time comes to slip them on and step hard on the gas pedal until the polyurethane indents with toe prints, and the car reaches the Pacific. We may only make it for a few months, or we may stay forever. Check the beaches of Los Angeles and San Diego and you will find a bunch of blond Scandinavians—the most easily identifiable former Minnesotans. An invitation to the West Coast is stapled to our birth certificates, a merciful birthright.

I took out my invitation, and flip-flops, a few years before going to Iran. Sanjar had moved to San Diego and would hard sell the idea of relocation to California during our weekly telephone calls.

This was not like Saleh's invitation to stay in Granada, Spain. It would not turn reality into a dream. California turns dreams into reality—the reality of a monthly rent you cannot afford. When you are staring down the cold, steel barrel of a January in Minnesota you don't always stop to do all the practical calculations. I loaded my young family into a 1987 Buick LeSabre in the middle of a snowstorm, scraped the ice from the windshield one last time, and watched as a flash of gold hit the accelerator. We were going to live in San Francisco.

At the time, I had been working at a school with no windows and many locked doors. It was a place one step below a residential treatment facility and the beginning of prison prep. Inside the school there were rooms that had been stripped of everything.

What remained were white walls, concrete floors, and heavy metal doors. These were "time-out" rooms.

Inside those rooms were black kids who would not stop talking.

Somehow the image of an idealized classroom was a place where people sat down and were quiet. This view has been especially devastating to kids who are the unwitting bearers of an African oral tradition. Verbal skills that could access a line of knowledge and transmission stretching back to the beginning of time were a "disruption" to the learning environment in American schools.

When I was manning the "time-out" room, sometimes up to seven young men would be crowded in there. All they had were two broken pencils, a beat, and a need to talk.

Their topics of discussion were ridiculous. The material junior high kids use to test each other—someone's shoes were broke down, someone's hairline was crooked—but the art of storytelling was still there. Often the talk was revealing—a kid would claim to have ridden his bike from 'over North to all the way over South," and every other kid would roast him for 'lying his ass off." Anyone from Minneapolis or America can tell you what he means by passing from "North" to "South."

Men in the generation ahead of them were always being hounded, locked up, or killed. Family stories so often interrupted were pulled apart even further on the streets. Their heroes were turned into outlaws—then only back into heroes if they could cut a record.

Kids would be let back into class when they showed they were "ready." As soon as the teachers or administrators thought people were shutting up, following "the program," the wellspring of words would start up again. Whether it was stories from grandmothers or uncles or from deep down within them, it just would not stop. In an institution, without traditional guidance, the young mouths kept running, skillfully, meaningfully and meaninglessly, with fragments of song hooks linking it all together. It was like watching samurais using their blades to chop and prepare a nutritious meal—then being told the sound of the cutting was too loud, the blade unsafe, the ingredients wrong. Without any cultural appreciation of what talking could do, could teach, trouble did not wait long for those who learned through talk and stories.

It was not hard leaving a school like that for California.

Even so, I learned a little while working there. That came courtesy of Nockiel, an insightful eleven-year-old who happened to be built like a nail. We were cooped up together in the "time-out" room. He paced around. I upheld my end of the morbid charade by keeping a poker face. He tested my spirit with a few insults about nonconsensual situations involving me and Michael Jackson. Finally, he said he was going to "spend some knowledge on me." He proceeded to tell me the history of his gang going back to the early 1960s. The story had an arc, side plots, robust characters, and honor codes nonexistent in much of American society. But it was something else as well.

Nockiel had told me the story of his father.

ONE MORNING, WHEN the "wind from Iraq" had settled, Javid, Sanjar, and I headed to the palaces of Reza Shah and his son, the Shah.

Taking a cab from Tajrish Square, we were dropped off at the gates. Inside the gates were a group of eighteen palaces on an island of green acreage in North Tehran called the Saad Abad Palace Complex. Many of the palaces had been turned into museums, but the grass and trees were indifferent to the reclassification and flourished like royalty.

The grounds are kept up, but the purpose of the place seems uncoordinated, the vision missing. Like the Presidio, the former military post on an incredibly valuable tract of land in San Francisco, the palaces are owned by the government. In the case of the Presidio, the Presidio Trust, suspected by the public to be too business oriented, is in charge of its future. The rustic barracks and roads, and the healthy surrounding forest, shiver under the prospect of some heinous development.

The Saad Abad Palace Complex also felt perplexingly undeveloped despite its grandeur. Many historical sites had been dealt with decisively, bulldozed and burned after the 1979 Revolution, but this one was frozen in limbo between a public and private place.

Structural neglect was another tactic to renounce the "opulence" of the Shah's lifestyle. A lifestyle that hit its symbolic apex during a party celebrating 2,500 years of continuous Persian monarchical rule—a party that cost $500 million to put on. The most expensive party in history began at the crumbling tomb of Cyrus the Great. The festivities went on for three days, with feasts that involved fifty roasted peacocks, a thousand pounds of Imperial Caspian caviar, and a profound misunderstanding of the humble and righteous nature of the Persian Empire's first ruler, Cyrus.

The kings of Persia may be gone for good, but not without having risen from the grave a couple times—quite literally.

When Reza Shah made his "Declaration of Neutrality" for Iran during World War II, he was forced to abdicate the throne to his pliant son after an invasion by Britain and the Soviet Union in 1941. He was pushed into exile in Johannesburg, South Africa, where he died a few years later. His body was then flown to Egypt where it was embalmed and entombed at a mosque in Cairo. It was later transported back to Iran and buried in a Shia shrine on the edge of Tehran, only to be flown back to Egypt before his Mausoleum was destroyed at the dawn of the Islamic Revolution.

Now, the huge bronze legs of Reza Shah's son, the Shah, greet visitors at Saad Abad. They have stood without a torso for over forty years at the steps of the White Palace, the royal family's main residence. The hollow leg trunks lead into giant boots. Though anchored to the ground, they seem ready to march again into the story of this land, flickering as it does between turban and crown.

Sanjar complained that the government could make Saad Abad so nice if it wanted to—a place with cafés that people would want to come to. As it was, the place was nearly empty, its purpose and meaning unresolved. That made it interesting to me.

I read in Ian Frazier's *Travels in Siberia* that the prison camps of the Soviet Union proved hard to locate. When he did find them there were no plaques that indicated Russia's verdict on the era.

There were the aging wooden watchtowers, rough-hewed fences of pine, absence, and whatever conclusions formed in the observer's mind.

THE PEOPLE WHO could not wait were wearing shorts.

My friend Dan and I watched the chapped pink flesh of the runners pass. It was late winter, a half year after returning from Iran. The temperature was below zero. From the window of Café Barbette I could see the plowed sidewalk. Layered in the packed snow that lined the sidewalk with white walls was a geological cross section of the long winter. The foot of snow from the first blizzard of the year had shrunk but was still there, pressed against the frozen grass of the boulevard.

Another runner went by towards a circuit around the lakes. Sanjar liked to brag about how he used to go running in tiny shorts through the snowdrifts of Minnesota. He would appear at high school parties in a T-shirt and bare legs, a big head of hair flying, having just run nine or ten miles, high-stepping through unplowed streets.

During some winters in Minnesota I figured I might as well be hibernating—time went by in a blur of bundled shapes. Steamy breath was captured in frigid poofs, forming blank speech bubbles that trailed these dreamy figures wrapped in Gore-Tex and down feathers. They shuffled along icy walkways and disappeared into buildings, like ghosts vacuumed into a warm oblivion.

Runners offered hope, but the whole place felt weary, waiting for the seasonal damnation to end.

"You know what I think?" I said, straightening up a little.

Dan ran a finger down his glass, clearing a path through the condensation, and waited.

"I think you have to go out of your way to make memories," I concluded.

Dan kept waiting.

"Sometimes the only things I remember from my childhood are family trips. You know, the times when we dropped what we were doing and did something else."

Dan looked over my shoulder at the tattooed arm of a girl, took a sip of his pint, and, like a great friend, agreed unconditionally. "Holy shit. That's right. It's the break in the routine. Even if it went bad, it opened a new part of the map." He took a pomme frite and dragged it across some garlic aioli sauce.

I lifted my pint glass against the harsh white light of winter coming from the window. Peering through it outside, I saw a golden August afternoon.

"The other day Khalil and I went to a park and climbed into a frozen waterfall. Inside, it was completely blue. A *blue* room." I got out my phone to show the video.

Before I could enter my password, I heard Dan whisper, "Beautiful."

Ordinary words had already taken him there, behind Minnehaha Falls, inside the blue room—the empty heart of winter's haunting specter.

IN THE SAAD ABAD Gardens, on our way from one palace to another, there was a row of large bronze statues. The people depicted were not in suits or military uniforms.

"Who are those guys?" I asked.

"Oh, *big* deal. It's some of the great Persian poets," Sanjar answered after a quick glance over.

"But …"

"Look, that one is Hafiz." He pointed to a statue. A contemplative man in robes sat behind a wild beard cast in a metal so durable I imagined cockroaches sheltering in its folds at the end of time.

"You don't think they should be here?" I asked, worried.

Sanjar kept walking, "Well, I mean, what's the point? Man, they could put a café there and then there would be some life here at least."

"But it's Hafiz!"

I RECEIVED A PACKAGE from my sister. It was postmarked "Malta."

I was now studying at a different university in the Midwest. Looking through my dorm-room window, I could see even-headed kids from Minnesota, Wisconsin, Iowa, and Illinois walking around in silence, carrying huge backpacks.

I ripped open the package to reveal whatever fantastic sample of the broader world my sister had sent this time. There was a book and a postcard. The postcard reproduced a surrealist painting of an old boat resting in the water alongside a dock. An antique-gold-colored sun filled the white sky above it with ten lines of light. On the dock was what looked like a cactus slouching toward the water. Next to it was an enormous spoon and fork. I imagined two weathered and hungry Maltese fishermen working together to lift the utensils above a giant tuna-fish filet, prying off some chunks to eat, and then napping in the dust under the shade of a cypress.

The handsome book was a collection of Hafiz poems. Between its tangerine orange covers were seven-hundred-year-old words translated in the required soft focus of New Age spirituality. I made a cup of tea using the portable water heater my mother had tucked into my bag. I tried to cuddle with the gauzy renderings of poems that I imagined had a lot more bite in the original Farsi.

On my desk was a stack of dense scholarly articles—my homework. Faced with pages of thoughts grotesquely deformed by the academic pressure on their authors to sound smart, I latched onto the irreverence of Hafiz, the ancient Persian master.

I have learned so much from God
that I can no longer call myself a Christian, a Hindu, a Muslim,
a Buddhist, a Jew.

In the back of the orange book there was a short bio. I saw that Hafiz was born in Shiraz, Iran. I didn't know where that was.

My mind ran slipshod over a map of Asia, like hands on the planchette of a Ouija board.

Two decades later I would learn that the poems in that orange book, titled *The Gift*, are not even translations of Hafiz. They are the original mystical poems of an American from St. Louis, Daniel Ladinsky. He claims that Hafiz is transmitting new material to him from the great beyond. It's unfair that modern physicists can casually sound off about the multiverse, but I cannot verify this poet's claim on romantic merit alone.

After all, maybe Hafiz, who has been called the 'Invisible Tongue of God' did find a way into the mouth of an early 21st century man. I'm sure he appreciates a full set of teeth—probably hard to come by in 14th century Persia.

SAAD ABAD WAS one of the few tourist destinations I went to in Tehran.

As such, I tried to apply myself. I kept my eye out for significance and photo opportunities as we selected structures in the compound to visit at random. Again, there were no tidy clues of how Iranians wanted to formally present this part of their history to the world. A line from the Polish poet Wisława Szymborska allowed me to span the uncertainty: "Every beginning, is only a sequel, after all, and the book of events is always open halfway through."

Inside the White Palace I saw Russian tourists with cameras so big I thought they were each filming their own IMAX documentaries. They swung their cameras like Kalashnikovs into doorways, conducting photographic security sweeps of each lavish Louis XIV–style room. The Shah's fixation with everything French displayed itself through picnics of furniture and objects spread upon Persian carpets measuring half the size of a basketball court. Sanjar claimed that neither the furniture nor the rugs were originals. Many items had been removed from the palace after the Revolution. Imitation Louis XIV decor had been replaced by imitations of the imitations.

Waist-high glass in the doorways kept visitors from entering the rooms, so we stood in groups peering in. Sanjar struck up conversations with fellow visitors. One Iranian told the story of how, in the 1930s, Reza Shah had hired Walter Aigner, an Austrian engineer, to build a railroad bridge in Veresk, Mazandaran. It would connect Tehran and the Caspian Sea region. When the bridge was complete the engineer presented it to Reza Shah.

"Is it strong?" Reza Shah was said to have asked.

"Your majesty, it is strong," Aigner answered.

"Okay then, bring your family beneath it, and when they are there, I will cross on the first train."

The bridge held, and eventually became the lynchpin of a supply line for Soviet troops in World War II—of such importance that it came to be known as the *Pol-e-Piroozi*, or Bridge of Victory, as was the entire country of Iran. Aigner asked to be buried underneath the bridge, confident that his work would hold as an exquisite tombstone, arcing above his grave.

THE MOST BEAUTIFUL palace at Saad Abad was the Green Palace. Built higher up the mountain than the others, it was constructed with a frosty stone, holding within it a translucent, meteoric green. It was a hint of the luxury that would be found inside the palace. For Reza Shah, who came from a village and spent his life as a soldier, it might as well have been kryptonite. He did not appreciate the years of work it took to arrange minute shards of glass in symmetrical patterns that covered each square inch of the walls in the atrium.

Famously, he abandoned the ornate bed built for him, settling instead for a mat on the floor. Reza Shah, a king who had risen from below, tried to avoid the luxurious element of power that immobilizes and neuters a man. He was somewhat successful—keeping his hands busy with all parts of Iranian society.

Advisors have sought to keep royalty inaccessible since the time of the first pharaohs. These are the notorious viziers and priests who secured the role of keepers of the realm while sovereigns hobbled around in robes, pinned under heavy crowns. Formalities related to interacting with kings, such as bowing and walking backwards, multiplied over time. Each petitioner became a captor as both king and subject were trapped in elaborate protocols. The common taboo against speaking directly to kings served nobles and priests well. They had an interest in keeping kings from engaging directly in affairs of state.

The long tradition of kings disguising themselves is a counterbalance to this power dynamic, and arose out of a desire on their part to escape the mediating forces and filters of the palace and see their kingdoms for themselves. Dressed in the clothes of common men, kings of the East and the West wandered among their subjects, some out of distrust of the nobility, others for love of the peasants. A few went to assess the conduct of officials. One—the Tiger King of Thailand—even snuck out to fight in martial arts contests in the villages.

Reza Shah, a king in a new age, wore no disguise when he drove an armored car into the holy shrine of Fatimah with a caravan of soldiers. A cleric had scolded his wife for exposing her face while visiting a mosque in Qom. Reza Shah got out of his car and slapped the man.

This gave a personal touch to his broader standoff with the Shia clergy. A modernizer, Reza Shah seemed to use his wife's humiliation to play his own version of "dress-up" with the country's women: he demanded that they adopt Western dress and had soldiers rip off their veils in the street.

THE ENTRANCE TO the Green Palace is split by a stone column with a smiling face carved nine feet up its height. Two frowning college girls were watching the door, books spread before them.

"What does the face mean?" I asked them.

One of the girls nudged an open book to the side. "It represents Reza Shah's happiness to receive his guests."

"Come in and you can look at the other side of the column," her friend suggested.

I stepped inside the palace, turned and looked up at a frowning face.

"This shows Reza Shah's sadness at the … departure of his guests," she added in near perfect English.

I hopped out again to look at the smiling face. The two of them stared at me and one touched a hand to her book.

Reza Shah seemed like a Teddy Roosevelt kind of guy—hearty, self-possessed, and stubborn. I made this comparison innocently and spontaneously, but like the political litmus test involving the kebab, I should have known better. It was Kermit Roosevelt, Teddy's grandson, who helped orchestrate the overthrow of Iranian Prime Minister Mossadegh in the 1953 coup d'état. This was Iran: political-historical trapdoors might open anywhere I stepped.

We walked dutifully through the ornate and stale rooms of the Green Palace, our shoes covered with protective slippers. I needed to use the bathroom. We sped through the last rooms, past the frowning face, and into the afternoon.

I thought that stepping off the stone pathway leading away from the palace and into the woods was the best option for a bathroom break. I figured regime jurists would be forgiving about urinating on the Shah's old land. However, I heard that the current presidential palace was adjacent to the Saad Abad Complex, so I did not wander too far. When I returned, I took a series of photos of Javid doing his best aerial double-kicks in front of the Green Palace with Tehran in the background.

In the stuttering picture sequence, Javid is a swirl of energy, a single man in flight, trying to clear a space for himself between kings, ayatollahs, and presidents.

WE LEFT THE SAAD ABAD COMPLEX feeling refreshed and loose—a little too relaxed for Tehran, because as we casually walked along a wide sidewalk, a Sepah soldier in a sharp uniform rushed over with his machine gun and told us to step back to the other side of the walk. An important conference was taking place in the building behind him. The gun caught my attention because most soldiers and policemen I saw in the city were not armed.

I kept remarking on this until Sanjar got fed up and knocked on the door of a little police outpost as we passed through Tajrish Square.

"Hi dears, my friend here thinks the police don't have guns in Tehran. Do you guys have guns?"

A familiar wave of self-importance struck me again, and with it the seed of a new waking nightmare. Inside my mind the seed germinates, "What if they think I am on a reconnaissance mission assessing the firepower of Iran's street police?" When the policemen read my thoughts, I am swept into a secret compartment of the miniature police outpost. Sitting behind a table in the dark room, a brisk hand is slapping down photos in front of me. In one, Sanjar and I are approaching the outpost. Then another photo is nailed to the table by a sharp finger jab: it is me peering into the police outpost.

The final photo is rested lightly in front of me, like the weight of a handful of dry Iranian soil landing on my coffin. In it Sanjar and I are walking away. My head is turned towards Sanjar but one eye is glancing back at the station. I lean forward until my face is a few inches from the photograph. I'm about to plead for my life when I feel Sanjar tap me on the shoulder. I blink once, then twice.

When I realized where I was, I shrugged slowly away from the cracked door of the trailer-sized station, but Sanjar pulled me back. The two real officers smirked and patted the revolvers on their belts. Sanjar and I looked at each other.

"See," he said.

"Okay, okay, you win. Let's go," I whispered.

A third officer slammed the door in our faces.

The afternoon was cooking now, and we no longer had the shade of a king's garden. Javid, Sanjar, and I tacked our way through traffic across Tajrish and folded ourselves into a minibus. The lunch Neda had made was going to get cold.

WE SAT IN HUNGRY silence in the minibus. The interior was a patchwork of coarse brown and orange upholstery. I pressed my back against an unforgiving seat and took a look out at the police outpost. Then we pulled away from the sidewalk. Just beyond it, several Afghans were taking their lunch in a decrepit tent on a construction site.

The frequency with which law and order had to be taken into one's own hands in Iran was surprising, given the number of security agents and the different levels of armed forces that were about. Examples of this were the spray-painted, handmade signs that warned about parking in certain places. After seeing them on garages and walls across the city I asked Sanjar to translate one.

"It says, 'Parking equals *swift* flat tire,'" he told me. This made me laugh out loud.

Part of the problem was that no one was really sure who was in charge. There is a theory in soccer: it is easier to dribble past two defenders than one—their attention is split. As various security agencies argue over who has what authority, the nuisance crimes and daily hustles carry on unchallenged except by people themselves.

One night, a taxi driver infuriated Sanjar so thoroughly that we jumped out while it was practically moving. A group of mechanics were hanging out under a light post near their garage. They watched, smoked, and prepared to make their ruling on the matter. The taxi sped away.

"Man! Eh! What an asshole! He wanted six dollars for a sixty-cent ride."

I was shocked by how angry this had made Sanjar. He and the driver had been screaming at the top of their lungs. They were about seven and half inches from each other's faces because Sanjar was in the passenger seat. The wiry, ratty-haired driver had changed his price along the way. Opening his mouth to argue, he bared his teeth, revealing a scale model of the Stonehenge ruins. He was making a play for a little more, just like most people. Sanjar would not stand for it.

"We're lucky those guys were here, or he may have hit me with a knife!"

"What?"

"Man, it's the whole thing. From the wimpy driver to the big guys in the government. If they can get it, they deserved it."

"What?"

"Everything."

ON ANOTHER TRIP, a taxi driver whom Sanjar trusted was driving us to Valiasr Street. It was funny to me to have to build a strong, loyal relationship with your taxi driver, as if he was your financial advisor or therapist.

The driver spoke of a friend whose car had been stolen a block from his apartment. A few agencies looked around for it but gave up. In the end, the victim's friends found it parked in another neighborhood—repaired and with a new stereo. They followed the thief to find out where he lived then told the investigators.

The response of the investigators was, "Okay, you got your car. Now, *why* do you want to make trouble?"

WE GOT OFF the minibus and strolled down the streets of North Tehran to the apartment. Since this was the middle of Ramadan, the mid-afternoon pace of the city had slowed. When we arrived at the apartment, Maziar and his father were napping in the living room, knocking a few hours off the fast in a state of unconsciousness. Sepehr was moving towards the kitchen where Neda was about to unveil a masterpiece. I walked past Maziar and Anoush and thought of my own hours with my father—the way we would wrestle hunger down in the late afternoon by pinning ourselves down on a couch for naps.

The smell of stewed potatoes, tomatoes, and lamb quickened my steps. I saw Sanjar and Javid tiptoeing ahead of me. We were all just evil enough to eat, and we took our seats next to Sepehr.

Neda was smiling at her audience, holding a big spoon in her hand like a conductor's baton. Her face was full and round, but was losing color as a result of her prolonged illness.

Before I had even taken a bite, she looked at me and asked Sanjar, "Does he like it?"

MY BIG TOE had a dead nail and Khalil was under the water with his scuba goggles trying to see if it had fallen off. When it finally did, he insisted on putting it in his little tooth-fairy mailbox when we got home. The next day, to Marie's dismay, a dollar would appear under his pillow. A reward for being the only person on Earth who would handle my dead toenail.

At the lake that summer day, a year after coming back from Iran, I had my eye on my own father. He was on the shore talking with an Egyptian friend, Yusri, who had spent the last five years moving his family from Cairo to Berlin, then Singapore, then Boston, and now to Minneapolis, trying to find a cure for his six-year-old son's illness. Yusri, as a Muslim, read the Qur'an but accepted earlier revelations, and could personally relate to ordeals of biblical proportions.

When we picked up Yusri and his family earlier that day I had asked him, "What's the latest adventure?" He opened his arms up wide, and then wider, as if to say, "Take your pick."

I was knee-deep in the water with Khalil and Yusri's son, Tamer, when I noticed my father's white shirt move across the sand and disappear into the beach house. My father is getting older. I worry about the toll of bugs and illnesses from his village years in the Nile Delta.

After a couple minutes I noticed a school of sunfish suspended in the water all around me. They had gotten close because I had not moved.

Lately, I had been watching many of the people I loved walking through doorways. Then I would wait and wonder if they would ever come back out. The white shirt of my father reappeared just as the lifeguards blew their whistles for a ten-minute beach safety check.

On the shore I urged my father, who was sitting next to Yusri, to tell the story of the poor shoemaker and the fava bean bowl. He had not told it in years, and here was a chance: Khalil and his friend were going nuts waiting to jump back in the water, and Yusri was taking a break while the next verse of biblical suffering was being written by doctors or immigration officials.

"What's the story of Maruf the Cobbler?" I prodded.

My father and Yusri shot some Arabic back and forth and settled on a new title.

"Al Sultania," they answered in unison.

"Hey Khalil! Come here. Grandbaba's going to tell a story." He and Tamer reluctantly dropped some artifacts in the sand and ran over.

Khalil stood staring at the lake. His arms were stretched behind him and his hands gripped a wooden wall: he was holding himself back from the water. My father began. He was a little rusty, but he warmed up as the tale went on. As he continued, Khalil slowly turned around to face him: the ocean in the story was becoming bigger than the lake in front of him.

"An old shoemaker was walking home by the docks thinking about the difficulties in his life. In his hand was a *sultania*, a bowl that he used to carry the fava beans he ate for lunch each day. He was very poor and the bowl was all he had, besides a wife who complained about their situation day and night. Her favorite way to abuse him was to compare him to their neighbor, a rich merchant.

"Deep in thought, he passed some fishermen loading their nets. They were short one crew member, so when they saw Maruf they called out to him. He pictured his wife waiting to belittle him at their tiny shack and decided to join the crew. He could earn a little extra money and spare himself some ridicule when he returned home.

"While sailing back they were caught in a storm. When it looked like the ship was not going to make it, Maruf said a prayer, tied his bean bowl on his head, and jumped into the ocean."

"Was he dead?" Khalil asked, half hoping the story was over so he could swim.

"No. By some miracle he washed ashore on a small island—alive. As Maruf picked himself off the beach, big, scary people appeared at the edge of a forest and came toward him. They grabbed Maruf and brought him to their chief.

"The shoemaker, thinking he was going to be killed, untied the bean bowl from his head and presented it to the chief as a gift. The chief took it in his hands and a big smile crept across his face. Then he placed the bean bowl on top of his head. He sent two men into his hut and they came out with a basket of rubies, pearls, and gold. It was given to the shoemaker. It was more wealth than the shoemaker had heard about in even the wildest stories told by sailors down at the docks. He touched his heart and bent very low to kiss the chief's hand."

The lifeguard blew her whistle and Khalil and his friend crept towards the water, then stopped. My father rubbed his hands on his knees.

"The shoemaker was given a small boat and somehow made it back to his own land. After a few weeks his rich neighbor noticed that Maruf's life had improved a great deal. Maruf, being a simple and honest man, told him about the treasure and how he had got it. When the rich neighbor heard this he immediately ordered a ship to be filled with rugs, the finest Egyptian silk, jugs of honey, and other gifts, and set off across the sea.

"After some struggles the ship found its way to the same island. The chief, with the bean bowl on his head, met the sailors on the shore himself. The rich neighbor bowed low, then presented all his gifts to the chief. The chief was overwhelmed by the stranger's generosity. He thanked the man and declared three days of feasting.

"When the three days ended, the rich neighbor was led to the chief's royal hut. The chief thanked the man again and said he would be presented with the most precious treasure on the island. The rich neighbor's eyes got big. He brushed his fingertips down his cheek.

"The chief then held out the crown jewel of his kingdom.

"The neighbor took it in his hands and started weeping, 'It's, it's … a *sultania*!'"

AT THE STINKY CAFÉ SANJAR once told a story about a king who had a royal poet. When the king won a battle, the poet would write heroic odes to him. When he lost a battle, the poet would write heroic odes to him. I wondered if I would do the same for my father and if Khalil would do the same for me.

What's left over from a life? What does it amount to?

When the plane of Minnesota Senator Paul Wellstone fell out of the sky, Sanjar and I were sitting by the fireplace at Caribou Coffee in Minneapolis. Sanjar said that Wellstone had done the best thing he could have done in this world: he was leaving his children a good name.

"You possess only what will not be lost in a shipwreck."

That was the line I had in my head when I kissed Khalil on the cheek at the airport en route to Tehran. The one thousand-year-old words arose not, as I thought at the time, from dread that I would not return, but from fear that I had not passed enough along to my son. Enough to hold on to when he was tested—when his ship bashed against the rocks.

Chapter Twenty-Six

SANJAR AND I were ready to head back to the apartment. We had spent an hour looking at souvenirs in the lower level of an upscale mall near Tajrish Square. Sanjar had tried on a full sultan getup, appearing from behind a curtain in an outrageous green- and gold-trimmed shirt and pantaloons. He had been flirting with the shop owner's daughter and had commanded her attention over by the shoji screen that formed the shop's changing room.

Dressing up reminded us of the Halloween parties at First Avenue in Minneapolis that we would crash. One year we arrived like the scouts of a bombastic Arabian caravan. En route, dressed in turbans and robes, we passed the mounted police downtown. To see three forces at work on the faces of the police—reflexive suspicion, frayed restraint, and knowing amusement—was a precarious luxury afforded some Americans and denied others.

Walking around the club, we would stop ax-murdering nurses drenched in fake blood. We would ask to see the health of their teeth, and then offer each other ten dirhams for their purchase, as if we were their owners. We called it our "coming-out party," indulging in the stereotypes for our own amusement. One girl, dressed as Cleopatra, said that it would be nice to have a sugar daddy with access to oil wealth, but what she really needed was a "good navy." A guy walked by dressed as USS Enterprise Commander Jean-Luc Picard, and she ditched us.

At the souvenir shop I had picked out two decorated mugs. On one was a picture of a Qajar-era palace, and on the other, an image of the *Faravahar*, a mythic bird, bending its wings around the cup.

Below the bird, along the bottom of the cup, was a Zoroastrian saying: "Think good, say good, do good."

We left the shop and began to discuss the price home with cab drivers. An old, white "official" taxi pulled over. It looked like it had been chewed, swallowed, and digested daily by the streets of Tehran since 1982.

"How much to Evin-Darakeh?" Sanjar shouted.

"Six dollars."

"I'll give you four."

"As long as you're smiling, I don't care about the money—nobody is smiling in Tehran these days," the driver answered, and we hopped in.

A long conversation began between Sanjar and the driver. I was in the back sitting on some cloth that was layered like two sheets of filo dough on bulges of metal. I sat wondering if my door would pop open, marveling at the instant flow of talk between these two strangers. It was not tentative chitchat, but a full-throated attempt to search the soul of a nation in the time it took to break through a midday traffic jam. Not impossible while trapped within central Tehran's coiled serpent of cars and trucks, which tightened its grip at the slightest hesitation. I narrowed in on the currents of their conversation, straining to make sense of the moments when they would glance at each other or motion towards a scene on the street.

One of these scenes was a commotion near a bus on the other side of the median. The arms of the driver, who was standing outside his bus, were electrified by the case he was making against a woman sitting behind the driver's seat of a small car. Indignation whipped through his body until his hand slammed on the roof of her car. The woman, whose window was half-open, clutched the wheel, eyes scanning ahead.

The man reached inside the window to pull the woman out or strike her. The man in her passenger seat stepped out. The woman, imploring with her hands like a mime pressing up against two invisible walls, stopped the men before they could yell toe-to-toe with each other. We were stuck on this street together, and I had the feeling that this woman needed to use our presence, not to help win the argument but so that we would temper the rage of the men with disinterested eyes. I looked at it as my jury duty in Tehran.

The reason for the altercation was that the driver had hit the bus and tried to drive off—a hard thing to do in such traffic. The bus driver, anticipating a slap to the face back at the depot, went for his own retribution. The tension of the standoff waned; no one wanted to wait until the police got involved. The cars all inched forward and away.

When we arrived at the apartment the heartsick cabby looked uninterested in Sanjar's money. He looked tired, traveling day after day through streets that might have held his youthful memories of fatal love affairs with women and ideas. His face was black and white with stubble and creased with sharp lines—as though a lion had tried to wipe away his tears with a claw. I squinted and imagined him stumbling out of a sculpture studio into the sunshine after working all night, a man whose dreams had been forged in a cosmopolitan Iran before the Revolution.

He tossed the *rials* Sanjar handed him into the nook where the broken speedometer sat behind a dusty plastic shield.

"There is no true love in Tehran," the cabby pronounced before he drove off.

These were the only words from the end of their conversation that Sanjar translated for me. It was not necessary to know what exact question or comment they were addressing. The cabby's eyes looked out his windshield, and he saluted us before heading back down into central Tehran—a man at sea, sails in tatters, who no longer curses the direction of the wind.

THE OLD CAB DRIVER made me think of Andrew. We had seen him one last time at a café in Darband, a neighborhood at the foot of Mount Tochal. He was leaving the next day. He handled the surprise of running into us with deft politeness, but there was an unease about his face.

When someone is dreaming, their eyelids ripple as they follow the wild action of the subconscious. When I looked at Andrew,

I saw his eyes moving in darts and circles. It was as if he were straining to reconcile the carefree catastrophe of some fantasy with the subdued and consequential reality at its root. I worried that he had broken away from the conference group without a guide and something bad had happened to him.

Sanjar and I took off our shoes and joined him on a dais covered in Persian rugs next to the river. When he noticed that we were in no rush he began to tell an epic story.

One night a small group from the conference was taking out to the Cinéma Café at Bagh-e Ferdows. When they were leaving a young woman heard them speaking English. She walked through the dark to Andrew. Having just taken an English examination, the girl was able to say clearly what she wanted. Flattered, Andrew accepted her telephone number.

The next day they met in Darakeh and stopped for tea at one of the mountain cafés. The girl, Zahra, had brought her cousin. Andrew was with his two Iranian friends, academics he met at the conference. Both of them were good-looking, educated, and polite, but there was one problem: they were Iranian. They tried to handle the attention Andrew was getting with good humor.

Listening to Andrew talk, Sanjar shook his head. This dismissiveness Iranians had towards other Iranians bothered him. The conditions in Iran could cause an unsettling, thinly-masked loathing between Iranians. It amounted to a sort of lingering accusatory resentment reserved just for each other. According to Andrew, Zahra and her cousin and his two friends skeptically eyed each other.

Andrew had an advantage beyond this mistrust among Iranians. He represented a way out. What is more, he had flaws unfamiliar to Zahra—the charm of every foreign lover. Still, the ease with which he had gotten her number and then a date must have hurt Andrew's Iranian friends.

Andrew described Zahra as a Persian beauty: big, dark eyes that were unflinching, the sensuous antithesis of Ayatollah Khomeini's sober stare. I thought immediately of a poem Sanjar would recite to women on occasion:

It's not that I don't want to swim in your eyes,
it's drowning in them that I am afraid of.

Sitting at the café in the shadow of the mountains, above the undertow of the Morality Police, Andrew invited Zahra to his side of the carpeted dais. The sun was setting, and Zahra had to fend off a cell phone inquiry from her mother. Lamps were being turned on in the café, and soon they were fixed in a warm orb of light, intimacy nipping and arcing between them.

Andrew let himself unravel into her. Intellectual that he was, he watched himself fall in love from a distance. "Action anthropology," he called it. He was heading back to Cairo, but he let his mind touch the idea of staying.

Andrew was already pressing his luck by straying from conference sanctioned activities. Across the darkening canyon was the silhouette of the Evin Prison wall, breaking the surface of the mountain like the zig-zag back of a giant serpent. Zahra, his clever companion, sat close to him, and they guided each other along with dialogue that fell like footsteps on a path that was treacherous and daring.

Zahra was asking him questions and he was answering them. If it was a love song, the precision of the answers didn't matter: simply passing notes back and forth created a melody. She brought up the location of his passport.

"Do you have it?" she asked.

"Yes, of course," Andrew answered.

"Can I see it?"

"Why?"

"It doesn't matter. I don't care. I just want to look at it."

"You want to see my documents!" Andrew teased.

"I don't care. Let's talk about something else."

Andrew's friends were laughing at him, just as Sanjar and I now laughed at him. Sanjar interrupted Andrew for the first time.

"I know that girl! I know her! She wants a PhD, wants it real bad, and will do anything. She wants a ticket to America so she can go to a good university there. She has it all planned. It's all in her head, man! I *know* her!"

Andrew had traveled enough to understand his worth—he knew the agenda. Zahra had a degree in engineering from one of Tehran's most prestigious universities. Her bluff about not caring about his passport showed she was also an artist.

Zahra, Andrew, and one of his Iranian friends, Shafiq, left the café and walked down the mountain. They jumped on a minibus. Shafiq took a seat in the front. Sitting next to Zahra in the back, Andrew checked the driver's mirror and assessed the tired people scattered in the seats ahead of them. He felt Zahra lift his arm over her shoulders and inch closer in the cramped seat. This was when he started to lose his scholarly perch above himself. His hand was on Zahra's shoulder, against the tight fabric of her manteau. He guided his eyes out the window to the lights of Tehran below.

Andrew wanted me and Sanjar to know that Zahra's flirtation was the greatest compliment he had ever received. He was worth that act of flirtatious courage. Any high-school girl in America scrambling out of her bedroom window gives this compliment to the guy waiting down the street. In Iran, it was not only the father, but the fatherland that Zahra was defying—and it filled Andrew with a sappy pride.

Andrew walked back to Hotel Enghelab with Shafiq. Andrew had given Zahra Shafiq's number and she was already sending Andrew texts. They both heard the messages rolling in. Andrew looked at Shafiq but did not ask to see the phone.

Shafiq wondered aloud whether Andrew should bother an Iranian girl, knowing what the likely endgame would be. Shafiq was not sure who needed to be protected from whom. Finally, he handed over his phone.

Andrew looked at the screen, "*Azizam* … my sweetheart, I keep thinking about you."

With each new text Andrew's face drew closer to the phone until Shafiq told him that the texts he was getting were from an online database of romantic lines. All the girls mined it. I remembered Sanjar complaining about the same thing.

Using Shafiq's phone, Andrew set up a date with Zahra for the next day. He wanted to meet her alone this time, and Zahra arranged to meet him at a roundabout called Shahid Shahriari Square near Shahid Beheshti University. It was close to Shafiq's apartment and Andrew could walk there easily on his own.

Andrew slipped away from the conference early and headed to the square. He waited near a line of people trying to catch rides. Spotting Zahra on the other side of the square at a bus stop, he walked along the street until he was parallel with her. She saw him and gave a quick wave. She was on the phone. Andrew then went rigid. He now remembered the name Beheshti from a magazine article he had read in Cairo.

BEHESHTI WAS AN AYATOLLAH who was the chief justice of Iran when he was assassinated in a bomb attack in 1981. The official version identified an operative from the People's Mujahedin of Iran as the assassin. As always in Iran, rumors took on magic shapes that resembled the truth and were hard to escape.

It was said that British agents facilitated the strike as a warning to leaders in Iran who had gotten too close to the United States. Beheshti had traveled to the US before the 1979 Revolution to mediate a conflict among Islamic groups. He allegedly went to a secret meeting with Reagan's closest campaign advisors. They sought, in exchange for arms, to delay the release of the US Embassy hostages until after the 1980 election, so as to discredit President Carter.

IN A CROSSFIRE of thoughts Andrew saw Zahra's hand waving again, their connection like another tormented strand of history reaching across the square. He felt the pause of self-consciousness as cars and people seemed to slow around him. Andrew could pass as a Tajik, or some other Central Asian, but his movements were unsure. In the coordinated chaos of Tehran's streets, where bodies and cars weave together, nimble and assured, like the hands of a carpet weaver, false moves stand out. He took some wobbly steps into traffic, but Zahra moved across the road to him, still holding the phone to her ear.

When they met in the middle of the square, Andrew did not know whether to shake her hand or kiss her cheek, so he gave a little bow. She handed him the phone.

"Andrew, how are you doing?" It was Shafiq.

"Fine, is everything okay?" He glanced at Zahra.

"Yes, I'm coming to you guys. Everything is fine, just wait with Zahra." Shafiq was talking fast. "Look, I was speaking with my friend, who is a lawyer, and he told me not to leave you alone."

Andrew took a quick look around the square. Cars tacked their way in and out of the circle; people jumped in and out of taxis, marked and unmarked. The bustle begat order, order begat a tempo, and Andrew regained his anonymity. The sun threw light over the mountains while tired, preoccupied Iranians sifted towards quiet apartments. Andrew, although frustrated, knew he had to trust his new friend. He stood with Zahra on the sidewalk watching Shafiq approach from halfway down the block.

Andrew looked up at Sanjar and me and sighed. He was cherishing the memory of those strange seconds alone with Zahra, before describing his conversation with her.

"Your friend is worried, Andrew," Zahra said.

"I'm not sure what is going on."

"He thinks it's not good for us to be alone like this."

"Let's see," Andrew replied, twisting away inside from the feeling that Shafiq was trying to stay between them out of jealousy.

Andrew leaned back on the worn embroidered cushion at the Darband café. "For *security reasons*," he said, joking to us, "Shafiq could not let us fall in love."

Sanjar chuckled and adjusted his thick white sports socks before straightening his legs out again on the dais. I watched Andrew's finger trace the line of a wolf's mouth, a symbol woven into the nomadic tribal rug. I didn't know if he understood its traditional meaning: protection for a traveler against wolves.

He looked at the river and did not look back to us when he continued his story.

When Shafiq reached them in the center of Shahid Shahriari Square, he relayed his friend's suggestion that they end their solo date. Shafiq had never been let down by his friend, and followed his counsel. Zahra was understanding, having to negotiate her own checks and balances set up by her parents.

Andrew felt her sinking a little as they walked with Shafiq to a café near Darakeh. She was an engineer seeing her blueprint revised before her eyes.

IT WAS ALSO NEAR Shahid Beheshti University that an Iranian nuclear scientist, Majid Shahriari was assassinated a few months after Andrew and I were in Iran. Shahid Shahriari Square was renamed to honor him. A bomb was stuck onto the window of his car by a man on a motorcycle, and just like that a mind that understood the inner workings of atoms was erased by a crude explosive.

I thought of this as Andrew explained the real reason Shafiq had joined their date.

When Shafiq told his friend that Andrew was comfortable meeting Zahra alone, the lawyer exploded, "How did he meet this girl?"

"Outside Café du Cinéma," Shafiq answered.

"What do you mean? She just walked up to him on the street, out of *nowhere*? Who is she?"

Even an urbane academic can be naive at times. Shafiq's friend told him a story of how the chief of police of Tehran was tricked. He was beginning to bother some politician or religious leader with an investigation. Then one night he invited a group of escorts to his place. The chief managed to choreograph a scene in which the ladies knelt in prayer in front of him—completely unclothed. One of the girls, or all of them, were agents, and a photo was taken of the party.

"If the chief of police can be tricked, who are you guys?" Shafiq agreed and made the call to Zahra.

Andrew was convinced that she was okay, and so was Shafiq, but the last two dates they had before he headed back to Cairo were threesomes. On one of these dates, they met at Jam-e-Jam, a renovated cafeteria on the second floor of a small shopping mall. Andrew and Shafiq noticed how Zahra led them to a table in back, between a pillar and large ficus tree.

"I guess it was the engineer at work," Andrew admired, adjusting the cushion behind him.

The table Zahra picked provided bad sight lines for other boyfriends and family members who might be around. This was a hilarious detail to me because Sanjar had just told me the tale of King Jamshid's magical seven-ringed cup: the Jam-e-Jam. It was filled with a potion that allowed him to observe the entire universe.

When the waiter approached to ask if they would be ordering anything, Zahra dispensed with him: "We're leaving soon, understand?"

Andrew's words began a fleshy climb into lust as he described her translucent black-and-white-patterned headscarf. Her manteau was fastened tight. The curves ironed out by day in a baggy, modest fit had returned by night.

Zahra wasted no time, "Tell me Andrew, what do you think of me?"

"If you had dressed more modestly, maybe I would be able to think," Andrew replied.

Zahra laughed, but quickly returned to the business at hand. "Okay. Then I will tell you. I will tell you what I think of you. I think you are a very real man."

Andrew asked her what she meant.

"You are not like Iranian men who think they can do what they want. You don't have the *Shaytan*, devil, look in your eye, always thinking trouble. You have kind eyes that don't look like they will take you."

"Yes, I'm American. We've been turned into weak men. I wish I had the *Shaytan* look!"

Zahra slapped his arm. A smile began to grow back on her face, but she was serious.

"No! Don't say these things. I don't like these jokes. I told you what I think about you, and you now tell me what I am to you."

Andrew did not know what this was all about, but she needed a good answer. He thought it might have been a proxy interview by her parents. It was possible she was more traditional than he thought.

He told her that after so many months in the ancient libraries of Cairo, she was like a dream to him. Zahra pulled back from the table, disappointed by Andrew's trivial analysis of her.

Sanjar laughed and inserted that it did not matter what Andrew said—she was already thinking of the graduate courses she would take in America.

Andrew ignored him and described how Shafiq, in a lighter mood, had grabbed both their hands and recited the *sigheh*—a few lines of Arabic that can join a man and woman together in a temporary marriage in Shia Islam.

Recognizing the Arabic, Zahra gasped and withdrew her hand, scolding Shafiq in Farsi.

By now she had received three calls from her mother. They left the cafeteria and Zahra found out she had a ticket on her car. She cursed the attendant she had negotiated with to park there, but he was not around to hear it. She paced until Shafiq suggested that she give them a lift down the street. Andrew was still rattled after her single-minded evaluation of him at the cafeteria.

Halfway down the block she pulled into a narrow side street and stopped. I pictured Andrew sitting there in the half-dark next to Zahra—an unmarried couple alone in Tehran. They were prime targets for the GuiDance Patrol.

Roy had told me about his struggles on dates trying to "wrench" a breast out from the tightly fastened manteaux of his girlfriends. Andrew, more of a gentleman, was less ambitious. He told Zahra that he needed one kiss. That would be his souvenir from the Islamic Republic. When Shafiq discreetly left the car, Andrew imagined a timer being hit. Like a technician scrambling to defuse a device, he took a breath, and slipped his hand underneath her scarf, taking hold of her dark curls. She leaned towards him. Each time her headscarf slipped, a hand would instinctually go up to adjust it.

Andrew and Zahra's lips met and for an instant they sealed off the harsh world of modern Iran. Zahra's veil slid to her shoulders and rested like tumbled, airy skin shed from a majestic serpent. When she pulled it back over her hair, Andrew said it looked heavy as chain mail in her hands.

I REMEMBER GOING to see some ancient petroglyphs in the prairie of southwestern Minnesota. A set of narrow, flattish mounds of granite rise gently out of the ground, barely visible from the surrounding grasses; on them are fossilized sand ripples from the bottom of a sea that once covered North America. Between the time-frozen waves were thunderbirds, bolts of lightning, and sacred buffalo-turtles, chiseled into the rock nine thousand years ago. During the middle of the day the images disappear. Then, when the sun is low in the west, they lift off the stone and come alive.

Only the earth endures, the native elders of the area say.

I wondered what fleeting mark on the earth Andrew's kiss with Zahra would leave, roughcast in flesh, in the half-light of a Tehran alley.

The Chilean poet Pablo Neruda said that "love is so short and forgetting so long." Andrew had a night left in Iran, then a taxi ride to the airport, where an exit stamp would be pressed into his passport—after that, stretching unbroken before him was time.

LISTENING TO ANDREW, I looked over at Sanjar, arms folded, guiding his skepticism through the story's end. I thought of our trips to First Avenue in Minneapolis. Stepping off the dance floor, I flirted with a girl who tried to scare me away by saying she was in medical school.

"You must be very smart." I gushed.

"I am."

"That's good. I only like smart women. But you have to prove it … what's the longest word in the English language?"

"Pneumonoultramicroscopicsilicovolcanoconiosis," she replied. A fake word, it turns out, but with roots in a real medical condition.

The word was a cock-block combo, hitting my throat so I could not speak, and my groin, which lost sensation. When I recovered, her friend had arrived, and they cut away. In so many ways failure is better than success when it comes to flirting. Flirting is an act of skepticism, according to the French, one that defends you from the whitewash of romance, and from sex—the oblivion and trap of success.

When I found Sanjar, he was sitting with two cups of ice water, taking a break from dancing. I described the rare case of someone who knew how to talk in the club. He slid one of the cups over to me and gave me the answer that I needed.

"No, no." He slowly raised his eyebrows twice and looked out at the dance floor. "Man, you should have told her that the longest word in the English language is 'love.'"

Another made-up word with roots in a real condition.

SANJAR COULD NOT resist telling Andrew that he was not special. Foreigners were preferred for these dalliances because the risk of being shamed, or gossiped about, decreased with an outsider. I heard this myself from women in Iran.

There was a twenty-three-year-old at Bame Tehran who told me that her one and only kiss had been in Dubai with a Lebanese boy. There was no telling what could happen in Iran if you fooled around with the neighbor boy and he decided to burn you. With a foreigner there was also the wild card of marriage and immigration papers.

ANDREW WOULD MEET ZAHRA one more time, at Café du Monde, with Shafiq and his cousin. Zahra had been forthcoming with her parents, and her mother was willing to open a small window of time for her strong-willed daughter. Zahra took a taxi to the café after work.

Shafiq and Andrew were at the Hotel Enghelab waiting in the red lobby for Shafiq's cousin to pick them up. When he arrived, he had been in traffic for three hours and raced to the bathroom. Shafiq ordered him some tea. Andrew paced and then sat down. Shafiq's cousin returned and began slowly sipping his tea. With his fingers Andrew tapped a concerto of impatience on his thighs.

Sanjar and I thought Andrew had thrown his dignity into the air long ago, but, of course, we were wickedly eager to see the places he went without it. Both of us kept quiet, and Andrew continued telling his story.

When they finally left the hotel, the car promptly took its place in an apocalyptic traffic jam. Andrew had Shafiq's phone and was getting texts from Zahra, who was waiting at the café.

I did my part. I am here. There were problems for me too, but I fixed them all so I could be here at the right time. What did you do to be ready?

I don't like this. I am sitting here alone. It's not good. People will start looking at me.

After they had been in traffic for an hour, she called. Andrew had no idea how close they were to the café, so he handed the phone to Shafiq. Andrew could hear her complaining through the receiver from the backseat.

"Lady, the only reason I haven't hung up on you is because my friend likes you," Shafiq told Zahra in English.

Shafiq's cousin pulled into a private alley and slipped the guard some bills. They walked a couple blocks in collective tension. Andrew was feeling guilty. He was ashamed of viewing his two friends as burdensome chaperones. He admitted that he secretly had hoped they would take another table at the café.

Turning to Shafiq's cousin, who had spent five hours in a car to get them here, Andrew said, "I'm sorry for the trouble."

"Okay, see, okay. Um … in Iran, in Persian culture, we don't have this. We don't use this 'I'm sorry,'" Shafiq's cousin replied.

When they joined Zahra at her table, Andrew promptly offered her some apologies. She had been working on her French and had drawn little illustrations next to words in her notebook. *Chateau. Oublier. La mer.* For *oublier*, to forget, she had made a tiny picture, in blue ink, of a heart with a question mark in it.

Andrew, cowed by the angry texts, ordered an espresso. The Iranians, a bit more used to conflict, ordered ice-cream sundaes. When the sundaes arrived, Shafiq sent his back because it was half-melted. The waiter, a young man in his twenties, could not fathom the complaint. The manager came over.

At this point in the story, a daydream formed in my mind. I was sitting there in Andrew's place at the café. I saw a renunciant, hearing the request for firm ice cream, silently alert the Revolutionary Guards to my presence with a touch of a hidden alarm. The Guards crash through the café, setting legs in tight jeans in motion. Gas torches tip, setting English menus aflame. The trial day arrives. A mullah is defining the bankruptcy of American culture, and the triviality of needing "firm ice cream" as the blood of believers flows worldwide.

SANJAR AND I surprised ourselves with our interest in Andrew's details—the details men do not care about.

A new ice cream was brought for Shafiq in a frosty bowl. When the time came for Zahra to go home, she set down her half-finished mango ice-cream drink, said thank you, got up, and asked Andrew if he would walk with her to the street. Shafiq and his cousin both looked down at the unpaid bill.

It was dark and they walked as slowly as they could to the curb, praying not to Jesus or Allah but to Zeno.

"Zahra, I wish that I had more control. But here I don't. I don't know the situation here like I do in Cairo, and I have to trust my friends."

"It's okay Andrew. I'm not thinking about it anymore."

"I don't have a phone or a car … if I did, I …"

"I'm happy that you are here now. We are together. It doesn't matter."

They were nearing Valiasr Street, where the taxis were. Zahra took a turn down a side street. A streetlight was nearby but they were in the shadows of some gated apartments and sycamore trees. Zahra was staring up at them. Andrew told us that he felt that she was inviting him to imagine their wealthy life together in America.

Then Zahra got a call from Shafiq. She handed the phone to Andrew.

"Where are you?"

"We're outside the café. Just down the block."

"Hurry up."

Andrew walked Zahra to a little space between the trunk of a tree and a wall. He put his hands on her shoulders. They looked past each other at the green screen of Iran, a backdrop that projected the supervising presence of the state.

As he tried to bring her toward him, Zahra stuttered some words, as bolts of fear circled around them. "In Iran, you always feel that there are eyes."

Later, near Darakeh, I would hear a woman whisper this exact sentence to Sanjar.

"Where? Up there?" Andrew looked towards the sky. "The eyes up there would be American—probably some horny Air Force pilot in a trailer outside Las Vegas. Don't worry about him," Andrew said, looking at Zahra so she knew he was joking.

They both looked up at the sky and tried to laugh. Again Andrew pulled her towards him. Zahra's phone rang. She handed it to Andrew.

"What are you doing? Let's go!" It was Shafiq.

Andrew did not want to anger Shafiq, so they hurried over to Valiasr Street. He faced Zahra, and saw a young street hustler looking at them from behind her. As she turned to catch a taxi, Andrew told her to text Shafiq, so that they would know she got home safely.

Andrew returned to the café through a lit, tented walkway, where tables were lined with books. Shafiq and his cousin were sitting in the café in silence. Andrew figured they were worried about Zahra's intentions. When he sat down to hear their conspiracy theory, he was surprised that what had doomed her in their eyes was that she did not offer to pay her part of the check.

Shafiq, Andrew's new and loyal friend, was blunt. "I don't like her. That girl is trying to come between us. And look," he held out the check, "no class."

NIGHT HAD FALLEN in Darband. It was a beautiful place. There were terraced rows of balconies and patios, each cluster a lit-up restaurant with high-end aspirations. The canyon of lights rose on both sides of the tiny Darband River, as if colossal cruise ships were lined up next to each other. At the bottom, winding its way between them was the river, like a shy water snake.

Sanjar's arms were still folded over his chest, eyes closed. Andrew was in a trance, rocking like a man reciting scripture or riding a camel.

I buttoned my blue linen shirt, inhaled a deep breath of cool night air, and asked a question to Andrew like I was handing him a knife: "Was that the last time you saw Zahra?"

ANDREW PASSED AN HOUR in the car ride home from Café du Cinéma listening to Shafiq and his cousin's subdued conversation. He looked out the window. From Shafiq's pocket he could hear the musical strum of incoming texts. He did not know why Shafiq kept it on, but as they entered their second hour in traffic the texts arrived in agitated waves, subsided, then resumed again.

Andrew felt his face was like a heavy wood block. He tried to carve neutral features into it like an ancient god in a temple. Gradually the default electronic tone of Shafiq's phone transliterated itself into Zahra's fury.

Andrew finally spoke to Shafiq. He used the words of American power brokers that he had heard a diplomat joke about in Cairo. During back-channel discussions with leaders of coups d'état, deciding the fates of millions in places like Argentina, Chile, East Timor, Iraq, and Cambodia, US consent or disapproval would be signaled by baritone-voiced men like Henry Kissinger, saying, "We're giving it the *green* light," or "That's a *red* light."

Knowing how Shafiq felt about Zahra, Andrew felt that even the question was a betrayal. Still, he leaned forward and asked, "Shafiq, if it's a red light, it's fine, I won't ask again. Can I use your phone?"

Shafiq reached for his pocket, then stopped. "For her … no."

Andrew leaned back into the darkness of the back seat. Unread texts accreted in Shafiq's in-box and upon Andrew's mind. The notifications, like relentless Pavlovian elevator music, sounded off as Andrew was transported to the lowest chambers of his mind.

They entered the third hour of traffic. Shafiq switched off his phone. Andrew visualized green hills across a river of fire. A small figure stood on the opposite bank. He knew it was himself, but he had no idea what would bring him to the other side, and how long it would take.

He had simply lost his head.

Still, Andrew wanted to look at that chain of texts. The radio-active bits in the inner coils of Shafiq's phone: a first message reassuring Andrew of Zahra's arrival at her house, the second one already weighted with doubt, the third hopeful again, the fourth before sleep, and every one after that when sleep was impossible.

I looked up at Andrew, a pale, exhausted figure in a brown tweed sport coat. He rotated his teacup counterclockwise and stopped rocking.

Row, row, row your boat,
gently down the stream,
merrily, merrily, merrily, merrily,
life is but a dream.

Sanjar, his eyes still closed, unfolded his arms and suddenly began singing. He told a story about his childhood, when his mother sang him a song in English that he did not understand. The melody, though, was always in his head.

"THE LONGEST NIGHT of the year scared the hell out of ancient Persian people."

In my classroom in Minneapolis, I had gotten my students attention with a bad word. It was a week before the winter solstice. The night before, I had received a message from Sanjar in Iran. No luck at the Foreign Ministry. It was the third year of trying to get a visa. If spring arrived without my having started the process, it would be another year gone.

My students were still paying attention, so I took a breath and continued. "It was the night of the greatest battle between the forces of light and darkness, the night when people would be farthest away from Mithra, the god of light. Mithra was the sun god and ..."—I raised my thick eyebrows at them a few times—" ... the god of love." Gasps of disgust were spat out on cue.

"On the eve of the longest night of the year, they would try to help Mithra by staying up all night, praying, telling stories, and keeping a bonfire lit. In the morning Mithra was reborn. The days started getting longer and the forces of light regained the upper hand."

I decided not to push things that day. Many of my students' favorite winter traditions came from a land that was now imagined to be the home of an archenemy. I did not tell them about the evergreen cypresses that were brought inside ancient Persian homes. Nor did I tell them about how children wrapped their wishes in silk and hung them on the branches. The Persian roots of the Christmas tree, and the gift bonanza that my students loved, would be saved for another day.

The winter after I returned from Iran, I created a bittersweet tradition of my own: I would sit and think of Zahra and her hunger to advance in life, a hunger that was so strong, and so thwarted, that she would remake herself as Andrew's beloved after hearing a few English words on the wind.

I thought about how strange it was that circumstances, and the seasons of the year, can alter the nature of gods.

Chapter Twenty-Seven

I THOUGHT A LOT about Andrew during my last few days in Iran. I pictured him in a café in Khan el-Kalili back in Cairo, smoking a hookah, incapable of returning to his ancient Islamic texts at Al-Azhar.

On a page in my passport was a light blue stamp and a scribbled message in red ink. I checked it each morning, making sure it hadn't faded like Dith Pran's forged passport photo in the film *The Killing Fields*. While he is seeking refuge in the French Embassy, the underdeveloped picture disappears, along with his way out of Cambodia, as the Khmer Rouge take over.

I began to wonder if I would be leaving Iran in one piece. I handled the letter from the Foreign Ministry. My fingers would be clipped to it in my pocket at the airport. If there was a long frown at my passport, I would pull it like a ripcord.

The departure date, instead of making Sanjar and me move faster, slowed us down. There never was an agenda, so nothing needed to be done. In fact, Sanjar had a watchword that he shared with me when I visited him in San Diego during the weekend he became a citizen. We were driving down Interstate 405 with nowhere to go and he said, "I don't care what we do as long as it's fun or productive." It had that easy-to-digest quality to it. It was freedom.

Yet, sitting in Tehran, trying to enjoy a cup of tea, my body was knotted with tension. All my little waking nightmares had sent waves of nerve signals to ready my muscles for impacts—baton blows, accusations—that never came. Now the phantom scenarios were balled up inside my limbs.

Even with this backbeat of stress I released some tiny muscle fibers inside my eyes and felt my depth of field expanding.

I started to see and hear the city without leaving Sanjar's balcony. Having been down to central Tehran and hustled around a bit, I found it easier to take in the dusty spread from a distance. Tehran is a city that is said to have no soul, no ancient history, no true love. If this was the case for the city, it wasn't the case for the people in it.

If Tehran was a vacant city, my memories would all be lies— dust waiting to settle on an empty plateau in the shadow of the Alborz Mountains.

THE NIGHT BEFORE MY FLIGHT, Sanjar, Javid, and I decided to go to Bame Tehran. I wanted to get there early so that I could take a picture of Tehran while there was still light. Javid put on his boots, camouflage cargo pants, and black Ninja Tehran shirt. Sanjar wore a T-shirt with surfboards that said "San Diego." I had on my blue linen shirt, the bland and inconspicuous outfit I settled on most days.

Incredibly, we found parking on a side street and started our way up. In the photos I have from that day, the sun has already moved on to shine on the west, and Tehran, below, is a mass of grey-black pixels.

The city disappeared for a few minutes at dusk, as lights started to be turned on and the last glow of day sifted below the mountains. We passed a café with a paintball course wedged against the mountainside in what looked like a giant fenced-in tennis court. It puzzled me at first to see a people who were coming off eight years of war, and who were now targeted by the aggressive focus of a superpower, playing at fighting.

Gunplay and paintball were understandable in America, insulated as it was by geography from any threat of a ground war from a foreign adversary. Of course, the toys and games of children foreshadow future activities, which makes me uncomfortable when I wonder which enemy Americans imagine as they play at fighting. Who is a worthy nemesis for a country with such a powerful military—but itself?

But if you are in your thirties in Iran, you are a child of war, fed heroic stories by the state; you may be thrilled from time to time by the cat-and-mouse games played at protests, but in reality, you are more likely to be struck with a wooden stick by a Basij militia member than gunned down. A conundrum, as Sanjar always claimed that Iranians were not the warrior type.

"Man, *Iranians*! They're a bunch of little guys running around singing poetry," he liked to say.

The American cultural talismans of badass violence appealed to hip young Iranians. We found this out when we saw a kid wearing a *Scarface* T-shirt. Sanjar stopped him on the way up Bame Tehran and asked him if he knew who was on his shirt. He had no idea. When we told him, he smiled as he walked away, puffed up by the Uzi-induced bravado of the gangster, like so many rosy-cheeked American teenagers.

We continued up the mountain, stopping at the bathrooms near the top. Complaints can be made about invasions of privacy in Iran, but the bathrooms cannot be included. There were no urinals and each stall had a full-length door and lock.

Near the bathroom was a boy chasing a soccer ball. I have heard that when get older you return to the hobbies and activities that brought you happiness in your youth—the ones forgotten during midlife. I was also feeling aged by the real and imagined dangers of Iran. When the ball fled the control of the boy I softened my body to receive it. It was a joyous instinct.

When Javid returned we went with the boy a little farther up to the ski-lift parking lot, his dad trailing at a distance. The boy was determined but not very good, which made my modest skills dazzling to him. We took turns shooting at Javid, who leapt into the air to catch the ball, slamming down onto the blacktop with his back and shoulder rounded to break the impact—his martial arts training coming in handy in a city with no grass.

A sharply dressed man was sitting on a bench, watching intently. My suspicions stirred. I was moving more freely then at any other time in Iran, running, showing off, not afraid of bringing attention to myself. Instead of a security agent, I imagined he was a soccer agent: Jose Mourinho, the legendary Armani-clad coach of Porto, Real Madrid, and Chelsea, scouting Tehran for untapped talent.

I thought of my country's crushing sanctions on Iran. The damage was akin to war. The pain was absorbed by Javid's generation, economically and socially. I spun and then backheeled the ball past him to the boy's delight. It was a performance not unlike those orchestrated in war zones, with occupying soldiers charming children whose fathers and brothers they have humiliated. The soldier forgets the weight of his gun as a handful of candy flies from his hand into a dust cloud of scrambling children.

Javid punted the ball high in the air and I raced to collect it, shaking my cynicism loose.

I felt safe, in truth; a part of the boy's world. It was constructed of the simplest materials, the ones I floated on through my own happy childhood: a ball and a father willing to kick it back. As George Clooney said in the remake of the Russian science-fiction masterpiece *Solaris*: "We're not looking for new worlds, we're looking for mirrors."

Sanjar had continued up the mountain but we knew where to find him. Javid and I walked towards the benches that look out over Tehran. The city was lit up below, farther away but more intimate, and willing to keep secrets from this distance. The anonymous lights were like a sky full of trustworthy stars, soothing us in a way the near and fiery sun could not.

We looked for a man sitting next to a woman and entertaining her. We walked through the darkness of the lookout listening for English. We found Sanjar sitting next to a couple. He was relaxed and friendly, demonstrating that, unlike Roy, he was not always on the hunt.

We greeted them in English and sat down. The man talked languidly about this and that. Boredom and its twin, tension, were always trading places in closed societies like Iran. Javid, affected by the man's malaise, got up and took a few steps away from us. He leaned on the waist-high chain-link fence and considered his city.

"I think of all the people down there ..." Javid began.

"Banging," I said, trying to distract him. I could sense an inward spiral, the motion of a young man circling his lot and finding it small.

"I think about it. I look there and think maybe they are not alive." Javid turned his back on the city, letting his elbows rest on the top of the fence.

"Take it easy, man, just try to enjoy the night," the man advised, before easing his arm around his girlfriend. At that point I realized that he was very high.

"Look at the lights and don't worry. It's a beautiful night," Sanjar remarked. Javid swung back around to face the city.

"This is the best place in Iran, and we are here," I said. "Man, you know, I'm jealous, there is no place in Minneapolis like this, *no* place."

I thought about something Sanjar once said in Minneapolis. He had returned from Iran for a visit, after finally moving back there. We pulled into the desolate HarMar Mall on a February day: Barnes and Noble was there, our favorite place to binge-read magazines.

The open acres of icy blacktop in the parking lot filled me with winter blues, but Sanjar remarked, "This is *so* nice."

"Are you crazy?" I asked him with no hesitation.

"You know how hard it is to just find a place to park in Tehran?"

To his eyes, the suburban wasteland was a precious vista.

WE GOT UP and left the couple on their bench. After all, the girl had a perrito, as Roy would say. We had not called Roy and wondered if he was heeding the ban on returning to Bame Tehran that the Mountain Police had levied against him. Sanjar maintained that Roy would not quit, even if it killed him. He was flirting with disaster. He was my kind of martyr.

The last time we saw Roy, he told us that he had brought two gold coins to the downtown police station to see if he could tidy up his record. He also planned to accuse the old woman of questionable political affiliations. Sanjar and I freaked out.

Roy answered us coolly: "Hey, if someone wants to fuck with me, talk about me, they're not going to get away with it."

Roy, not interested in politics, tested the authorities and the limits of freedom by following his sexual instincts. In America, people get in the habit of assuming they are free for so long, that they never bother checking. When they finally get around to verifying if they are free, often sometime in middle age, they have affairs or participate in weird swinger contrivances, just to see if the freedom they are feeling is real. Freedom is an opening with sharp edges that disfigures some and refines others.

For many white Americans, freedom is something they possess, like money or property. It is banked and the fear is that someone might take it away from them. They get preoccupied with a brand of reality that promises safety for what they own and never find out how much space there actually is to live in. Black Americans often think of freedom as something they are working towards, not a possession but a hope, that in the future might be fulfilled. As usual, a thing is seen more clearly from the outside.

In the streets of Tehran, freedom and its lack are visceral and acted out on the bodies of its citizens. It is a touch-and-go relationship with freedom that is at times akin to what African Americans experience.

On the surface some of the struggles for free expression were trivial. I remembered the teenager wearing the ragged "Got Jesus?" t-shirt on Bame Tehran, like a battle flag raised in the air. A tool for agitation that, like a punk, he collected from a second-hand store. For the guitarist singing a song on the park bench until taken away, the struggle was less trivial.

Then there was the woman who let her breasts bounce under her open manteau as she crossed a street in central Tehran. Each movement under her thin white shirt was a foolhardy statement of her survival as a sensual person. To accept her own body was provocative, rebellious, and a test. It was deadly serious.

An airplane's "black box" is actually bright orange. In the wreckage it can be spotted more easily. Wherever the woman was now, I wondered when a member of the Basij would be provoked by her thumping beacons, her defiance, at the crash site that is freedom in Iran. She was Sanjar's hero for a few days as he fondly recalled the brash sway of her bosom.

DRIVING AROUND DOWNTOWN Minneapolis years ago, Cheb Khaled's song "Aïcha" came on the radio. I hesitated to turn up the volume. We were idling in traffic among the weekend influx of suburban SUVs. The song is in French and Arabic, and it was the era of "Freedom Fries," so I demurred—my fear of patriots was intercontinental. Hocine, an Algerian friend riding along with me, better at testing for freedom, gave the dial an emphatic twist to the right. Singing even louder, he screamed, "It's good for the spirit!"

In Iran, when Roy passed the Basij in his car blasting Enrique Iglesias, I steeled myself. I loved how pop triviality was transformed into an act of courage, depending on who might be listening.

The opening lines to the song "Escape" flowed out of the open windows. I sank a little in my seat.

Another track began and Roy swerved into an opening, sidling up to a car filled with young women. From out of the open windows the words licked at the air as though the car interior were on fire: *"I like it ... "*

In Tehran, people like Roy grabbed freedom for a moment and rode it through the small spaces between the boredom and vigilance of authority, slivers of release that appeared at traffic circles next to strangers. Idling in the gridlock with speakers maxed out—not long enough to be condemned or identified, but long enough to institute a car-bound flash disco with like minds.

Ducking unpleasant and violent outcomes with a combination of savvy and luck, Roy was *refined* by freedom.

A look at the energy and drive of many young black men in America reveals a similar point of view: you live fast when you know it could all be taken away from you at any moment. It must wear a person out, but it hones something powerful within them.

I was told as much by Frank McCrary, a young black man who worked at the same terrible school where I met Nockiel in the "time-out" room.

Frank sighed and said, "Man, I can't *wait* to be an old man." He then smiled and went about the business of keeping the school from burning down.

AT BAME TEHRAN, Sanjar finally found a woman sitting alone and alighted beside her. She was tall, skinny, and in her late twenties. Sanjar made her laugh a few times. When she began to enjoy herself, she quickly mentioned that she was waiting for her American friend.

"What's his name?" I asked, doubting that there was another American around.

"Roy."

"Roy?" I repeated. Javid and I looked at each other. It was like two detectives finding out that an old and respected thief had pulled off another heist after years in hiding. It could only be him. Sanjar called him as Javid and I celebrated his resurrection.

"Hey man! We are at Bame Tehran sitting next to a pretty lady who says she knows you."

Roy's answer was muffled except for his last words, which slipped out of the receiver. "I'm going to get my shotgun, you sons of bitches."

He was on his way up. We all laughed and the three of us decided to let them meet in peace. In my mind I saw Roy put the phone back in his belt holster without slowing his pace. White pants, sandals, and a short-sleeved silk button-up, gliding forward on a slight frame. He was a man with someplace to be. The Doc Holliday of the Alborz—a reputation as a desperado, but in reality, genial and a great companion.

As the evening wore on, we stopped at one more bench. This time it was the English being spoken that attracted us. A British-Iranian woman was in Iran to visit her sister. Her twelve-year-old daughter had come along and was giggling with her Iranian cousin as we approached. They had been in London the girl's whole life and this was her first time visiting. The husband had stayed back, and it was not long before Sanjar had winked at her and persuaded her to think of her time in Iran as *her* time.

Her daughter was taking the visit in stride. Her hijab rested easily on her head. Sanjar was making the two girls shriek by turning and hissing at them. Sanjar loved children because they laugh at anything, and being a grand host, he was happiest when everyone was having a good time. As they smiled, he even got up and performed a rare piece of physical humor, which he generally despised. I do not remember what it was—an off-pace walk or a funny dance. It was simply a grown man upsetting the hulking stillness expected of men, to the relief of all.

We walked down the mountain with them. The girls, young and old alike, smiled and whispered the whole way.

I exchanged social media information with the mother and daughter because she was the age of my students, and I hoped she could put me in contact with her teacher so that our students could be pen pals. Months after returning from Iran I checked my Facebook page and saw the image of the girl. A mask of bright red lipstick and heavy eye shadow was her "face" to the online world.

A twinge of deviousness hit me.

It was not out of lust for a child-bride. I felt devious in terms of my own societal norms: I wished she would put her manteau back on, and the thin floral scarf I had seen hanging around her angelic face on Bame Tehran.

Chapter Twenty-Eight

OUTSIDE OF THE MOSQUE I was looking for Pasha. It was my last month of university in Wisconsin and I wanted to invite him to a celebration I was having in a couple days. I found him talking to Abdul-Samad: Pasha with his gray-white goatee, Abdul-Samad with his thick red-purple one. Their mouths moved in conversation, like gaps in two flowering bushes wavering open in the wind.

As soon as I joined them, Pasha flagged down a young black man walking by on the sidewalk. The next thing I knew, Pasha had left and Abul-Samad and I were sitting on very high stools at a café. Abdul-Samad hands over a Koran to the young man who is perched next to us.

"I have to sit down in a room with this," the man humbly replied as Abdul-Samad leaned forward and asked him if he knew where his family came from.

I am a bit allergic to the idea of trying to convert people head on. I guess my trust is in people's ability to find out more about an admirable person's way of life. I didn't know what Pasha was thinking setting us up on this religious blind date. Abdul-Samad had lived in India and returned a man of deep faith. Now he was asking the man if he had ever looked for the truth.

"My whole life," the young man replied.

The questions made me cringe, asked as they were from a position of certainty, but the man's answers were genuine. Abdul-Samad was offering an invitation to Islam. I sat there squirming, piping up to say things like "Think about it on your own" and "It's no one else's business." (Which, in Islam, is technically true. There is supposed to be no intermediary between you and the Divine).

I looked deep into the young man's face. West Africa, East Africa, the Sudan—I could not quite place where his ancestors originated. I knew one thing: his ancestors had not been invited to America. This was part of the appeal of Abdul-Samad's offer: an invitation to a brotherhood, to a circle where he was wanted.

The day of the party I was walking up a hill. It was early afternoon, the spring sunshine flowing clean and light through the air. I saw the young man as I was walking down the hill. We exchanged greetings.

"You should come tonight. I'm having a party. People are showing up around eight."

"I'd love to man, but ..." He smiled and looked down.

I looked down too.

He lifted up the leg of his pants. I saw a black electronic device. It was his ankle monitor, otherwise known as a *tether*.

SANJAR CALLED his personal taxi service the night before my flight. It was the same driver who had picked me up from the airport, and who had driven us around the next day to chase down a visa office that never existed. We had been avoiding this driver because Sanjar said he misbehaved on the fare that day.

I was convinced that there would be some hassle at the airports both in Iran and in the US. What concerned me more was that Sanjar was also convinced of this. Nothing terrible was expected— just enough to allow me to commiserate with Sanjar the next time he had to pass through security in the U.S.

I had brought only a backpack and small carry-on, but for the return flight I would be checking a bag full of pistachios, figs, walnuts, apricots, and mulberries to deliver to Sanjar's brother in the States. Any imprecision of claims at US customs, especially since I was coming from Iran, would result in confiscations, and a strike against me.

It was hard to imagine that these were items unavailable at some import grocer. As with the sesame bundled back from Egypt when someone in my family returned from there, the idea, biased by sentiment, was that the goods carried back from the homeland were better.

Sanjar prepared the black suitcase stuffed with dried snacks. Yes, I thought, these walnuts are nutritious. They could be used to sustain a terrorist sleeper cell in the eyes of Homeland Security. I made an accurate list of the contents, so I could declare everything correctly on my customs forms. When we could not find the English or Farsi name on one bag of dried red berries, Neda and Anoush got involved to help identify them.

As we were on our way out of the apartment, Sepehr rose from his table to say goodbye. The table that was filled with volumes, quotes, and refutations, stacked in threes and fours, spread out like ingredients on a chef's countertop. It was a chaotic mélange managed by the private logic of the author.

In a V-neck T-shirt and pajama bottoms, the uniform of a man who understands the sanctuary of the home, Sepehr shuffled over. Having lived a large life, he still found the energy to take on projects; he was like Will Durant reshaping his *Story of Civilization* opus in his nineties, or Doris Lessing declaring that in old age all one has is their work—if they are lucky enough to have found it.

Sepehr's life took place against a backdrop of kings, war, service, and revolution. He was a grand figure, but he met the quotidian with grace each and every time. The callers who would arrive by day knew he would listen to their complaints and requests: the list of minor and major favors he had done stretched back decades.

The families that arrived at night unannounced knew that tea, fruit, cookies, and backgammon would transcend any magisterial work in progress. In the end, this was just Iranian hospitality, of which he was an exemplar.

It was this noble man who lived close to the earth, and was not shy about its pleasures, who met me at the door on my way out of Iran.

"Did you have a good time?" he asked.

"I have had such a good time. I have made great memories, some that I don't even know I have yet."

"Good."

Sanjar, at times stingy with his translating, obliged fully this time. He reformed my words into Farsi. I kissed Sepehr's cheeks twice, then once more, and left for the taxi. It was four hours before departure.

AS THE FREEWAYS opened up near the edge of Tehran, our driver pointed out a stretch where he had seen two men roll out of the back of a police van earlier in the day. The van was speeding to the prison, and the men had opened the back door, or perhaps it had just popped open. Handcuffed, they bounced on the road, got up, and started running.

"They were both overweight, but they were giving it their best shot," the driver chuckled.

His passenger at the time, a middle-aged woman, was mortified. I tried to picture the chubby fugitives trying to jump the guardrail to enter the neighborhood streets, gambling on a safe house emerging out of the thick air of general discontent with any authority.

It did not occur to me that they may have been guilty.

IT WAS NOT long before we left Tehran behind. I did not look back but let my eyes roll out upon the great Dasht-e Kavir, the flatlands. My eyes, which for weeks had been confronted with people, buildings, the sides of mountains, and lights, now glided across layers of alluvium stretching into the distance.

There were scorched fields matched with crumbling mud compounds. An abandoned firing range appeared on the roadside. A humble wooden watchtower overlooked a dozen busted tanks. Their turrets were rusted in place, pointing towards Iraq.

As with the half-finished apartment buildings in the capital— incomplete shrines and mosques, abandoned through lack of funding or favor, stood in resignation along the highway.

Near the *Behesht-e Zahra*, or Paradise of Zahra cemetery, we passed the mausoleum of Ayatollah Khomeini. Under construction for over twenty years and developed across five thousand acres, this shrine has both favor and funding—over two billion dollars have been devoted to the project. The fountains, grass, and trees that cushion the structure make it easy to overlook the ongoing construction, which has perhaps been paced and lengthened to keep the juice of the revolution fresh.

On a thick strip of raised grass between two parking lots sat the calming sight of a family picnicking.

WATCHING THE PLANES flying low overhead, Sanjar spoke of the effects of a new round of sanctions as we neared the airport. Without the ability to buy new planes, or to get parts to repair older ones, Iran had a dismal air safety record. The country had been the victim of relentless rounds of nineteenth-century geopolitical moves, and now its fleet of creaking and sputtering twentieth-century American, French, and Russian planes struggled to keep up with the volume and pace of twenty-first century travel.

In the terminal Sanjar was able to walk with me up until the first checkpoint. I scrambled to get my book out so he could write down the full name and title of Mr. Mostafavi. On a desk set aside for preliminary bag checks, I set my backpack down and pulled out my book. Sanjar assuaged the impatience of the security agent, and wrote down the name of the man who had made my extended stay possible. My plan was to take it to one of the senators or representatives from Minnesota and see if they would write a thank-you letter to him.

A quixotic agenda item of staggering naivete—but one I pursued.

I hugged my friend goodbye and timidly took my place on the fringes of a swarm of East Asians, South Asians, and Iranian nationals; I then squeezed through the metal detectors and braced myself for the coming interrogation. I managed the bottleneck and walked around aimlessly, looking for Emirates Airline. It was a small airport—at least it seemed that way, judging from the parts that were open.

When I walked past the same potted ficus tree for the second time I just sat down.

An Emirates sign materialized behind a counter, and a long line started to form, so I joined it. The Emirates flight agent was well chosen. Yet another Persian exemplar to swoon over. Sanjar would have said, "Iran is such a beautiful country, with such beautiful *people*," and winked at her, but I tried to be as boring as possible.

The impulse that had been stirring since I sat with the Ethiopian woman in Dubai flared as I lost a heartbeat in the agent's steady gaze. In fact, it had been there since high school, when I found myself staring through a window at a katana sword with a waitress outside Amarillo, Texas.

Is travel inseparable from seeking a mate?

Although I tried to deny it the question had been developing in my mind about why these brushes with women while traveling were so sexually charged. There were the intentions for my trip that I voiced—seeing a friend, adventure, cultural exploration. Then there was something ticking deep within me, something evolutionary. The noble and chaste reasons plastered over a biological fact. We evolved to roam over unfamiliar terrain and not get lost, but why? Once we found somewhere new our purpose for wandering into the unknown was clear: Make sure life goes on.

At the Emirates counter I turned myself into a cog of some company's sales force numbly rounding the circuit of global commerce and slid the agent my identification.

BOARDING PASS IN HAND, I approached hurdle two as I stood in line waiting for security officers to check passports in the "Foreign" line. I evaluated each agent. Observing their faces, I worked up an algorithm: amount of facial hair, amount of time spent looking at each traveler's passport, zeal in the eyes, insecurity in the mouth. I chose the least studious-looking one and stepped up to the counter.

I passed over my documents and noticed that he had turned to the page with my initial visa, which read "seven days," and which would mean that I had overstayed my visa by many, many days. He asked me a short question that I missed. I began mumbling and excusing myself, asking for forgiveness.

Then I went on about how if he turned the page he would see a note about the extension.

He stopped me. "You don't get me," he said.

I kept blundering, "I have a letter, and the stamp is on another page."

"No, you don't get me. I ask if you have a *green card*."

Thinking that this was some probing intelligence question, maybe a subliminal trap to see if I supported the Green Movement in Iran (which arose after the 2009 election). I set about trying to manufacture the correct answer.

"I never needed a green card ... I don't have one, or, I guess I do. I don't know. I was born in America. I guess I was born with one, kinda. A US citizen just ... *has* one." Stumbling, I exposed to myself how little I needed to know about bureaucracy as a middle-class American.

"If you have a passport you get a green card!" He was putting together a puzzle for himself and his own future, and I was simply a source of information.

"It sounds correct," I stuttered.

He then passed me through with a wink. It's true that if you look for trouble, you will find it, and more often than not it comes from within you.

The last hurdle was a final bag check. The metal detector, like a freestanding gray portal leading to other dimensions, filled the hallway leading to the departure gates. Machine guns appeared, held by fresh-faced young men. It was a low-tech, and cheaper, mode of intimidation when compared with the gadgets designed to dissuade people from plotting at American airports. (In my hometown airport, I once had a sweat sample taken from my palm and analyzed, after which I passed through an x-ray tunnel and then had a non-ionizing radiation body scan).

BOARDING THE PLANE, I literally became a hurdle—to the other passengers. Empathizing with the need for people living with a billion compatriots to nudge ahead when possible, I could not help finding myself cursing a fat, sloppily dressed Chinese man in flip-flops who barged past me on the jet bridge. Then an Indian man jostled around me in the tiny plane aisle as I was walking forward. As India and China regained their wealth, they were becoming as ugly as Americans. Their nouveaux riches could now afford trips abroad, so the rest of the world witnessed each country's quota of brutes from among the ordinary masses.

Worrying about these microscopic annoyances must have meant that I had made it. I felt like the Australian reporter Guy Hamilton from the film *The Year of Living Dangerously*: a foreigner, an outsider, witnessing the trials of a developing country. Except I added a new scene to the movie's ending that matched my ungrateful attitude: Guy makes it onto the last airplane escaping a chaotic revolutionary Indonesia. With bloody gauze over one eye, he hugs Jill Bryant, the British attaché, and settles in to watch the country descend into violence from a safe height. As the plane hits cruising altitude, he complains about the lack of a beverage service on the outbound flight.

WAITING FOR THE PLANE to Dubai to take off, I read about a man who biked eighteen thousand miles from London to Thailand only to slip in the shower of a Bangkok hostel. He had to be airlifted out.

My plane taxied to the runway. I felt fingers of euphoria crawling up my throat but swallowed them down. It was time to make a map. I wondered when the journey to Iran had begun; I suspected it was like a baby's teething: happening continuously, but in different degrees of intensity.

I had been preparing to go to the East since becoming aware of my father's accent. Other parts of the beginning: lonely nights reading Persian mystics at the University of Wisconsin, a photo of the Milad Tower in Saleh's photo album in Granada, Spain, meeting Sanjar.

I had waded through the middle of the journey, which consisted of walks, stories, and tea. The respected word of Mr. Mostafavi had carried me over a political labyrinth made out of documents and ink and guarded by male secretaries. I had witnessed a few confrontations on a mountain without getting so much as a scratch.

Besides the three hikers who were still in Evin Prison for crossing the border by accident, the closest an American had come to getting harmed in Iran while I was there was when Andrew fell in love with Zahra.

Outside the window the scenery sped up, and then the Emirates plane lifted above a vast blanket of alluvium.

Soon I would be able to count my fingers and toes on a US tarmac. In my mind a doubt began to form. The ending to a journey could not be written with the black rubber streaks of plane wheels on American concrete—that was just a contract with an airline being discharged. Without an ending the movement from one destination to the next could not be a story.

Chapter Twenty-Nine

AFTER DEPARTING FROM DUBAI, the Emirates flight to New York flew over Iraq. High-definition screens mounted on the back of the seat in front of me gave me live shots from cameras mounted on the front, back, and bottom of the aircraft.

It was night, and the darkness surrounding us was fed through all the lenses.

With five hundred in-flight channels to choose from, the steady void of these shots served as a meditative salve. Tipping my sight out of the window and down, I strained to get a firsthand account of the simmering war zone. It was impossible to see anything. It could have been Utah.

There was a digital map on the monitor, tracking a path over a quarter of the Earth. I saw that we were gliding near Baghdad. Crisscrossing the paths of bombers and tracing the whiz of a cruise missile in a commercial airliner above the city fulfilled the logic of war, I suppose.

The beverage service passed by. I wondered whether I was entitled to the whole can of ginger ale. The almond-scented hot towel that had rested on my face before takeoff was now stuffed in a metal drawer in the back of the plane, cold, but still perfumed.

MY RENUNCIATIONS at thirty-five thousand feet drifted helplessly towards the ground where the magnificent war machine of America had gone to work. The wimpy hands of pacifists had tugged apologetically on the brake of the broad metallic combine.

It would claim a harvest of progress and freedom after fertilizing the land with confusion, blood, and uranium.

It had rolled into and over Afghanistan and Iraq, and it now idles, awaiting its part in creating the borders of a remade world.

SITTING WITH DAN in downtown Minneapolis a few days after my return, I opened a plastic wrapper that held a toothpick inside. A breeze blew it to the sidewalk, and I lurched to catch it.

"What's the point?" Dan said to me, his nostrils beginning to flare with an oncoming guffaw.

I looked up from the concrete. From there my eyes followed a steel-and-glass structure rising fifty-seven stories into the sky. It was the IDS tower.

"Look what we've done to the place already!" he shouted, and we both fell into hysterics.

WALKING AROUND his neighborhood in Iran, Sanjar spoke of how people looked at him funny when he said "hello." He had done this for months when he first moved back to Iran. After some time, he stopped. Remembering small moments is easier in a troubled land. Moreese Bickham noticed the first gray hair he got in Angola Prison. It was right in the right so he could see it.

I remember standing outside Sanjar's apartment when a cab passed by slowly. It was the same spot where the cab driver had said there was no true love in Tehran. The driver was another scruffy old man—fitted inside his cab as if the steel body had been shaped around him, and the contours of his soul.

He leaned out the window with an ice-cream cone and gestured "cheers." His tangled eyebrows arched like the vine-covered gates of paradise.

When he was sure we were looking, he corkscrewed the entire cone toward his grizzled face, took a huge bite, and sped off.

IN THE THIN air above Baghdad, ten hours of flight ahead, I reviewed the items packed underneath the plane, the ones I had to describe to the customs agent in the United States:

dried mulberries
apricots
figs
pistachios
cashews

DRIED FRUIT AND NUTS memorized, I was ready to land. Arriving at JFK, I made my way over to customs and immigration. The immense room resembled a huge maze made of line dividers.

American citizens can pick from among thirty lines. Another ten lines are for those with green cards. The last twenty to thirty lines are for "foreign visitors."

It sounds like a statement, but it's a question: "You don't look American." It shakes the legitimacy of one's very right to be present. At JFK, it formed in my mind. For many children with parents from continents other than Europe, the question can affirm or condemn. It was affirming when I worked on a film one summer. The seasoned lighting director listed the characters I could play by continent. He only left out Antarctica.

I learned to take it as a compliment, a boon of international appeal granted to children whose parents were of different races. I adopted the imperial view of the dubious Englishman, who traveled the world and was stunned whenever he was considered a foreigner.

At JFK, I tried to study what an American looked like by watching several lines of people and blocking out the signs above them. It was impossible to tell what an American looked like. I thought of the disappointment of the young lady in Sanjar's garden when she saw that I was not a tall blond with muscles.

Immigrants forget to report back to their friends and family that America is *them*.

The use of cameras and video devices was restricted in the customs hall. The one story that needed to be documented and shared, the confusion over which is the "foreign" and which is the "American" line, is stored away on Homeland Security servers.

THE PASSPORT-CONTROL AGENT waited in his cubicle as I stepped over the yellow line on the floor and walked over to him. Without my noticing, my suspicions and anxieties shifted smoothly from the Iranian authorities to these new ones.

I had chosen the right line—US citizens—and had my passport in hand. Still, because of my international complexion I expected to hear the question I have heard my whole life in America: "Where are you from?"

When the first Gulf War began, I was in London with my soccer team. Being twelve years old, I had ignored the mutterings of adults. My teammates and I did not realize war had broken out until we arrived at the airport to fly home: a group of us walked into a gift shop and saw the large, thick font of a British tabloid announcing "WAR!"

A few minutes later, while I was checking in, an airline agent walked me away from my teammates and held my passport open. "Where is your family from?" he asked.

I found myself stumbling over my words. My mind went in two directions: east and west.

Years later, I was trying to find some way to make the bombing of Afghanistan seem more real. I looked down at my feet, then the dirt, and imagined an unbroken stretch of land rolling and bulging across America, under the Pacific, up out of the South China Sea, tracing lightly over brutal peaks, and then stopping in a dusty Afghan village still shaking from an explosion. And that became my answer from then on to the question: Where are you from?

"The ground beneath your feet."

THE PREJUDICES AND FEARS buzzing in my head made me incapable of hearing the passport-control agent's question at JFK, just as I had been incapable of communicating with the Iranian agent at Imam Khomeini International. It was like being stuck in the windpipe of a ranting talk-radio host. Sounds gushed past my ears, but they were meaningless. All I could taste was bile, all I could feel was the spray of dry spittle.

"How was your trip?"

Squinting into the cubicle I saw the unflatteringly lit face of the agent. His eyes were bloodshot and his hair was greasy, but his demeanor was implausibly amiable.

"Pardon?" I braced as I waited for him to repeat a barbed inquiry that I had refused to process. He had seen the visa from Iran— what could there be in his mind but trouble?

"How was your trip?" He repeated.

"Wha-, ah, good. Very nice."

He returned my passport with a tired smile. He had coffee-stained teeth, but they were all there, like an off-white picket fence. I definitely was back in America. I smiled back and went to collect my checked luggage.

I STILL HAD to pass through customs with the fruits and nuts.

Stepping up to a round uniformed man whose mustache must have been confiscated from an Iraqi, I handed over my customs form. I bowed my head.

A clean metal operating table was placed at his left, waiting for my bag. Then it happened. A miniature waking nightmare of Tehrani vintage. I saw the zipper of my bag yanked around. Inside, the contents breathed upward against the loosened canvas. The top was flipped open and a pair of white gloves plunged inside. One hand peeled off a thin layer of T-shirts to reveal the contraband.

"What's this? On your customs form you wrote *raspberries*, not *mulberries!*"

Picking up two large tomes, the white gloves dumbly picked through the pages of Sepehr's books of medieval Persian, nearly impossible for most Iranians to read.

"What's this book about?"

"It's the science of—"

"Destruction. I know. And here, I don't see any declarations about walnuts."

"But I did, I wrote …"

"You know what happens when you lie to Uncle Sam?" The mustachioed man grinned and swirled his finger around a bucket of water.

MY MIND REEMERGED into reality: the man with the mustache was before me, his plump body crowded behind a podium.

He had set down my form and was waving me on, in effect saying "don't bother checking this guy." I walked forward, confused and embarrassed, into the American world of bustle and preoccupation.

I tumbled into anonymity, darkly craving a little more attention from Homeland Security. I had cleared the efficient system, and now, since I was not a celebrity, I was able to move freely—to do what, was another question. This was the welcome to a life so many millions around the world clamored for: No hassle and no love. America: come in, make money, and, if you wake up and do not know who you are anymore, start shopping.

I looked around for the people I had seen in the "foreign visitors" line. Finding a few of the young men, some scrawny, some jacked, with shades hanging from polo shirts, I was certain I knew when their journeys to America had begun. Whether they were from villages in Uttar Pradesh, or shantytowns in Lagos, it was all the same: their journeys had begun when they saw their first episode of *Baywatch*.

My evidence for this claim is based solely on my experience with Nyasha, my Zimbabwean college roommate. We drove from Des Moines to Minneapolis one day and he made me spend an entire afternoon taking pictures of him in front of my father's red Acura Legend—his arms around a blonde friend of mine who was game for this diorama of the American Dream. He sent the pictures back to Harare as proof that he was making it.

I collected my charge of dried fruit and nuts and dragged the bag towards the doors. Arrivals to New York City spun off in different directions on trains and buses and in cabs and limos. No one cared about who anyone else was until they were told to by popular demand.

I would have to make that most American of transitions in the vast country: from anonymity to loneliness, then solitude, on the homely streets of Brooklyn and Minneapolis. Eating its way out from within was a longing to be known by someone, anyone.

I looked back at the foreign studs. They had their shades on, a good first step in the mechanization of their lives as they became Terminators relentlessly chasing success. I wondered when they would start to miss the poverty and brotherhood they had left behind.

MY FATHER LOSES PATIENCE when I complain about America. It results in unspoken pacts to not discuss anything except the Minnesota Twins or Liverpool FC for weeks. What I am really doing is trying to get him to admit missing something he never noticed he had in the village. Something I feel and "taste" in the East: a real culture. I cannot verbalize what makes this culture more real, so I bitch about America, hoping my meaning will take shape by describing what it is not.

I remember sitting in the back seat of my father's car some years ago after a fishing trip. My father was dropping off his friend, the Egyptian musician, and noticed that the house next to his friend's house had a nice garden.

"My neighbor was up at sunrise doing his work on it," his friend explained.

My father nodded and asked: "Do you know the sign of a good gardener?"

We waited as he scanned the terraced front yard before continuing: "It's what you don't see."

WHEN I AM HEADED home after a trip, the safety of home becomes mythical. At JFK I started to wonder about just how quiet and peaceful those streets of Minneapolis really were.

When my sister and I were children, we would sit in the dark on the living room rug after evening prayer and listen to my father. I never thought much about it. It was just a time when we did not get up right away to do something else. Muslims end their prayers on the ground, and we would all be kneeling on our prayer rugs. Maybe a lingering submission to gravity had something to do with our not getting up.

He would share a few stories or translate the lines of a verse from the Qur'an. Our South Minneapolis neighborhood drifted off one house at a time into the sweet harmony of sane and boring routine. I had a foreboding that this was a life without the inspiration of risk and danger, and that fate would get its revenge on a neighborhood playing at perfection through a life that simulated death—each family sealed up in its own tomb. As if everyone thought that by keeping quiet at night, playing possum, hardship would pass over our block and we'd wake up to all our privileges.

Rumbling inside me all those years was volcanic activity. All the joy, fear, and anger that keeps people stumbling ahead. And I hear my father's voice now in the dark. It is there—the risk, the assurance, that life would be more than what I saw around me. That around each corner there was a surprise, a test.

"Who knows what tomorrow will bring, or what land you will be buried in?" he told us one night.

It was a question but it landed in me like a promise—a falcon feather dropped from the balcony of a king.

AT THE PAY PHONE I dug in my bag while listening to the Caribbean English of two New York City taxi drivers. I had seven units left on my cheap salmon-pink phone and called Rob in Brooklyn.

My flight home was the following day and I was happy to get a chance to see him again. His voice was heavy. I was separating myself from the throes of self-conjured calamities in Iran and I wondered what real one had befallen Rob.

I had begun to be embarrassed by the frightened figure I struck in Iran. "Die before you die," Al-Ghazali had instructed. In Iran I had died about a hundred times over, but not the right way.

The great Eastern tradition of contemplating death was to absorb it into the normal cycle of awareness, to transform life into something wildly precious, with incredible stakes that must be teed up and met moment to moment. I had not learned this. My thoughts of death in Iran were shallow, fearful stirrings about immediate pain—or a premature collapse of a foggy life agenda into the grave.

Getting on the train to Brooklyn I took deep breaths.

Being a Midwesterner in a subway system usually made me feel like a steer in a corral: anxious, but barely conscious of what was going on. I would feel dim and wary. Now, I found that I was taking the mean underground in, open chested, looking up sharply at my surroundings where I would once have passed in glossy-eyed timidity.

I guessed that these were the fruits of passing out of danger, real or imagined.

The world moved around me in an orderly and rhythmic way. I got out in front and around people and things. It was like being on a stage where props and actors move in predictable patterns. I was apprehending my own culture, and it appeared in slow motion.

When a muscular man with tattoos and a huge duffel bag—the kind carried back and forth from prison, war, or cage fights—asked me for directions in the station, I glanced at a map and gave a long, confident answer, with clear diction. We wished each other luck.

REACHING BROOKLYN, which was quiet in the late afternoon, I bought a pineapple juice at a bar and looked upon the ease with which people carried on. New York City had a reputation so strong and secure that it carried people along like bits of glitter in a self-contained waterfall.

A city largely balanced, with pace and features set, despite the perpetual construction and influx of dreamers. It subsisted on its own steady yield of style, its capacities staggering but fully accounted for, fulfilled, and weirdly stagnant. The soul of the city was pickled.

Its energy seemed to swirl aimlessly when I compared it to Tehran, a place always on the brink. In Tehran, people had nothing to do, but they did it with grace and intention, urgency and desperation. Iran was on the precipice—it was already over the edge—and Iranians worked furiously to maintain life on the face of a cliff.

Tehran, because it was a city with no soul, required its citizens to cling to their own souls with everything they had.

IT TURNED OUT that Rob was fine. When we met up he took us in his light blue pickup to a pizza place. Shining as ever, his soul was fresh, reaching out and warming me. He was just in the middle of a marathon writing session, working on a grant proposal due the next morning. He was stressed out and I had not slept for two days, but we laughed over balls of fresh mozzarella and basil.

We ate our pizza fast and I shamed myself by gloating over my irresistibility as an American over there. Rob was forgiving, mentioning his own experience in West Africa, where he declined the role of a Western witch doctor with the magic to transform a native's life with a kiss and a document. He had gone to make a documentary on cashew farms for an aid organization.

Being well traveled, and not zealous about details, Rob was the right person to meet after a trip. I had been passed along to him from the loving protection of Sanjar, and I was grateful for the gift of a small international network of true friendship.

Back at his apartment we made some tea, coaxing the last few leaves from the folds of a plastic bag and dropping them in the strainer.

Rob was typing his proposal, turning to me from time to time for help in selecting words. His longtime roommate, back from a music gig, popped his head in and sneered "fucking *cashews*," and disappeared back into the hall.

I sat in the corner dipping in and out of sleep. Remembering Hamid, I had gotten up two or three times to get Rob more hot water. There were no more leaves. The tea got weaker as the night went on. My head was bobbing now, going up and down every minute or so. In my dreams, a school of sunfish was either going to strip my hook or take me under.

When I woke up it was time to turn my shoulders towards Minneapolis, the city of lakes.

FALL, WINTER, SPRING, and then summer arrived. I was back. I was happy to enjoy the good life—as it could be—back home. On an overcast day, I was sitting at the computer in the sunroom of our house. It was early afternoon, humid, and I was frittering it away in half-conscious mouse clicks.

Our house is in a quiet part of a quiet city, a block off Lake Street. The river blocks traffic on one side, and old train tracks turn traffic away on the other. As I looked out the window, a passing biker caught my eye. I then noticed a young man walking quickly to my door.

He put one foot on the steps and saw me. Immediately he turned around and shuffled to the alley that cuts at an angle through the block across the street and outlets in front of our house. Once nestled in a shadow in the alleyway he turned around and put his phone to his ear.

He believes that I cannot see him.

I watch him leave, then I get up, walk to the kitchen, and look out at the backyard. A figure moves past the garage and onto the sidewalk.

That night I catch myself standing like a cyborg at the window. I am looking into the pool of light cast by the streetlight, then into the shadows at its edge.

Chapter Thirty

THE RADIO ANNOUNCED that US Representative Keith Ellison would be meeting with the public at Midtown Global Market in Minneapolis. It was winter break and Khalil was with me. Snow was falling hard that Friday night. Headlights and storefronts lit up the fresh powder all around in a cozy orange glow. We turned off Lake Street and pulled into the ramp.

The lobby of the building was filled with the hard stares of police officers. A restaurant was being set up with the artifacts of a memorial, and the scent of fresh flowers was in the air. On each circular table was a picture: a young girl, an elderly man, a couple.

We walked to the central food court and saw it packed with citizens determined to keep up the tenuous connection with the elect. It was one week after the attempted assassination of a politician, and the murder of eight others, including a judge. This was the first time a politician was holding a public meeting since.

I looked down at my son, and thought: if this is America, next time he will visit Iran with me.

KHALIL AND I had gone to the Global Market to get a letter from a representative in the federal government. I felt the Iranian gentleman who had helped me, Mr. Mostafavi, needed a show of appreciation from a higher-up in my own government. I thought I could persuade Keith Ellison to thank Mr. Mostafavi for aiding one of his constituents abroad. I knew it was a stretch, but grandiose only in the way a compliment about shoes can inoculate a woman against the day's forthcoming indifference, the way a tap on the brake for merging traffic averts fiery doom. I decided to throw my faith behind small gestures.

Being late to the speeches, I took Khalil by the hand over to the first place in line at the restaurant to which the "Congress in Your Corner" event would soon shift. The representative's assistants labored to make the atmosphere casual and welcoming, while the police did their conflicted best to project safety to the good and menace to the wicked—a fun-house mirror of public service.

A hundred people were eventually waiting in line behind us. When the event opened, we walked over and took our seat at the table with five Minnesotans and the politician.

Being the first Muslim ever elected to the US House of Representatives, Ellison had been threatened himself. I appreciated his bravery. As the first citizen to speak with him in front of the cameras since the shooting in Tucson, Arizona, I knew that I was supposed to say something about the tragedy. With my son on my lap, I leaned in, and sensed everyone around me—aides, citizens, reporters, police—turn and look.

Above the congressman's head I noticed a tense face peering through the circular window of the kitchen door. There was a bristling of restrained violence at my back, some of it from the police, and some from the zealous aides. They were waiting for me to make my move. The same tense conditions from my meeting with Mr. Mostafavi prevailed, this time in my own city.

I began by saying that I wanted to tell a story of "a man who kept his word." A strong-armed tactic to be sure, but this was something I wanted done. The other supplicants looked on in confusion as I recounted the story of meeting Mr. Mostafavi in Tehran.

I had read that the Battle of Gettysburg began over a search for decent shoes. Couldn't this mean that a war could now be prevented with a thank-you note? After all, wars are driven by obvious forces—money comes to mind—but the crank handle of peace is powered by a million hidden graces: weird reversals of feeling and action playing out on a pedestrian scale.

Sanjar once told me a Mullah Nasruddin tale that imposes itself on my mind when I think of sitting in that restaurant mumbling about Iran in the middle of an all-American disaster. It begins with Nasruddin smacking his son before sending him to the market to buy milk. When the mother complains, Nasruddin responds, "What good would it do if I slapped him *after* he spilled the milk?"

ONE THING CAN be said for most politicians: they mind their manners in public. As my request tapered off, I was surprised at how easily Representative Ellison responded. The request was, to use a word I hate, awkward, but he listened intelligently.

With a quick glance over my head, at an aide perhaps pointing at her watch or nodding, he agreed: "Sure, I can do that."

"That would be great. How will it work?" I pressed.

"You could write out a letter and I could sign it. Or I could write it myself. Just get Marjorie's card here and we'll set it up."

A politician's talent is to cast a spell of trust long enough for a citizen to be shuffled off and plowed under by the concerns of their daily life. Our group rotated away from the table, and we tried to find our way through the cordoned-off restaurant, already starting to forget what we had asked for.

A tall reporter, with milky and greedy eyes, stopped us as we passed a row of plants.

"Hi, is it all right if I ask you a few questions?"

"Okay."

"What did you talk to the congressman about?"

He pulled the microphone farther and farther away from me as I spoke, beginning with the word "Iran." The attack in Arizona was not on my mind, but I told the reporter the real reason I was there, and it was unusable in the story he wanted to tell.

ENVISIONING A LETTER written on US congressional letterhead making its way to Mr. Mostafavi, I even indulged in a waking nightmare that had a Hollywood ending. Standing before an Iranian judge, I feel him glare at me before he asks his question: "So why did you return to Iran?" My answers only make things worse as the room fills with skeptical turbaned heads. They begin shaking side to side after hearing my next answer: "Because I love it."

The guards are preparing to take me to Evin when Mr. Mostafavi, dressed sharply, appears in order to intervene on my behalf. We walk out of the courtroom together and he invites me to his office for tea. While we are waiting, I notice a framed letter above his desk. It is a thank-you letter signed by US Congressman Ellison.

AT THE MARKET Khalil was quiet at my side. The conversations had dipped in and out of his interest. He can point Iran out on a map, he has met Sanjar many times, and his head pops up from his Legos when news reports on the radio mention the country.

I wonder if, decades from now, he will have some strange, specific longing for Iran, or just a general imprint of longing for other places.

Ian Frazier, the journalist drawn to Siberia, once tried to trace his desire to go there. He recalled listening to early radio reports about the Cold War, and his father's long-lost commentary on the Soviet Union and people called "communists." Traveling icy roads built by miserable political outcasts, Frazier was stunned by the silence of a former prison camp. The site was not marked by any historical plaques containing paragraphs summing up the tragedy and hope found in a Gulag. Only a layer of frost separated the past and the present.

Another writer, the crusty old bard from Michigan, Philip Levine, picked through his past by reading a journal his father had left for his mother. While reading it, he noticed a distance growing between him and his father. He was not a son circling back to become his father in old age because, as he discovered, his father had held *other* circles inside of him. It was not clear which one he had wandered along the farthest. The poem he wrote about it is called "The Return" and in these few lines I saw his sense of his father changing, the radius doubling:

At first my brothers and I tried conversation, questions
only he could answer: Why had he gone to war?
Where did he learn Arabic? Where was his father?
I remember none of this. I read it all later,
years later as an old man, a grandfather myself,
in a journal he left my mother with little drawings
of ruined barns and telephone poles, receding
toward a future he never lived, aphorisms
from Montaigne, Juvenal, Voltaire, and perhaps a few
of his own: "He who looks for answers finds questions."
Three times he wrote, "I was meant to be someone else,"
and went on to describe the perfumes of the damp fields.

IN THE DEAD of the winter after I returned from Iran, I was
making a fire at my parents' house. It wasn't the winter solstice,
Mithra wasn't at risk, but the nights were getting long. My father
caught me reading newspaper articles before I threw them into
the flames.

I was told that my grandfather in Egypt had done this. He seized
on bits and scraps of information and strained them of use, before
the paper was finally used as fuel, or to wrap a feta and olive oil
sandwich.

When my father left the village for Cairo, he was guided by a
centralized state system into an agricultural college, where a series
of biology and chemistry texts landed like fist blows on a literary
mind. After a career working in a greenhouse, my father finally
began to write during his retirement.

The Egyptians in his circle do not read all that much, and just
want to talk politics. Joining book clubs, he has found more than
once that every other member was a Jewish "brother or sister,"
as he says. He often takes a chair and fishing pole down to Lake
Harriet on summer afternoons, hoping someone will walk by with
the time to talk about books.

One time he read a book review in a magazine three times, until
it finally occurred to him to go out and buy the book. His is a
portrait of someone making up for lost time.

I HAVE A STRANGE PICTURE in my mind when I think of the past and of what future generations may take from old stories: Lake Vostok. I was doing the dishes in Minneapolis, fencing with myself as I tried to scrape peanut butter off one knife with another knife. A radio report came on NPR about the work of a global team of scientists in Antarctica.

Vostok is a huge lake discovered nearly three miles beneath an Antarctic ice sheet. Water effectively sealed off from history—the rest of nature—for millions of years. A Russian scientist at Vostok Station used seismic soundings, measured the thickness of the ice sheet, and suspected something was underneath. A few years later, a British team using ice-penetrating radar surveys detected fluid, indicating the existence of a subglacial freshwater lake.

For decades their report sat in a drawer, but now Lake Vostok has become one of the most carefully managed research sites in the world.

Everyone wants to take a look at what might be living down there, claiming it is akin to studying the icy oceans beneath the distant moons of our solar system. NASA has taken the lead on the project. The fear is that capsules sent down the drill shaft to look will destroy the purity of the environment. Any confusion between what was originally there and what was introduced would corrupt the findings.

The other feature of Vostok is this: every thirteen thousand years, the weight of the sheet melts enough ice so that the water of the lake is completely renewed by itself. Inside this self-contained world life has survived—as scientists have discovered hundreds of species in water samples they have taken. Evolution may have invented a self-sustaining world, living off and sharing a recycled scrap of solar energy from before Antarctica was frozen over.

Sometimes I plunge back in time to study eras of my life. When I do, I worry about disturbing a balance within the past that my mind has managed to keep with new hungers, new experiences. I read about a woman who will not listen to blues records she loved in her twenties, lest her moody early-adult mindset return with the chords.

There are weird similarities between us and the waters of Lake Vostok. We, the living, are standing on a sheet of ice three miles thick. Somewhere beneath us is the future, and created in its blindness are unknown forms of life like the hidden world of Lake Vostok. We're protected from the paralysis of knowing the true results of our actions: what will we find there? We drill down to penetrate the future—and when we arrive, contaminate it with our nervous desires, that slide in from the present.

We have stories and they have saved us from the mucky doom of reconciling the past, present, and future. Stories have beginnings, middles, and endlessness. The storytellers all die but there is no art where the name matters less. Tell a tale and be with us always.

There are the stories I tell Khalil about my life, but also the ancient stories retold in my own words. Their wisdom is not subject to contamination because it lives in a special chamber of the human heart, protecting and purifying itself like the waters of Lake Vostok.

Remembering ordinary life, and even momentous historical events, has its warping and rotting effects—its oblivion. But the stories that my father passed on in the dark to me and my sister, and that I now pass on to Khalil, have a timelessness all of their own.

They live even when we are not looking. Visiting Iran made me remember their value because, in a way, what has helped Iranians to survive through their ups and downs is the sharing of poetry and stories. The stories are like little worlds, breathing examples of life, that can be referenced—lighting up the darkness of the individual and the state when logic and thought burn out in both.

IT WAS A SATURDAY night at the Stinky Café. Sanjar and I had known each other for a couple of days, and I was trying to get used to his playful style of conversation. After an hour he hopped up because he wanted to grab something from his apartment.

Two blocks later we arrived and ran into his friend Paul, who could memorize an entire newspaper before his first cup of coffee grew cold. We stopped in Paul's room, which was a like a fourteen-year-old boy's, filled with the detritus of a month's worth of enthusiasms and carelessness. Among the underpants and Pringles containers was a framed diploma from MIT.

Sanjar and Paul sat down at a laptop that rested on a pile of pre-Copernican issues of *Popular Science*. They played a game in which a snorting, snickering devil would appear and reappear on the screen between machine-gun massacres perpetrated by some wicked army. It unsettled me for some reason, and I squeezed my eyes closed.

Paul was crazy. He looked at me and said things like, "A dichotomy in the mind is how it usually happens." Then he would burst into laughter until I could not tell who was laughing: Paul, or the devil on the screen.

I did not know what Paul was talking about. I assumed crazy people meant something important when they raved. I deduced that the theme was having parents from the East and West, but as for what he meant by "happens," I had no clue. Sanjar, on the other hand, berated him for being silly and rude. We got up and left.

"I hate it when he acts like that," Sanjar said once we were outside.

We decided to walk to another café nearby called Muddy Waters. As we passed an alley, I saw the shards of a broken bottle shining under the streetlight. I started to pick up the pieces one by one.

"What are doing man?" Sanjar asked.

"Someone might walk on these," I answered.

"Okay, then take the whole street," he pointed down the alley where suddenly about ten galaxies of shattered bottles sparkled under the orange streetlight.

I finished picking up the big pieces in front of me and joined Sanjar, who had crossed the street to the café. He was sitting on a picnic table outside.

"What can I say? I want to help out," I apologized.

"Man, are you going to clean the whole world!"

"But I had the time to pick a little glass up."

"Let me tell you, if you want to help, fix yourself first."

I was looking down into myself to see how I was broken when I heard a honk and jolted up. Ferris had showed up in a huge Buick, and Sanjar ran over to his window. He invited me over and we were introduced. Ferris sized me up like he was a general inspecting his troops.

Looking at me he said to Sanjar, "Is this individual *trainable?*"

There was an odd essence that Sanjar and Ferris shared. I noticed it right away but couldn't put my finger on it: Some lightness, some sense of power arriving and departing in a healthy way. I put it aside, it may have been the simple ease of two old friends. But I would notice it again when we were with Ferris in downtown Minneapolis playing chess with ex-cons. It was midnight and Ferris was sitting next to me waiting to take back his seat at the board after a loss.

Suddenly he turned and said, "You know, sometimes I wake up and say, 'Fuck everything.'"

I was a little afraid of him still but he had Sanjar's knack for making this kind of vulgar statement sound like a Buddhist meditation on non-attachment. I even felt like giving it a try the next morning.

Standing on the street next to his Buick the first night we met, I could only let Sanjar take the lead.

"Man, who are you?" Sanjar said, mocking Ferris' words by growling, "*Is he trainable?*" Then he challenged him, "Mister, would you like to receive a whipping?"

"From a man like *you?*" Ferris replied.

Soon they were sitting at the picnic table like two titans with a chess game in full swing. Each move was followed by an insult about Arab or Iranian inferiority, hurled with such abandon that I knew I was in the presence of a strange brotherhood. I stayed low and quiet, trying to not get hit in the crossfire.

On the board there was a whirlwind battle between darkness and light that was beyond my comprehension. I watched Sanjar concentrating with every fiber of his being, glancing up at pretty girls as they walked by with a passion and a levity that were hard to reconcile.

IF KHALIL DOES eventually have a longing to visit the East, I wonder how it will appear to him in thirty years. Media images will vilify, or at least frame as abnormal, the people and their beliefs—making it hard to remember with dignity the identities of his own father and grandfather.

I hope he remembers that he was once a little boy who pointed to a random region on a map, thought about what he knew, and said, "Everyone in the world farts, even in Afghanistan and Iran."

THE WINTER AFTER returning from Iran, I was sitting on a couch with Khalil. A home movie played on a large, flat computer screen. In the movie a baby wiggles on the carpet. He arches his back, turns his eyes to the ceiling, and pushes the huge mass of his head upwards with puny arms, only to collapse to the floor facedown.

I turned to Khalil. "Look, you were trying to crawl."

"Baba, I wasn't trying to crawl! I was trying to *walk*."

The things we do as animals—pooping, fornicating in the dust, burping, birthing, dying—can humble us as humans. The things we do to become human should humble us as animals.

AT BEDTIME THE LIGHTS go out. Rumpled clothes bunched in dark corners gather themselves up into horsemen and giants, and bookshelves and curtains shudder to life. All the forces of night take turns making gestures of aggression and danger towards Khalil. The energetic child lies still under the covers. Moving from the back of his mind, and progressing through the windows, air vents, and doors, are monsters.

I give Khalil a stuffed animal. He cuddles with it for a few minutes before letting it go at his side.

"It's still too scary. I need one with a real heart."

One summer I was in the middle of the Boundary Waters, a large wilderness in Minnesota, camping at the edge of a deep glacial lake. My Indian friend Prithvi had woken me up with a short burst of words spoken in his sleep. I opened my eyes and saw him sitting up in his sleeping bag. We both heard a pop and scrape of sound coming from outside the tent. I felt my hand dig for the jackknife in my pocket.

When Prithvi was a child in Bombay he would have terrible night frights, leaping out of bed and shaking his brother awake. Hybrids of Hindu gods from the *Mahabharata*, Bollywood, and his own imagination loomed and snatched at him.

As he settled himself down in the tent, he told me what he had learned as an adult.

"What I wonder is this: when I was a kid, I knew the monsters were coming from my own head—I knew I was making them. So why didn't I ever make up magical weapons too, ones that could protect me?"

For better or worse, I never acknowledge the monsters in my son's room. I do not say the word. I do not go through a goofy mock monster hunt under the bed or closet. I sure as hell never tell him that they are not real. I tell a story, then usually leave without saying another word except, "Goodnight." Twenty minutes later when I go up, he is sleeping, without having yelled out again.

I would look around his room. He had chosen his own weapons: the light would be on, the aftermath of a Lego battle with dark forces will be on the floor, or a half-finished drawing would be on his desk. Like an ancient Persian lighting a fire on the longest night of the year, he has found a way to answer fear.

I HAVE A STORY I can tell Khalil about his grandfather. I hope he remembers it when they try to place a monster in front of him and tell him it came from the land of his ancestors.

My father, a small brown man, was with some volunteers at an Islamic center, planting flowers around the building. Some kids, bored by the task, chased each other around and into the street, where a minivan screeched to a stop a few feet from them.

A woman rushed out of the passenger side. She marched towards the doors of the Islamic center and my father met her halfway.

The first thing she said was this: "My sixteen-year-old son was driving. If he had hit those kids, do you know what it would have done to my insurance?"

My uncle and I, observing from a distance, dug in on our haunches. Before our teeth could show, I saw her disappear into the building, following my father. A few minutes later I saw her walking in the street towards the minivan, holding a tray of purple and red perennials. My father was next to her. His head was tilted because he was listening to her; his hand was reaching out because it was opening the door.

ON THE WINTRY DRIVE home from Midtown Global Market, my son dictated his own story to me. I was excited about having met Keith Ellison, the politician, and expected to see Khalil and I bravely sitting at a table next to him on the front page of the Star Tribune.

Khalil started to tell his story several times, each time adding new details. The streetlights showered us with bright bursts of light every few feet as we glided home through the slush in my gold Mazda Protege. His story ended with some lava-fueled destruction, close calls, a mother and a son, and a brand-new landscape.

"And baba," he added.

"Yes?"

"Everything was as clean as a wish."

Chapter Thirty-One

JUST AFTER DAWN I rolled my bike down the small grassy hill of our front yard in Minneapolis. Two strong pedal strokes later and I was off the curb and into the street. The air was cool. My favorite white short-sleeved dress shirt was open and starting to lift behind me. It was my third day in a row wearing it. I had plucked it years ago from a mountain of used shirts dumped on the concrete floor of a shop in San José, Costa Rica.

That's when I saw it: long yellow ribbons crisscrossing the street, tied hastily around trees, light poles, and street signs. There are many running races along the river road, and this was my first thought: another charity, another race.

I gave the pedals one more pump, and that got me close enough to see the writing: "Police Line Do Not Cross."

Turning at the corner, I headed past the back of our house, looking for another way to the bike path along the river. At the far end of the block I saw strands of yellow stretched everywhere like a sickly spider web. A man was standing in the street next to his car.

A young couple approached him and asked, "What's going on?"

"I don't know, but it looks like I'm going to have cross a police line to go to work."

Never wanting to be bloodthirsty, I turned around and found a street that was open. I pumped hard for a minute and was soon gliding along West River Parkway. The crew team from the University of Minnesota was pushing through the water down on the Mississippi. Barks of encouragement from the coach's megaphone echoed to the shoreline and up the river ravine.

The blank, grassy riverfront of Bohemian Flats was still fuzzy with dew as I coasted under the Interstate 35W bridge. Then I was downtown, the stone walls and ruins of lumber and flour mills sprouting up here and there like the crumbs of an old, dry cake. Tokens of history next to a solid batch of condominiums.

I stopped on the Stone Arch Bridge, above the crisscross of locks, dams, and concrete spillways—all the productive manhandling of St. Anthony Falls stretching back a hundred and fifty years. Before that, the Dakota, who call the falls *Owamniyomni*—turbulent water—lived with the waterfall, with neither the means nor the desire to try to make its power their own. Their descendants still share its power—letting the whirling energy heal them, even now.

What has never changed is the fact of a river flowing towards the sea. I stared hard at the raging waters. Somewhere deep beneath the surface of the Mississippi, just off the bridge, were the stone roots of Spirit Island: a place sacred for its own reasons, dismantled by the Army Corps of Engineers to make room for cargo boats.

WHEN SOMEONE is in a panic, they fall back on what they learned first. They teach you that in karate anyways. The story goes that when Master Funakoshi brought karate to the mainland from Okinawa, it was not long before officials wanted it integrated into the school curriculum. Damaging strikes to the head became safer blows to the chest. Many of karate's self-defense applications were neutralized or not taught. Benefits of the lethal art as an exercise were promoted.

Knowing that most students would not get to the advanced katas, Master Funakoshi decided to pick the beginning kata of most practical worth—*Heian Nidan*. The first action of this kata resembles the flinch reflex people experience when something suddenly comes towards their heads. It is natural. Everyone does it. The training just refines it, bringing fluidity and purpose to hands thrown up in shock.

HEARING A NOISE in the middle of the night, the young man, who lived across the street from my family, grabbed the knife he kept on his bedside table. In his living room were two intruders. He swung the knife once. A bullet was fired. It was experienced as just a louder-than-usual thud in the night by the neighbors next door. The wounded hand of the intruder left a trail of blood out the back door.

The police dogs lost the scent on the stretch of street that passes our back door.

SOMETIMES MORE is called for than a first instinct, even one that has been honed through training. At my dojo, Sensei Fusaro knew this, and told a story during class that I have not forgotten.

A long time ago in Japan a man was careless and insulted the skill of a great warrior. Since the fool did not have a weapon, it would have been dishonorable for the samurai to slay him right then and there. The samurai gave the man one day to train, after which they would meet on the bridge in the center of the village to settle the matter.

Desperate, the man hustled around the village looking for someone who would teach him how to wield a sword. Everyone refused, saying it was a lost cause, and that he was doomed. He came to the edge of the village where there was a tiny shack along the river. He rapped hard on the door and waited. An old man opened it and invited him in. The fool, close to giving up and throwing himself in the river, begged the old man to help him escape.

"I will teach you what you need to know," he said calmly, "but you cannot question the training."

The fool agreed.

The old man then had the fool practice pouring tea in a smooth, graceful manner. He poured through the afternoon and into the night, only stopping to heat more water. It went on right up until dawn, when pink streaks started to stack up on the eastern horizon.

As the sun rose into the sky, the man, trembling and furious, set the pot down carefully one last time. He turned to the old man and yelled out in hopelessness, "How is *this* going to help me?"

The old man looked out of his tiny shack towards the bridge. "When your opponent draws his sword, *first pour tea*, then reach for your own sword."

Weeping, the man left and walked slowly to the river's edge, and then to the bridge.

EVERYONE IN THE LONGFELLOW neighborhood was haunted by what happened. A strong young man, in his own house, had been shot dead by strangers in the middle of the night. The mayor of Minneapolis and police chief even showed up at the neighborhood block party for National Night Out. The kids inspected a fire truck, played games, and won coupons to the Dairy Queen on Lake Street. The adults sat near an enormous saucer of paella. The mayor and I crossed paths on my way out and he said, "You know, this is a good neighborhood, and we want to keep it that way." What plans they had to keep a neighborhood 'good' I chose not to reflect on.

That night I caught myself glancing through the trees and bushes in my backyard at the house across the street. After laying Khalil down to rest, I went into the backyard and insisted upon the safety of my world by sitting in the dark on a wooden lounge chair.

In a phone call earlier in the day Marie heard that her friend's six-year-old son had drowned on a day camp swim trip in a quiet northern town. That night, as I sat in the lounge chair, gray shapes reached and pulled themselves out from another world. It was death unraveling from a fold in our world into the air above my lawn. It was reaching for our house.

I regained control of my own mind, and the shapes retreated like genies back into their bottles.

A similar vision had struck me once before, at the Stinky Café. The skull of a man across the room became visible to me, like the aliens in the movie *They Live*. I was holding my breath when I caught a fragment of a conversation Sanjar was having with a girl about her psychology course: "The mind is a very, very powerful thing."

As I sat in the backyard, with the spirits put in their place, the last minutes of the young man's life preoccupied me. Had he had fear or courage in his heart when he picked up his knife from the bedside table? I thought of the single swing of his blade in the dark as though it were a clue.

The clue worked itself within me until it found a story in my mind.

Once upon a time there was a wandering holy man making his way across Arabia. Some nomads found him deep in the sandy wilderness and he was taken prisoner. They were suspicious: "You are a spy and we are going to cut off your head."

The old man replied: "I am not a spy. Before you kill me, I want to ask you for a favor. Give me a sword from one of your men so that I can kill one of the guards. Then, when you execute me, you will be doing it out of revenge. Your honor will be saved."

A star muscled its way through the city sky, like the dropped flashlight of a canoeist shining from the bottom of a lake. The boughs of my favorite tree in our backyard, a mature red pine, spread above me—not protectively but indifferently. The old tree never misses me but is always waiting. I peered over the back fence across the street again: In the dark of night courage and fear can't be told apart.

SOME DAYS WENT BY, all of them sunny and beautiful. I figured the drops of blood had set in the asphalt before turning gray, flaking, and vanishing in the heat. Out of my living room window I watched a large, sloppily dressed boy. He walked with duck feet towards our house, a yellow bag in his hands. Then I saw his father following in a rusty station wagon, the back swollen with yellow bags, his bloodshot eyes troubled by money. Across the street his younger son tossed a bag onto a doorstep.

Inspired, I hauled the kitchen garbage bag out to the bin by the garage. I saw people gingerly walking by the house where the murder had happened, as if to avoid disturbing the dark meditations of the spirits occupying the shadowy temple the house had become.

Rituals would take place away from the scene of the crime: an investigation, an arrest, a mug shot, and a trial. There would be a funeral. I had a longing for some other ceremony too, some curl of sage smoke floating to the sky from the steps of that house—words with magic in them.

A week would pass before a man with a bandaged hand and his younger friend were taken in. They had hit the wrong house. It was supposed to be a drug house and it all went bad. Nobody was supposed to get hurt. Somebody got murdered. It was all true.

For me, it had led to several days of reconsidering where danger existed in the world. Then, when I thought of Iran, *how* danger existed.

With the assailants in custody, a secular ritual would begin. Pictures of the two criminals appeared in the newspaper. A flimsy glance at their lives established only that they were bad men. I did everything I could to not look at the photos. There was a chance I would see the face of the man that had come up my front steps and met my eyes through the window.

If I recognized the face of one of the killers in the newspaper photo, I would know I had been lucky. My house could have easily been the "wrong house" that the intruders entered that night, and it would have been me surprising them in the dark hall. My reaction to them and the flash and pop of the gunshot would have happened all at once. I would have been lying on my back, dying from a single bullet. Out of the corner of my eye I would have seen the blurry chaos of two men running away from a mistake the size of a house and length of a lifetime.

It's only because it wasn't me do I have these moments to philosophize, where I can choose to embrace the killers as part of this strange world. Do the killers or the killed need to humble themselves? No, that was a task for me.

You always find death in the last place you look—so be always looking at love.

*

A FEW YEARS AFTER I was born, the infamous "Down With the USA" mural was painted on the side of the US Embassy in Tehran. It is fading now. The image falls on exhausted eyes. There are hundreds of murals in Tehran, portraying figures such as the twelve-year-old Palestinian boy Muhammad Al-Dura, female suicide bombers, and countless martyrs from the Iran-Iraq War. Most of them are not gory. The people in them are shown in their prime, smiling.

Other acts are afoot in Tehran. Men in blue coveralls water bushes and flowers on boulevards and along highways at all hours. This is the beauty-loving strand of the national character that gave us the word paradise, after the ancient Persian word for the walled enclosure of a garden: *pairidaeza.*

Another story about the Iranian obsession with beauty comes from next door in Iraq—specifically, the fall of Baghdad during World War II. With bombs landing everywhere, and amid rumors of imminent executions, a few hundred British and foreign nationals sought refuge behind the barbed wire of the British Embassy. Reports state that through the ordeal, the Embassy's Persian gardeners watered the verbenas and kept the grass a bright green.

William Faulkner, in his novel *The Unvanquished,* describes the scent of verbena as "the only scent you can smell above the smell of horses and courage." I wonder about the effect of this aroma, when it fills the nostrils of youthful coffin bearers in Iran and the rest of the Middle East, chanting with perhaps too much courage in the face of death.

In Iran, the gardening regiments of men in blue coveralls work on the landscapes in between buildings, but the buildings are changing too: some of the old murals are being replaced. Scenes from the *Shahnameh,* or *Book of Kings,* the epic poem telling the history of Persia, are painted next to classical Persian patterns and quotes from the Qur'an.

Specific martyrs, transposing the grief of a single family into the meaning of a nation, have been covered by abstract scenes, or turned into faceless martyrs oriented towards a glowing paradise. It is a semi-official concession to lift the spirits of a nation full of young people looking for a future, not glory.

THE BOOGIE MASK of communism has been exchanged for the mask of Islamism, with nationalism, as always, standing by.

"The 'isms' and their schisms," as Sanjar would say.

I do know we were together once. Was it a million years ago? Was it less? One group became two. A bold monkey-man dropped from the trees and walked far out into the savannah. Others followed; their shapes, their movement, blended into the grasses, and they disappeared.

If you want to be technical, you can say this: as speakers of Indo-European languages, Iranians and Europeans—and, by extension, Americans—are ethnically, culturally, linguistically, inextricably linked. These connections do not run deep enough. It is not the type of information I turn to for an answer when people ask me, "What are you?" I prefer to tell them, "I'm human."

It is scary when people laugh at that answer, or dismiss it as cheeky and evasive.

Sometimes I say I am African. This is usually met with a mixture of skepticism and appreciation by my junior high students who are black. I trace my beginnings to one of those wanderers who went beyond the savannah, leaving signs and symbols in caves, in skyscrapers, on the moon, and in altered genetic codes. Marks that would add up and become what we think of as the story of civilization.

Global circumstances have led to the day when ancient dispersed tribes are meeting up again. The people of each tribe have changed color, and upon first glance they run from each other or kill each other. Some bunch up along borders to seek refuge where the air is sweet, or at least not on fire.

We end up at a wall, one that grows and pulses, an amalgam of our varied experiences, which over millennia hardened and remolded into stone and mortar, tattoo marks, electronic IDs, preferences, denied visas, tethers, sanctions, restrictions. Sometimes the wall is within a tribe; sometimes it is between the old and the young. People on each side describe those on the other side, but not with enough words—and a story can't be told in one word.

The first coat of paint is always in blood; the one that follows is never enough.

What should I do when I become bitter about the way things are?

Crumple up the map of the world and redraw it? Things done at the tables of great empires should be done by my own hand.

Sanjar, leaving the Stinky Café one night at closing time, saw a mop bucket and thought out loud, "We take ourselves *so* seriously—but what are we but those bubbles on the surface of the water?"

The foam of the surf. Rising and falling with the water, masters of a tiny globe that may pop with our next breath. We can be a presence in there—an eye in motion waiting to peek over the next wave, riding lightly in this world, taking nothing, adding nothing, and telling the tale of its bounty, before disappearing into the ocean again.

I thought it was impossible to take a trip to Iran. Thinking back, I had not really tried. I do not know what they say in Farsi, but in Arabic they say *nam selka*: the true intentions were not there. The failures I had before my success were just feedback: you do not really want to go yet. Now I think there are a million ways to get into Iran, each one leading to a different place. They are the people of Iran, wherever they may be, each one offering to be your guide.

IT WAS THE MIDDLE of the night. Sanjar and I were walking through downtown Minneapolis.

We had whirled and jumped around for hours at "Too Much Love," First Avenue's weekly dance party. We found a bench to rest on at the edge of Loring Park. Across the street the outlines of giant outdoor sculptures at the Walker Art Center competed with the honest silhouettes of ordinary trees.

This was the age before everyone had a cell phone, and the two of us faced the ambient feelings and sensations in the air together. To pass the time he told me a story.

Once upon a time, in a land ten thousand miles from here, there was a master poet whose apprentice listened to and memorized all of his words. Though he never said it, the apprentice was impatient for the day when his turn would come to be the master.

Once a year the old poet went away to a festival in the countryside, where he judged bards from throughout the realm. While he was gone, the apprentice boasted about knowing all the verses in the old poet's repertoire. Many of the poems, including the longest and most challenging epic, were about the king, who was happy to let the apprentice recite them while the old poet was gone.

A full royal audience gathered in the throne room. Once the student began, his voice became confident, and he built triumphantly to the final word of the epic poem. The king, overwhelmed, decided on the spot to appoint the apprentice as the new royal poet.

Months later, the old poet returned to the castle and found that his student had taken over his quarters. The situation was explained to him, and he agreed to accept his fate on one condition: that everyone come to the throne room once more so the new royal poet, his former apprentice, could recite the epic poem in his presence as well as the king's. Without hesitation, the former apprentice agreed.

The king gave the order, and the entire royal court was assembled to hear his praises sung once again. The young man began strongly. The beauty of the words cast a spell on the entire room.

The old poet, his eyes watering, listened as the poem unfolded.

Then, as the last word of the epic left the lips of the apprentice, the old poet picked up the line—and continued.

⟶

THE LAST THING the Iranian government wants is for foreigners who visit the country to be writers. People who have gone to Iran and subsequently written books are now banned from the country. I did not go to write a book. I went to see a friend.

I have always guarded my own world as closely as a government wants to guard theirs. I have held my flame close. Most secrets remain so. It is all very normal and all very silly. After all, our minds are filled with secrets, and there will always be more left untold than what we reveal. New mysteries are born each time I sit down with others. We help each other uncover thoughts and feelings we did not know we had or forgot we had. It shows on our faces. It is why old friends stay interesting.

Sanjar shared with me and I learned from him. I am telling as much as I can, knowing that as soon as I tell one secret, three grow in its place.

THESE DAYS THE STINKY CAFÉ is tamer, like a museum. The cast of characters has dispersed. I have not been there in years. Other places are alive now. The place that is most alive is usually wherever Sanjar is when he is in town.

I will hide in my song so that I may take kisses from your lips as you sing it.

What I have done is what we all have done and promise not to do even after we have done it: kiss and tell.

I GOT A POSTCARD from my sister. The windows are frosted, and I can't see outside. I do not want to see outside: a brutal regime of snow and ice has ruled for the past three months. It's February and there is no reason to think anything has changed. The combination of being skinny and easily chilled and not having decent boots has left me in a terrible mood.

I look at the picture. It is a photo of a sunny café in Istanbul, Turkey. Old men blend into the worn chairs and tables. Cups of coffee bloom white from their rough hands like little jasmine blossoms. In front of the old men is a board for backgammon—a better game than chess. It is more like life. You do your best to plan, but you still have to roll the dice.

On the back are two sentences:

"I have a good name for your baby: Khalil. Find out what it means."

Glossary

adhan: literally means "to listen" in Arabic. The Islamic call to prayer. Ubiquitous sound in Hollywood movies trying to set a tone for a story in the Middle East.

agha: Farsi word meaning "sir" or "mister."

Ahura Mazda: literally means "wise lord" in Avestan. The supreme deity in the ancient Iranian religion Zoroastrianism. See Avestan, Zoroastrianism.

Al-Azhar University: preeminent center for Islamic and Arabic learning for over one thousand years, located in the medieval quarter of Cairo, Egypt.

Alhambra: palace built in thirteenth century Granada, Spain, by Muslim rulers. Its garden is influenced by Persian garden philosophy and style.

Alhamidillah: "thanks be to God" in Arabic.

Artesh: the Army of the Islamic Republic of Iran. The regular military of Iran. Men are conscripted at the age of eighteen and must serve for eighteen months to two years.

ash-e-reshteh: bean and noodle soup.

Avestan: Old Persian, the language used in the sacred book of Zoroastrianism, the Avesta. Probably not used in everyday life since the fifth century BC, but passed on through oral tradition.

azizam: literally means "my dear" in Farsi.

baba-joon: Farsi word of endearment, literally "dear father."

Sardar-e Bagh-e Melli: literally "National Garden Gate." Magnificent brick gate leading to the Ministry of Foreign Affairs in Tehran. Once the symbol of Iran, before Azadi Tower was built.

Bagh Ferdows: "garden of Eden," a historical complex dating from the Qajar dynasty; where the Cinema Museum of Iran is located.

Bame Tehran: literally "roof of Tehran." One of the most popular mountain paths and hangouts for city dwellers below Mount Tochal. Lookout with benches allows for a full view of the city.

Basiji: paramilitary militia below the Sepah and Artesh. Often engaged in upholding Islamic norms in society and controlling major urban areas.

Behesht-e-Zahra: largest cemetery in Iran. There are sections for martyrs of the Iran-Iraq War, people who died on the pilgrimage to Mecca, and, touchingly, the Iraqi Kurdish victims of the gas attack in Halabja, Iraq. They have recently added a section for martyrs from the conflict in Syria.

Darakeh: outer suburb that is quickly becoming another neighborhood of northern Tehran. Sits at the skirt of the mountains where a popular hiking path follows the Darakeh River, past cafés and picnic spots.

Dasht-e Kavir: literally "low plains." Also known as the Great Salt Desert, it stretches across the middle of Iran.

djellaba: an ankle-length robe with long sleeves. A version of it is worn throughout North Africa and the Middle East.

Esteghlal: "independence," also the name of a soccer team in Tehran.

Faravahar: Assyrian representation of the deity Ashur, later adopted by ancient Zoroastrians. The symbol is an open-winged bird with a sun disk in the middle from which the head of a male figure emerges. No one knows what it actually represented to ancient Persians, but modern interpretations suggest that it signified divine grace, divinity, and royal power. Found on the tombs of ancient Persian kings, such as Darius the Great. See Zoroastrianism.

Farsi: language spoken in Iran.

gheliyun: water pipe, often called a hookah.

Heian Nidan: literally "stable peace, second level" in Japanese. Second kata or form in traditional Shotokan karate. (Chinese interpretation of the first character is pronounced "pingan," meaning "journey safely.")

Jame Jam: In Persian mythology the "Cup of Jamshid" allowed the ancient rulers of Iran to see all seven heavens of the universe, reflect the whole world, and reveal truths. Those who sipped from it gained immortality. Appears in Persian texts before the first mention of the Holy Grail.

khoda hafez: literally "may God be your guardian." Vernacular meaning in Iran is "goodbye."

kuh raftan: Farsi phrase meaning "go to the mountain."

lavash: round, thin bread popular in Western Asia.

Lors: tribe in southwestern and western Iran. Lived as pastoral nomads until mid-twentieth century, when they were forcibly settled and compelled to take up agriculture by Reza Shah.

maast-o-khiar: cucumber yogurt.

Mahabharata: ancient Indian epic written in the second century BC. Story of two families battling for the throne, interwoven with shorter stories and philosophical discourses. Contains the Bhagavad-Gita or "Song of God."

Mithra: most important god in pre-Zoroastrian Iran. God of the rising sun, covenants, oaths, and friendship. Mithra is judge, protector of truth, guardian of the harvest, waters, and even cattle. Romans found a lot to like about it and formed a cult, the Mithraic Mysteries, based on their perception of Mithra.

Milad Tower: tower in Tehran, and one of the tallest buildings in the Middle East.

Morality Police: uniformed patrol that acts as a kind of vice squad. Tasked with enforcing dress codes, especially the hijab for women.

Mullah Nasruddin: kind of like hummus, the chickpea dish, he is a medieval folk hero claimed by everyone—from Central Europe, to Turkey, to Iran, to the Xinjiang region of China.

nam selka: Arabic phrase meaning "the true intentions are not there."

nemi-doonam: "I don't know" in Farsi.

Nowruz: a celebration rooted in Zoroastrianism, literally "new day." Dates back at least three thousand years and falls on the first day of spring. Time of reflecting on the possibilities of new life after washing away the old. See Zoroastrianism.

Owamniyomni: the Dakota name for St. Anthony Falls in Minneapolis. Means "turbulent water, whirlpool, eddy."

Pairidaeza: Ancient Persian word meaning "walled garden." Did the linguistic shuffle through the millennia—passed into Akkadian, Greek, Latin, German, and French, and is the root of "paradise" in English.

paneer sabzi: Persian platter that includes mix of fresh herbs, mint, walnuts, feta cheese, and radishes.

perrito: "puppy" in Spanish.

Pol-e-Piroozi: "Bridge of Victory" in Farsi. Known since Second World War as Veresk Bridge for the important role it played in helping Soviet troops resupply.

Republic of Mahabad: the Soviet Union created this country at the start of the Cold War in an attempt to attach the northern part of Iran to itself. Lasting only a year, it was a bittersweet taste of political independence for Kurdish people.

sangak: literally "little stone" in Farsi. Bread baked on a bed of small river stones.

Shahnameh: "The Book of Kings" in Farsi. Epic poem written by Ferdowsi in the late tenth and early eleventh centuries. Tells the history of pre-Islamic Persia.

Simurgh: giant, almost timeless, benevolent bird from Iranian mythology. Purified the land and water, and was the link between the sky and earth.

sigheh: "temporary marriage," or "pleasure marriage." A renewable contract of marriage for a defined amount of time. Touted as a religiously sanctioned answer for single, economically insecure youths who desire sexual relations, it has been criticized as exploitative of women. The practice is not accepted as legitimate by the majority of Muslims.

Shia: there are two main branches of Islam: Sunni and Shia. The majority of the Muslim world is Sunni, but Iran is predominantly Shia. The difference boils down to a dispute about the rightful successors to the Prophet Mohammad, the founder of Islam.

sultania: "a large bowl" in Arabic.

tether: a slang word for an ankle monitor.

toman: former currency of Iran, replaced by rial. In daily life, however, Iranians often still speak of prices in toman. A seller requesting one hundred toman would expect to be paid one thousand rial.

Qur'an: the sacred book of Islam. The Angel Gabriel recited its verses to the Prophet Mohammad over a period of many years.

Zoroastrianism: ancient Persian religion that predates Islam and Christianity and likely influenced the development of Judaism. Founded by Zoroaster in the sixth century BC—though some scholars date the founding of the religion as early as 1500 BC. Views forces of goodness, truth, and light as involved in a constant battle with evil, lies, and darkness. This struggle rages across the universe; humans, endowed with free will, must choose a side. Possesses a refreshingly simple and unassailable adage: "good thoughts, good words, good deeds."

SELECTED BIBLIOGRAPHY

We wish to thank the publishers of the following works for their permission to use passages. While we have made every effort to contact copyright holders prior to publication, we will be happy to correct any inadvertent errors or omissions.

Buchan, James. *The Persian Bride*. Mariner, 2002.

Faulkner, William. *The Unvanquished*. Vintage Digital, 2013.

Frazier, Ian. *Travels in Siberia*. Picador, 2011.

Hāfiz, and Daniel James Ladinsky. *The Gift: Poems by the Great Sufi Master*. Arkana, 1999.

Lessing, Doris. *Time Bites: Views and Reviews*. HarperCollins Publishers, 2005.

Lessing, Doris. *Shikasta: Re, Colonised Planet 5: Personal, Psychological, Historical Documents Relating to Visit by Johor (George Sherban) Emissary (Grade 9) 87th of the Period of the Last Days*. Vintage Books, 2014.

Levine, Philip. *The Mercy: Poems*. Alfred A. Knopf, 2003.

Shah, Tahir. *In Arabian Nights: A Caravan of Moroccan Dreams*. Bantam Books, 2009.

Szymborska, Wisława. *View with a Grain of Sand: Selected Poems.* Translated by Stanislaw Baranczak and Clare Cavanagh. Harcourt Brace and Co., 1993.

Wawro, Geoffrey. "Our Special Correspondent." *Naval War College Review* 55, no. 1, article 7 (2002).

About the Author

KAREEM AAL is a writer living in Minneapolis. When he was in Spain on one of his "American Trips" a vagabond told him he would be guilty of a crime if he didn't keep writing. To avoid any consequences, he has continued to write. He is grateful that he doesn't live in a place where it might be a crime if he did write. *No True Love in Tehran* is his first book.